THE KLEIN–WINNICOTT DIALECTIC

THE KLEIN–WINNICOTT DIALECTIC

DIALECTIC

Transformative New Metapsychology and Interactive Clinical Theory

Susan Kavaler-Adler

KARNAC

First published in 2014 by
Karnac Books Ltd
118 Finchley Road, London NW3 5HT

British Library Cataloguing in Publication Data

A C.I.P. for this book is available from the British Library

  ISBN 978 1 78049 124 0

Edited, designed and produced by The Studio Publishing Services Ltd
www.publishingservicesuk.co.uk
e-mail: studio@publishingservicesuk.co.uk

Printed in Great Britain

www.karnacbooks.com

CONTENTS

ACKNOWLEDGEMENTS

I want to acknowledge the tremendous help offered to me by Dr Inna Rozentsvit, in all my current professional activities, and especially for her assistance in finalising and publishing this book. Since this book, and another current one, both being published by Karnac, are related to all my work as an object relations theorist who teaches through my role as the founder and executive director of the Object Relations Institute (ORI) for Psychotherapy and Psychoanalysis (since 1991), I want to also thank Dr Rozentsvit for her superhuman efforts in helping the Object Relations Institute grow and thrive. Dr Rozentsvit (Inna) is the jewel of administration, marketing, and comradeship that has reinvigorated all the faculty, graduates, candidates, and our communal professional network at ORI. Dr Rozentsvit entered my world as a student in my Melanie Klein course at the Institute, after having practised as a neurologist for most of her professional life. Her quick attunement and insight into the world of psychoanalysis, and the clinical contributions of the object relations theorists, including those of my own and of my now deceased colleagues, Dr Jeffrey Seinfeld and Dr Joyce McDougall, has allowed Inna to be a wonderful companion along the road of my continuing professional journey.

I also want to thank Catherine Sanguinetti for her earlier assistance in developing this book. I wish her the best of luck in bringing up her two beautiful little daughters. I want to acknowledge, as well, all the help she gave to the Object Relations Institute during her period of administration.

I would like to thank all my professional colleagues, who discussed with me the themes related to my theoretical and clinical ideas as I was creating this book. I particularly want to recognise my dear departed friends: Dr Jeffrey Seinfeld, Dr Joyce McDougall, Dr Conalee Schneidman, Dr Fayek Nakhla, and Dr Jerry Raphael. I also want to thank my current friends and colleagues who respond to my thoughts and, thus, inspire me: Audrey Ashendorf, Charles Bonerbo, Dr Albert Brok, Janet Burak, Nasir Ilahi, Raphael A. Javier, Dr Jeffrey Lewis, Harriet Pappenheim, Madeline Price, Dr Jeffrey Rubin, Lisa Shuman, Dr Jack Schwartz, Anne Rose Simon, Harriet Wald, Marc Wayne, Dr Lawrence Wetzler, and Dr Margaret Yard.

ABOUT THE AUTHOR

Susan Kavaler-Adler, PhD, ABPP, NCPsyA, D.Litt is a practising clinical psychologist, psychoanalyst, and a scholar of the object relations clinical theory for over thirty-five years. She offers psychotherapy and psychoanalysis for individuals and couples, while in therapeutic groups she utilises unique techniques of psychic visualisations to engage all participants in discovering their internal world's relationships. Her supervision groups for mental health practitioners are very popular, and include creative approaches of interactive role-play, case studies, analytic-session-as-a-hologram, as well as the analyst-as-instrument techniques.

Dr Kavaler-Adler is the co-founder, executive director, senior teaching faculty, training analyst, and supervisor of the Object Relations Institute for Psychotherapy and Psychoanalysis (ORI) in New York City. ORI is a non-profit New York State chartered educational institute, which has started its third decade of making mental health professionals and educating them about British and American object relations clinical theory and technique.

Dr Kavaler-Adler is the author of four books (two of which had been re-published in 2013 by ORI Academic Press) and over sixty peer-reviewed articles and edited book chapters, many of which are related to her view of mourning as a developmental process ("developmental mourning"), which is fundamental to self-integration, healing, and transformation throughout one's lifetime. Her unique integration of British and American object relations theory can be seen throughout her writing, fully defined as a theoretical perspective related to "developmental mourning" in her first book, *The Compulsion to Create: Women Writers and Their Demon Lovers* (Routledge, 1993. reprinted by ORI Academic Press, 2013). The focus of this book and her second book, *The Creative Mystique: From Red Shoes Frenzy to Love and Creativity* (Routledge, 1996, reprinted by ORI Academic Press, 2013), is on well-known brilliant women writers and artists. In these books, Dr Kavaler-Adler explores how the creative process can lead to progressive developmental mourning, self-integration, and reparation or, alternatively, it can be the captive of pathological mourning and psychic arrest in those who fail to mourn. This failure to mourn (or demon-lover complex) is usually related to developmental arrest from trauma in the primal stage of self-development.

Dr Kavaler-Adler's third book, *Mourning, Spirituality, and Psychic Change: A New Object Relations View of Psychoanalysis* (Routledge, 2003), the Gradiva Award winner (from the National Association for the Advancement of Psychoanalysis in 2004), further explores the clinical arena of the object relations phenomena. This book extends the clinical application of Dr Kavaler-Adler's theories that can be seen in her first two books through in-depth descriptions of the developmental mourning process in dialectic with analytic transference work, and with the interactive engagement of the psychoanalyst and patient.

Some other difficult but important topics of Dr Kavaler-Adler's writings are: self-sabotage, fear of success, envy, seduction, grief and loss, erotic transference, spirituality and psychic transformation, creative compulsion *vs.* free motivation, resolving blocks of creativity, along with the opening of creative self, finding one's voice, as well as the capacity to surrender—in life and in Argentine tango.

FOREWORD

It is a privilege to write this foreword, not only because of the importance of this book, but also because of my respect for Dr Susan Kavaler-Adler. Over the course of her career as a clinical psychologist and a psychoanalyst, I have often marvelled at her ability to integrate theories from the American and English schools of object relations into a coherent whole. That work is reflected in the curriculum she designed for the Object Relations Institute for Psychotherapy and Psychoanalysis in New York City—where Dr Kavaler-Adler is cofounder and executive director—and in her four other books, beginning with *The Compulsion to Create: A Psychoanalytic Study of Women Artists,* first published in 1993.

In her latest book, *The Klein–Winnicott Dialectic: Transformative New Metapsychology and Interactive Clinical Theory,* Dr Kavaler-Adler accomplishes what no one else has. She demonstrates how the contrasting and competing theories of Melanie Klein and D. W. Winnicott converge and complement each other theoretically as well as clinically. Most clinicians are unaware that Winnicott implicitly addressed many of his papers to Klein and that, though she overtly rejected them, they would influence many of her theoretical formulations.

Dr Kavaler-Adler discusses Kleinian theory and describes many of its strengths and weaknesses here. Like many clinicians, she believes that Klein's notion of the death instinct is unnecessary, and therefore recommends that it be discarded. What she finds most clinically useful is Klein's phenomenological theory, particularly its paranoid–schizoid and depressive positions, along with their accompanying defences. Acknowledging that as a developmental theory, it needs expansion, she recommends using it in conjunction with Winnicott's developmental focus, particularly with the emphasis on the role of the real mother or analyst in the formation of the psyche. Dr Kavaler-Adler uses rich clinical illustrations to demonstrate how the contributions of these two theoretical giants can work well together and can provide the psychoanalytic practitioner with numerous clinical possibilities.

In writing this book, Dr Kavaler-Adler has even further added to her standing as a major contributor to the field of psychoanalysis. Two years ago, her friends and colleagues, Dr Joyce McDougal and Dr Jeffrey Seinfeld passed away. Psychoanalysts worldwide felt their loss. Both of these eminent, highly esteemed psychoanalysts and object relations theorists had been very responsive, dialectically, to Dr Kavaler-Adler's writings. Her themes of developmental mourning, the demon-lover complex, and erotic transference had deeply resonated with them. Through her writings, Dr Kavaler-Adler has proved her stature as a psychoanalytic theorist alongside her two friends.

Richard M. Alperin, PhD

A developmental theory of psychological health based on the Klein–Winnicott dialectic and related object relations thinking

British object relations theory since the time of Melanie Klein, Ronald Fairbairn, D. W. Winnicott, Michael Balint, Hanna Segal, and Wilfred Bion has made enormous theoretical contributions to the clinical practice of psychological healing in all of humanity, and particularly in those with developmental arrests who develop character disorders. These theorists have made their contributions without discarding Freud's enormous contributions to the practice of psychoanalysis for neurotic patients. However, due to the politics of psychoanalysis as it has been practised in Britain, those who have been influenced by the Kleinian tradition—including the profound contributions of Hanna Segal, Paula Heimann, Rosenfeld, and Wilfred Bion—have seen themselves as directly in conflict with those followers of D. W. Winnicott, who have called themselves the British "Middle Group".

Housed both literally and metaphorically within the British Psychoanalytic Society (since that organisation was first run by Melanie Klein's friend, Ernest Jones, and then was perpetually dominated by Melanie Klein and by her successor as president of the organisation, Hanna Segal, who was also a chief biographer of Klein), those who have explicitly espoused Melanie Klein's theories have rejected the major theoretical contributions of Winnicott and his followers. These include Adam Phillips (1988) in the current psychotherapy literature in England, and those from the Tavistock Clinic, such as Michael Balint, who called their anti-organisational tribe, existing without a psychoanalytic society since the time of Winnicott's fireside chats and musically accompanied seminars in his own living room ("Mi Casa es Su Casa"), the "Middle Group". Both the psychoanalytic society camp and the outside "revolutionaries" of the Middle Group have seen themselves as diametrically opposed to one another, and, therefore, have often politicised their theory of clinical technique into polarised statements that have belied the profound degree to which their separate contributions could be integrated on a phenomenological basis.

I have attempted to integrate their theoretical contributions to clinical practice through the use of the conceptual term "dialectic", a term that has been formerly utilised in the American scene theorising of Thomas Ogden (1986, 1994) and Sheldon Bach (1985, 1994, 2005). In order to do so, I have had to make the case in this volume of thinking that the major polarising factor in the contributions of the two camps has been Melanie Klein's metapsychology of the "death instinct", rather than Klein's clinical theory with its brilliant phenomenology. Part of making this case has been to preface my clinical illustrations of the integration of Kleinian and Winnicottian theory from their contrasting, but also complementary, dialectical perspectives with some studies of Klein's psychobiography.

In doing so, I have particularly drawn on the biographical research of Phyllis Grosskurth, who published a major biography of Klein in 1986, quite a time after the briefer biography by Segal (1964). Grosskurth's (1986) psychobiographical insights are unique in having utilised formerly unearthed letters of correspondence between Melanie Klein and her mother, Libussa. It was the generosity of the British Psychoanalytic Society that allowed Phyllis Grosskurth to have access to the critical archives that housed the wealth of letters that she proceeded to study for her biographical work.

In drawing on the biographical resources of Grosskurth (1986) to look at Klein's life experience to understand the underpinnings of both her metapsychological and clinical theories, I have also faced the other side of the Klein–Winnicott dialectic by drawing on two biographies of Winnicott, with some minor references to the short biography of Kahr (1996) and more vivid and detailed references to the extremely comprehensive study of Rodman (2004). It is my belief that, just as many in the arts have come to admit today, no work of art exists in isolation from the biographical past of the artist (including the literary writer), which has allowed autobiographical influences to be valued rather than eschewed, as formerly in academic circles. They have come to admit that the artistic product of the psychoanalytic theorist, which is her or his written works on theory and their clinical applications, is inevitably stamped by the life experience of the theorist, and, as with the artist, and with people in general, the heaviest stamp of all comes from the formative years of infancy, toddlerhood, and childhood of the theorist. If this is admitted, the contributions of those who dare to indulge in biographies of psychoanalytic theorists can be greatly valued, and can be mined for their jewels of insight into the mind and its internal world within the psychoanalytic theorist. In writing this volume, I feel an immense sense of gratitude to Grosskurth (1986), Kahr (1996), and Rodman (2004). From this sense of gratitude, I can begin this journey into a discussion of the theories and theorists who inhabit the interactive, rather than polarised: *The Klein–Winnicott Dialectic*.

The theories

Klein's phenomenological theory of paranoid–schizoid and depressive position experience, which differentiates the pre-symbolic and symbolic levels of human experience, and which emphasises the internal world of psychic fantasy, will be seen in this book's journey to offer a developmental evolution. This developmental evolution can be formulated in terms of self-integration and/or separation individuation. This is a developmental and clinical theory that is not dependent on Klein's metapsychology of the "death instinct". Rather, regression or fixation into the more primitive and more dangerously aggressive paranoid–schizoid position can be understood in terms of a "developmental arrest" trauma in relation to primal maternal bonding, maternal presence, and maternal responsiveness, as opposed to being interpreted as the innate manifestations of a "death instinct". Through the Kleinian perspective of the internal world, with both its visceral and symbolic levels of experience, we understand how the internal world of psychic fantasy evolves and colours our experience throughout life.

Winnicott's theory operates in parallel with this phenomenological perspective. However, Winnicott focuses on the external world experience of development, and on the transitional world of intersubjective phenomena. The holding environment and its developmentally facilitating functions are all aspects of Winnicott's external world that interact with the internal world of Klein in self-development (see Winnicott, 1971a,b, 1986). The facilitating functions include the "subjective object", maternal mirroring that can be internalised and that can build in a sense of self for self-development, transitional space, and transitional phenomena. The intersubjective terrain of Winnicott's transitional space has been shown to operate alongside the paranoid and depressive fantasies (phantasies) of Klein's internal world, so that mature development involves sorting out what is inside and what is outside through evolving capacities for self-reflection. This dialectical interaction between internal and external worlds evolves along the lines of theoretical contrasts between Kleinian internal world psychic fantasy and the Winnicottian external world experience that becomes internalised. This Klein–Winnicott dialectic creates a comprehensive psychological framework within which to understand human development.

I will now comment on how the British theorists Ronald Fairbairn, Michael Balint, and Wilfred Bion, as well as the Americans, Margaret Mahler, Peter Fonagy, Thomas Ogden, and myself, fill in the gaps of this fundamental psychic dialectic between Klein and Winnicott. They offer differentiating concepts that elaborate the Klein–Winnicott theoretical domain.

Through an understanding of the Klein–Winnicott dialectic in relation to development, some of Kohut's theorising can be called into question. This does not detract, however, from Kohut's (1971) major theoretical contribution in terms of defining the specific nature of narcissistic transferences: the "mirroring, twinship, and idealizing" varieties.

Ronald Fairbairn's theories

Fairbairn's (1952) work on the nature of psychopathology of pre-oedipal trauma offers us the concept of the "bad object", and of the "addiction to a bad object". These concepts help us define primal object relations that are not, in Winnicott's words, "good enough" to facilitate ongoing development, or good enough to be internalised in representational form to fortify the primal or potential true self for developmental evolution. An object is "bad" if it disrupts or ruptures the self and other connections that need to be internalised from birth for development to proceed. The "bad" object, as a primal parental object, stemming back to the original real mother, can be inadequate, unavailable, mismatched with the child, or can be actively abusive and abandoning. In any case, it is "bad" in terms of being a malignant object that disrupts and arrests development, rather than being a facilitating object that allows psychological development to proceed.

Fairbairn's (1952) "bad object" would, in Winnicott's sense, fail to respond to the pre-oedipal child in a way that would foster the psychological nurturance (through internalisation) of a potential true and spontaneous self. But even more so, it is generally intensely sadistic and filled with hostile aggression. So, the "bad object" that fails to be Winnicott's "good enough" object provokes the kind of persecutory fears, visceral attacks, and persecutory fantasies that Klein would refer to as part and parcel of the paranoid–schizoid position. There is one important distinction, however. Fairbairn's bad object, which he first spoke of after working with traumatised children who were placed in foster homes during the Second World War, is a real parent who exists in the external world. Unlike Klein's instinctual hostile bad object of psychic fantasy, which could be hypothesised to be innate, Fairbairn's (1952) "bad object" is an incorporated parental object, which is too aversive to be psychologically digested through cognitive processes of symbolisation that build symbolic representations in the internal world.

Fantasy distortions and elaborations can be due to one's own internal aggression, but the malignant nature of the "bad object" is still highly tantalising and addictive for compulsive repetitions of trauma because it is the first object that the child has been attached to, since, and even before, birth, that is, the mother. Since Fairbairn believed that we are driven to connect with another from the time of birth, never entertaining Freud's fantasy of a primary narcissism, he also believed that we are overwhelmed by our needs for this primal other throughout life. In fact, we are haunted all the more since the "bad object" cannot be digested in the form of symbolic representations, representations that would allow us to have the resources we need in the internal world so that we can move on to new, and perhaps better, attachments.

For Fairbairn (1952), the child who has this early developmental disruption of internalising a pre-symbolic object in a globally incorporated form is unable to survive without taking this object inside its internal world to control it. Consequently, the child's internal world is poisoned. The child then denies the malevolent nature of the object, so as to psychologically survive in a world controlled by the malevolent one. To protect the image of the parents, and to idealise them, allows the child to avoid continual re-traumatisation from the true nature of the parents upon whom she is totally dependent. To protect the image of the parent, however, the aggression that is felt in relation to the abusive or neglectful parent is turned against the self. Consequently, the child is afflicted with "internal saboteurs" (Fairbairn, 1952), or with a consolidated structure of such internal saboteur malevolence that Fairbairn (1952) named the "antilibidinal ego" structure. The child turns against herself, perceiving herself as bad, and attacks herself—all in the service of protecting the image of the parent. Of course, she has been taught to revere the very parent who is depriving or abusing her.

In terms of Winnicott's theory, the very transitional space and corresponding internal psychic space that one needs for the spontaneous evolution of the feelings and thoughts that form a true self— and a true self in relation to another in an intersubjective dialectic—is foreclosed by a Fairbairnian "bad object". Such an object persists in the internal world psyche after traumatic parenting in the pre-oedipal era of development when the self-structure is just forming.

In terms of Klein, the "bad object" is so intolerable that it must continually be projected out into another so that vital elements of the psyche are lost and self-integration fails to take place. The persecutory fantasies of Klein, reminiscent of the paranoid–schizoid position, can be seen in Fairbairn's (1952) perspective as fantasies of actual bad object persecution from the time of primal connection with the mother. Klein's depressive fantasies might then be interpreted, from Fairbairn's (1952) perspective, as a form of spurious guilt, as opposed to actual existential guilt. The spurious guilt would be related to a defensive blaming of the self for the assaults of the parent (i.e., rationalising that "I deserve to be beaten") to protect the image of the parent, and to defensively idealise the parent, so as not to see the actual parent's failings. We need to distinguish Fairbairn's (1952) defensive or spurious guilt from the genuine grief about one's regret for our own destructive aggression that Klein refers to, without, I believe, jumping to the conclusion that the fantasies of parental persecution or abandonment is all a projection of our own aggression. We need to become conscious of the actual problems of our parents, and of the primal mother. Otherwise, we can remain addicted to an idealised primal parent object that we project on to others, or to an eroticised primal parent object that we project on to others.

Michael Balint

In *The Basic Fault*, Balint (1979) speaks of a pre-oedipal traumatic fault in mothering that we can compare to the more modern concept of "developmental arrest", as spoken of by Stolorow and Lachmann (1980) in their book, *The Psychoanalysis of Developmental Arrest*. Balint (1965) also speaks of a "primary love" in infancy, which relates to Fairbairn's (1952) idea of a primary craving to connect with a human other. Both the idea of primary love and primary connection are substantiated by modern infant research (Beebe & Lachmann, 1988; Beebe & Stern, 1977; Stern, 1985). Such research gives visible evidence of how babies are intimately aware of their mothers and related to their mothers from the beginning of life. Balint is, thus, one of the theorists who accurately disputes Freud's writings on primary narcissism, and would support his views only on secondary narcissism. Balint (1965, 1979) would assign pathological narcissism to secondary causes related to failings in early pre-oedipal mothering, as he would assign all character disturbances to such causes.

Wilfred Bion

Bion was an analysand and student of Klein's who helps us define further her views on the developmental course of emerging from protosymbolic to symbolic relations. He speaks of beta elements in the psyche that are like impulsive reactions, which are visceral, somatic, or behavioural in nature. These are differentiated from alpha elements that are cognitively and symbolically defined elements of experience, that is, ones we can put into words, and do put into words in the psychoanalytic situation (Bion, 1963).

Bion (1959) also speaks of "attacks on linking", a phrase which defines the disruptive disconnections that occur with early trauma, disruptions that can continually be repeated in the psyche over time, so that life and experience is necessarily fragmented or deadened. When one's mind attacks its own links that one cannot connect, beta elements or regressions occur, reducing alpha symbolisations to beta. Bion (1959, 1962) was a proponent of paying attention to the realities of mental phenomena, and to looking into overlapping areas of psychoanalysis, science, mathematics, and theology (Grotstein, 1996).

Peter Fonagy (after Mahler and Ogden)

Fonagy and colleagues' (Fonagy, Gergely, Jurist, & Target, 2000) concept of "mentalization" is another way of trying to get at the distinctions between protosymbolic and symbolic level experience. Fonagy and colleagues (2000) relate insecure attachment in infants and children to the failure of the mother's mirroring responsiveness. Related to Winnicott's (1971b) theories on mirroring, Fonagy, Gergely, Jurist, and Target (2000) speak of the ability to form representations in the mind of feelings and thoughts, which is the essence of the developmental achievement of self-reflection. He also theorises along lines congenial to what Ogden (1986, 1994) has called the development of the "interpreting subject." The "interpreting subject" is one who knows one is interpreting one's own experience. Fonagy, Gergely, Jurist and Target (2000) would see responsive and attuned mothering to be responsible for such developmental achievement.

The deconstruction of two theoretical misconceptions

The *first misconception* that is addressed throughout this book, and particularly in the first several chapters on Klein, is related to Klein's death instinct metapsychology. I believe that Klein was mistaken in believing that her theory of an innate "death instinct" is necessary to support her clinical and phenomenological theory of progressive developmental movement from a paranoid–schizoid to a depressive position. This Kleinian "death instinct" was not like Freud's entropy or nirvana, but was related to hostile aggression towards the mother, which was innate and had psychic fantasy predispositions. Such a "death instinct" was later described by Klein as envy from the primal oral era of infancy, which was experienced unconsciously as a threat to the mother, and would appear in psychoanalytic treatment in the transference. This envy was supposed to have an innate instinctual base, and was not necessarily reactive to actual frustrations during development.

As will be shown in the first three sections of this book, Klein's theory of the "death instinct" is not required for, and it should be separated from, her extremely clinically relevant phenomenological theory. With the background of the biographical reasons for Klein holding on to her "death instinct" theory, I proposed that hostile aggression, which can exist as disruptive beta-particle phenomena in the psyche, need not be presumed to originate from innate death instinct energy or from innate aggression, although there is more evidence to indicate that innate aggression does exist, as seen in the theory and clinical work of Winnicott, and in the predispositions to certain forms of innate psychic fantasy, as proposed by Ogden (1986). Nevertheless, I am proposing that when innate aggression, or, alternatively, aggression from primal frustration, disrupts the psyche (as it does in character disorder personalities), then primal developmental trauma occurs. This primal trauma then enacts a continuous rupture of the psyche through mental dissociation, based on a pathologically pervasive form of splitting, and it manifests in the dynamics of the Kleinian paranoid–schizoid position. This developmental trauma has been spoken of by Masterson (1976, 1981, 1985, 2000), following the work of Balint (1965, 1979) on the "basic fault", and Fairbairn (1952) on the parental "bad object". Primal trauma is the trauma in the first three years of life, prior to the integration and consolidation of an adequate self-structure. Such primal trauma disrupts the development of a "secure base" in the core self-structure (Fonagy, Gergely, Jurist, & Target, 2000).

Mahler's (1967, 1971, 1979) linear view of developmental stages indicates that character pathology originates during critical stages of separation–individuation, resulting in the kind of psychological phenomena which Klein outlines in her view of the paranoid–schizoid position and its pre-symbolic mode of enactment. The schizoid personality often suffers the critical primal trauma during the "differentiation" period of separation–individuation. Critical breakdowns in maternal responsiveness often occur in the rapprochement period of separation–individuation for the narcissist and for the borderline, with narcissists regressing back to the practising period to defend themselves with the fantasy of self-sufficiency. However, the paranoid fantasies can only be symbolically defined when one has entered the depressive position. One also encounters regression from depressive fears and fantasies to the paranoid or paranoid–schizoid position. (The schizoid aspect of the paranoid–schizoid position refers to the splitting off of the pre-oedipal aspects of the self, and the affective sealing off of the internal world within these split-off parts.) Once Klein's metapsychological theory of the "death instinct" is surrendered, the Klein–Winnicott dialectic outlined in this book can be seen to operate within all clinical experience on the basis of early developmental phenomena. The internal world of psychic fantasy and the transitional world of internalisation interact.

The *second theoretical misconception* which has haunted the world of psychoanalysis since its embrace of British object relations theory is that offered by Kohut (1977) in his second work, *The Restoration of the Self*. Kohut's developmental theory is severely flawed despite his contribution to the field in defining three forms of narcissistic transference (see Kohut, 1971). His three forms of narcissistic transference can be seen in character pathology. They are distinct from the neurotic forms of whole object transferences that employ symbolic representations of the internalised parent. Aside from this theory of narcissistic transference, Kohut's theory presents problems. Kohut (1971) proposes that when the early mother is psychologically inadequate to promote an object-related development of the self, a more benign or healthy father figure can create an adequate compensatory internalisation. This view has already been challenged by Masterson (1981), who has explicitly stated that the early trauma with the mother must be dealt with in object relations psychotherapy in order to resolve the character disorder pathology, despite any more adequate input from the father or from other later relationships. Such compensation for early mothering cannot be accomplished sufficiently to avoid developmental arrest, even with the "maternal father", a term coined by Masterson (personal communication, 1995). I applaud this countering of what seems like a naïve assumption on Kohut's part. I agree with

Masterson's thinking. I have become acutely aware as a clinician of how defensively the father can be used as an idealised object when the primal mother disturbance is not dealt with (see Kavaler-Adler, 1985, 1986, 1988, 1989, 1993a[2012] on the "demon-lover complex" phenomenon). In fact, the father can never be experienced as an adequate transitional object, let alone as an adequate oedipal object, when pre-oedipal trauma disrupts self-development (see Balint's *Basic Fault*, 1979), resulting in an ongoing disruption of later relatedness and its mode of internalisation.

The assumption that the father who is engaged with the child from the pre-oedipal era or/and also engaged during the oedipal era can adequately compensate for critical developmental failures in mothering during the primal first three years of life (which includes the critical separation–individuation era that is so infamously disrupted and distorted in the character disorders) has encouraged followers of Kohut to propose a rather limited form of treatment for those they define as "self disorders". They also generalise the category of "self disorder" to everyone, even though Kohut (1971) originally distinguished the "self" disorder from the neurotic (oedipal level) patient. Kohut also confused narcissistic and borderline character disorders, calling them both "self disorders", and assuming that borderline patients were borderline psychotic if they were not treatable in the same manner as the narcissist. Dismissing borderline patients as close to psychotic allowed Kohut to avoid knowledge of how borderlines need a totally different form of treatment than narcissistic characters. Kohutian view lacked critical differentiation in clinical approaches to character disorders when he lumped narcissistic character disorders and borderline character disorders together as "self disorders".

Given all this, followers of Kohut can be naïvely led to believe that a compensatory form of internalisation in treatment is adequate through therapeutic mirroring and empathy to cure character disorders. They can naïvely believe that treatment can cure without the tremendous grieving process, which I have called "developmental mourning". This "developmental mourning process" (Kavaler-Adler, 1985–2012) has repeatedly been shown through clinical case examples to deal with the primal trauma promoted by the mother. To believe that in character disorders, in particular, the mourning of "abandonment depression" (Masterson, 1976, 1981) can be bypassed because of the compensating input of the father is a faulty theoretical assumption that severely undermines clinical work. This is particularly true with those character disorders that have suffered pre-oedipal trauma with the consequent dissociation of a whole area of the self that is tied in with the "bad object" constellation.

As did Masterson (1976, 1981, 1985, 2000), Kernberg (1975, 1980) has notably countered Kohut's (1968, 1971, 1977) view when he spoke about how necessary it is to engage the primitive defensive processes of the character disorder conditions, which stem back to the psychic input of disturbed mothers. He explicitly stated that it is always necessary for the narcissistic character patient to suffer the breakdown of the "grandiose self", which is defensive and rigidly contrived, and pathological in nature, stemming from the paranoid mother, who must be defended against. Kohut (1977), on the other hand, naïvely speaks of the "grandiose self" as though it is a natural early omnipotent state, one that might be compared to the child's self-sufficiency during Mahler's (1979) "practicing stage", which precedes rapprochement in the developmental era of separation–individuation.

In contrast to this, Kernberg (1975, 1980) is very clear that the "grandiose self" in the narcissist is not just the persistence of natural childhood grandiosity. He is clear that the "grandiose self" is a rather rigidly contrived psychic structure, one which wards off the pain of the early object loss, and early object lack, in the face of a cold, detached, or actively paranoid and attacking mother. Given this rigid character pathology, as well as the severe character pathology of the narcissistic, borderline, or schizoid personalities, compensation by better mothering through the childhood father, or through a therapist later on, is far from sufficient to resolve the traumatic disturbance of the character disorder. In fact, it can result in better functioning personalities who sabotage interpersonal enjoyment and intimacy with compulsions to control others.

I believe, as do James Masterson and Otto Kernberg, that the original trauma must be opened up. Further, the dissociated area of trauma in the psyche must come forth in ego consciousness through painful affect states, which include primitive rage, and which can eventually evolve into the profound mourning of object loss. This mourning, which I call "developmental mourning", is for the absence of the love needed in childhood, the love that failed to be responsively offered during the first three years of life.

Mourning, which is needed for a healthy object relations development and internalisation, involves grieving the internal "bad object" situation. This situation must be experienced within the "developmental mourning process", rather than be repeatedly acted out. Only in this way can such a traumatic "bad object" situation be symbolically defined, so that separation from the bad object relationships takes place (the "bad object" situation perpetuates dissociation of the self through perpetual splitting). Only by symbolically defining the bad object situation—and, when possible, linking it with memories—can understanding of the trauma in conscious representational form be achieved. Then the patient can develop the capacity for self-reflection through the mourning process experienced with the presence and witnessing of the analyst in treatment.

The result of Kohut's naïve assumption that the father or therapist can compensate for the lack of good mothering in the primal years (without the breakdown of the defensive grandiose self in the narcissist, without resolving defensive splitting of the borderline, without resolving the defensive sealing-off of the schizoid) is that his theory produces better functioning narcissists. The better functioning narcissist develops ego capacities to better, in the words of the Kohutians, "get their self-object needs met" in the world as an adult. This view that someone can leave treatment as if cured when they still turn to others to support their self system from the outside by narcissistic mirroring and other forms of self-object responses is evidence of the shortcoming of the Kohutian approach. Although certain ego functions can be improved by new internalisations without reaching the area of core developmental trauma that has caused a character disorder at the time of primal mothering, the pathological defensive operations continue. Then the patient leaves treatment still looking for external self-objects. Such a patient cannot independently receive the self-regard, self-esteem, and general sense of being loved and worthwhile from the inside of him/herself, since the core self area has not been opened to new connections in the world. To open to new and healthier modes of connection, one must endure the mournful suffering of the pain of the primal trauma.

It seems to me that Kohut (1968, 1971, 1977) rationalised his misconception by proclaiming that there are two lines of psychological development, rather than one. He proposed that there is a narcissistic line of development that is independent from the object relations line of development, as the "self" evolves in childhood. This theoretical rationalisation for his original premise about the father or other compensating for the primal mothering has caused significant confusion in the world of psychoanalysis, especially in those attempting to grapple with the treatment of character disorders. By proposing that there is a narcissistic line of development apart from the input of object relations through internalisation, Kohut (1977) denies that the early problems in internalising the other as an adequate (full and not split) object is totally determinant of the health or pathology of psychological human being.

Consequently, when his followers attempt to treat "self disorders" without opening up the primal trauma and allowing the breakdown of the primal grandiose defence structure, they can declare their work is done if they build new and superficial internalisations. They can deny that these new and superficial internalisations will be used defensively by the person to ward off the primal trauma. Although these new internalisations might promote ego functioning which is in the service of appealing to external others for self-object response (like the narcissist's audience), the ability to perceive others in depth or to sustain true intimate relations will continue to be severely compromised. (Creativity too, will lack a depth and integration, as was shown in *The Compulsion to Create* (Kavaler-Adler, 1993a[2013]) and in *The Creative Mystique* (Kavaler-Adler, 1996[2013]).) Kohutians can say, then, that these people are developing along narcissistic lines, if not in object relations lines (and not in the external interpersonal relations, which stem from internalised object relations). This will be done at the expense of these "better narcissists" lacking in-depth human empathy or in-depth compassion for themselves; lacking a sustained internal dialogue with themselves, a dialogue which would allow them to engage with the spontaneous affect states of the true self. This will be done at the expense of these "better narcissists" lacking a fluid psychic dialectical flow between self-experience and attuned awareness of the other (Bach, 2005). These "better narcissists" would leave the "accomplished" treatment when still lacking the necessary intuitive input required for them to operate and make decisions on their own. That is what Kohut's (1977) theorising would imply, despite his contribution to understanding the narcissistic transferences and the nature of empathy.

Furthermore, the "better narcissist" that might evolve from Kohut's form of treatment does not have an expanded or expanding psychic space. Since such patients cannot allow sufficient transitional space between themselves and others, they lack reflective thinking within the self, and, furthermore, cannot engage with others without trying omnipotently to control all interpersonal transactions.

Psychobiographical, phenomenological, and clinical perspectives to counter the misconceptions

To counter these theoretical misconceptions, and to offer an integrative developmental theory, I present the following studies of Melanie Klein and D. W. Winnicott from three perspectives: the psychobiographical (a form of study extending back to Freud as written about by Coltrera, 1981), the phenomenological, and the clinical. Throughout these studies, I draw on the dialectical relationship between Klein's and Winnicott's theoretical perspectives. Similar to the ideographic growth of psychic dialectic within the individual, I picture an evolving theoretical dialectic for the larger group of practising psychoanalytic clinicians. I am naming this broader based theoretical dialectic *The Klein–Winnicott Dialectic*. In this volume, I shall define both the theoretical rationales and the clinical applications of this Klein–Winnicott dialectic. I believe that a theoretical playground (in the tradition of Winnicott's concept of play) based on Klein–Winnicott dialectic, can provide a great deal for the clinical treatment of our patients, and particularly for those with early developmental arrests (see Stolorow & Lachmann, 1980, on *The Psychoanalysis of Developmental Arrests*, as well as the work of Heinz Kohut, James Masterson, Sheldon Bach, Thomas Ogden, Jeffrey Seinfeld, and Althea Horner). This integrative theory combines Winnicott's ideas on transitional space and the internalisation of the other, with the ideas of Klein on the developmental movement to self-integration through the mourning process of the depressive position (extended in my theory of "developmental mourning", Kavaler-Adler 1985–2013).

In addition, the Klein–Winnicott dialectic includes Klein's ideas on reaching a level of symbolic interpretations related to the projected internal fantasy world which harbours the experiences of both the paranoid and the depressive positions. As the early traumas are experienced through memory, as well as through the transference, they are defined as symbolic fantasies rather than continuing to operate as provoked enactments (through projective identification). Real progress can be made towards a core self-integration, which involves a fluid interpersonal dialectic beginning to operate between separation from others and connection with others. This dialectic transmutes any former polarisation around separation–individuation and self–other connection. This clinical work takes time, but the evolution of the human life can be quite clearly seen.

The last part of this volume illustrates how a major perspective on the whole human developmental journey can be seen in relation to Winnicott's views on transitional space. By offering biographical and clinical examples that contrast the biographical foreclosure of transitional space *vs.* the opening of transitional space, I hope to translate to you, the reader, the overall gestalt related to my theoretical commentary. Let the dimension of transitional space serve as a hologram for all the other dimensions of human growth spoken of in this text.

*To my husband, Saul, who has been an extremely loving and
supportive partner through over thirty years together,*

*To my father, for his generous applause of all my creative potentials
and efforts, who sadly passed away when I was only ten.*

*To my mother, who always supported my education
and creative adventures.*

*To my friend and colleage, Dr Inna Rozentsvit,
who has made this volume possible.*

To all my psychoanalytic students, who always inspired me.

*To all my objective relations psychoanalytic patients and
analysands, who continuously inspire me.*

CHAPTER ONE

Melanie Klein, like Moses on the way to the Promised Land: a case of pathological mourning

The Bible records Moses as having led the Israelites through the desert for forty years. Moses is reported as having spoken to G-d on Mt. Sinai, and as having vented his retaliatory rage at his people, on the night when he encountered their sin (in the episode with the golden calf). The Bible also reports how Moses paid dearly for his retaliatory rage. Moses' own precious vision for the Jewish people would never be completely his. According to the Bible and its myth, Moses would spend the time of a generation in the desert. He would watch the children of his flock grow to adulthood. Only in old age would Moses view the holy land that he himself could never enter, due to the impulsive rage attack upon others. Consequently, Moses' vision was both his greatest gift and his greatest curse, for Moses could foresee what he himself could not participate in. He would stay behind, while the second generation of Israelites, the children of those he had parted the Red Sea for and had entered the desert with, entered the land of Israel.

I believe that one of the greatest ironies in the history of psychoanalytic theory is its biographical analogy to this biblical account and myth. It is the story and legend of Melanie Klein, who, I believe, similar to Moses, foresaw the vivid outlines of a promised land, a psychic land, which she herself could not enter or could enter only to a minor degree. It is the land of the fruits and honey born through the journey of the depressive position, a journey that entails an in-depth developmental mourning process. Klein was the first psycho-analytic theorist to believe in the necessity to mourn in order for psychic development to continue throughout life. She believed in mourning as a critical clinical and developmental process, and a way of processing all object losses, not just those related to bereavement. Wherever there is a psychic gain, wherever there is a choice in life, there is a psychic loss as well. Klein began to envision this as she spoke of the early loss of weaning from the breast (Klein, 1975). We speak today of the loss of the concrete object in favour of the gain of the symbolic internal object in the process of developmental separa-tion–individuation.

Klein (1975) revealed her new thinking about mourning in her classic paper, "Mourning and its relation to manic-depressive states", published in 1940. Yet, my reading of Grosskurth's (1986) scholarly biography on this woman–theorist has given me the impression that Klein was psychically arrested in a pathological mourning state (stemming from her early pre-oedipal childhood), which preven-ted her from going beyond the initial stages of her own mourning process.

I propose that like many of the women writers and artists whom I have studied and written about (Kavaler-Adler, 1993a), Klein could not succeed in reversing her own blocked mourning process. She, like many highly creative women, attempted to face her internal life on her own, despite her brief periods of psychoanalytic treatment with Sandor Ferenczi and Karl Abraham when she was in her thirties. By the time Melanie Klein discovered the critical significance of mourn-ing, she was a leading figure in the British Psychoanalytic Society in London. She conducted many training analyses for up and coming analysts such as Susan Isaacs, Paula Heimann, Wilfred Bion, Joan Riviere, and John Bowlby. She supervised, taught seminars, and treated adults in psychoanalysis, and children—from the perspective of her original form of play therapy. According to Grosskurth's (1986) biographical studies, Klein faced negative transference rage in her treatment with Abraham, and might have begun a necessary grieving process at that time as well. Apparently, she was capable of being conscious of aggression with Abraham that she never encountered with the more idealised Ferenczi, with whom she had entered psycho-analytic treatment when she was young and just divorcing her husband. Yet, it seems that after her two early psychoanalytic experiences, Klein never paused to return to analysis for herself. This appears to be true despite her belief that countertransference was something an analyst returned to treatment to face. In fact, she never viewed countertransference as something conscious that could be used in treatment, as Heimann (1950), her own analysand, began to suggest.

Nevertheless, Klein was forced to pause and reflect on the overwhelming necessity to face the rage and hunger behind her grief at the point when her elder son, Hans, died in an accident in the mountains when he was an adult. She not only paused, but, during this time, she developed a whole theory of the developmental necessity to mourn, which she then related to her earlier phenomenological theory on the paranoid–schizoid and the depressive positions. She was the first to speak about unconscious aggression as a block to feeling loss, and, thus, as a block to feeling grief, regret, renewed longing, and the refined symbolic memories of a lost primal love.

With all this, however, Klein could only go so far in her own personal mourning process. Based on Klein's (1975) description of her own mourning process (see Case of Miss A in "Mourning and its relation to manic-depressive states"), and on the biographical research of Grosskurth (1986), I concluded that Klein's tenacious clinging to the metapsychology of her own version of the "death instinct" can be seen as a symptom of her own arrest in a state of pathological mourning. Although in my earlier works I have cited contributions by Segal (1964, 1986) and other biographers of Klein, in this study I have drawn particularly on Klein's biographical research done by Grosskurth (1986), because she is the only biographer of Klein who had access to the letters of Klein's mother, Libussa Reizes. I will try to demonstrate why Klein clung to her "death instinct" metapsychology. I believe that she needed that in order to psychically cling to her mother. The subject of the death instinct was one Klein touched on, relinquished to some degree, and then returned to. I believe that her resistance to giving it up is, in itself, a diagnostic sign of Klein's poignant and evocative pathological mourning state. Grosskurth (1986) helps her readers imagine the maternal and fraternal relationships that contributed to this state of mind in Klein.

The death of the narcissistic mother

Relying on the letters of Klein's mother, Libussa, Grosskurth (1986) portrays a vivid view of her mother. Grosskurth's view might be one that Klein herself needed to deny, in loyalty to her mother, and it generated a great deal of controversy among Klein's followers. However, Grosskurth's view is based on historical and biographical data, which had never before been available. Her view also seems to have an internal consistency, particularly when one combines knowledge of the narcissistic character with the research data and some rather astute biographer's interpretations.

As Grosskurth (1986) points out, when, in 1937, Klein writes "Love, guilt and reparation", she speaks of coming to terms with the hate, rage, guilt, love, and reparative needs for forgiveness that each individual feels in relation to their most primal parent, their mother. In this paper, Klein discusses the difficult and, ultimately, meaningful psychological work necessary to come to terms with psychic truth within one's own internal world, and within developmental process of self and psychic integration (in the depressive position) (Klein, 1975). Nevertheless, Grosskurth must ask, in allegiance to biographical truth, to what degree did Klein do this work in relation to her own mother, and in relation to the massive impact her mother had on Klein's internal world? Asking the question opens a can of worms, for here lies the great contradiction in Kleinian theory and Klein's own personal thoughts. Klein's conscious report of her mother is one too beautiful to reflect the woman whom Grosskurth (1986) discovered in the mother's letters to her daughter. Grosskurth, therefore, declares that Klein held an idealised view of a daughter in relation to her mother. The term idealisation takes on quite a valence when it is put in the context of this daughter's own ground-breaking psychoanalytic theory. Whenever Klein herself spoke of idealisation, she spoke of its defensive function; she spoke of it as of psychic mechanism employed unconsciously to ward off rage towards a love object that arouses (unbeknown to the conscious mind) the deepest paranoid terrors.

Grosskurth (1986) tells us that Klein cried in secret when she discovered that her mother had cancer. This is the mother who had been living with her not only in childhood, but also throughout Klein's entire life. This is the mother who took over her household, even though Melanie was married and had three children of her own, the mother who suggested that Melanie leave home for lengthy periods to visit health spas, to soothe her "overwrought nerves". Libussa most certainly would have rejected the notion that her daughter's "nerves" could have arisen from an internalised anger she herself had caused. And what would Libussa have said if anyone had suggested that Melanie's anger was proportionate to that of a repressed childhood rage arising from the unspoken despair of a young woman who unconsciously believed that she would never find any form of fulfilment? Could Libussa Reizes ever have understood that the tension in her daughter, which she had called "nerves", was actually a symptomatic reaction to Melanie's lack of conscious concern and grieving for her own potential competence? Could Libussa ever have grasped that by religiously and narcissistically imposing a regime of pampered invalidism, she effectively opposed her daughter's potential competence, which was nearly cut off all together? Or ever acknowledged how convenient it felt to have Melanie take an extended leave, while she herself remained in Melanie's home to dominate her daughter's husband and children?

Melanie periodically returned home from the health spas. She even separated from her mother for some time, through the strength of her friendship with her female friend, Klara. She might even have begun to fight back against her martyred, efficient, and guilt-provoking mother when allied with Klara. Nevertheless, prior to any psychoanalytic treatment, Klein seemed to believe that she could not survive without her mother. From Grosskurth's (1986) biographical report, Klein seems to have experienced her mother's death, when it came, as a trauma, not just as a loss. I would suggest that the loss was so traumatic because Klein had never adequately separated from her mother in childhood, had never had tolerable degrees of loss in a separation process with an emotionally available mother. Klein seems to have reacted to the trauma of her mother's death with an idealising defence, denying who her mother had truly been to her. According to Grosskurth (1986), Klein never stood up to her mother, a woman who had competed with Melanie for her brother's affections and, later, positioned herself between Klein and her husband. Denial brings its own form of obsession, and it seems that for Klein the artful ways of the construction of her mother's memorial (in her own mind) were attempts at creating psychoanalytic theory. Through her psychoanalytic writings, Klein found a powerful vehicle for the articulation of her prolonged attachment to her mother. It could be that Klein constructed a mother in her mind in the intellectualised form of theoretical beliefs, which she would never decisively deconstruct, especially since her brief psychoanalytic experiences did not allow her any kind of full mourning and grieving process.

Klein eulogised her mother in her writings by reporting a scene at her mother's deathbed, a scene that Grosskurth (1986) finds hard to accept as factual. Melanie asks for her mother's forgiveness. Her mother replies that Melanie has at least as much to forgive her for as to be forgiven for. Klein writes of her mother's benign generosity at this time. She reports her mother's resignation to her approaching death, to have spoken well of all, with not a criticism in sight. No wonder Grosskurth harbours doubts about the veracity of this report. The report could have been symptomatic of Klein's unconscious guilt about repressed rage and accusation towards her mother, for Libussa's nature (as shown in her letters) was the one prone to hostile criticism and an attitude of contempt (Grosskurth, 1986). Did Libussa relinquish such an attitude during the last days of her life, or was her daughter exaggerating so as to preserve her mother's image? Ironically, Grosskurth (1986) reports that Klein avoided all her feelings towards her mother at the time she wrote this death scene, as she was turning abruptly, with a manic twist, away from her depressive concerns. She turned towards the condemnations of her older sister, Emilie, whom Melanie had always envied for receiving her father's affections, while such affections were denied to her. Emilie seems to have served as the displacement figure for all the split-off rage and aggression Melanie felt towards her mother, which helped her maintain her defensive idealisation of her mother.

Consequently, when writing of her mother's benign tranquillity as she lay dying, Klein simultaneously berated her sister's way of handling the situation, and maintained that her mother's attitude of benign regard for Emilie was superior to that of her sister. Klein assumed that her mother had considerable reason to resent her sister Emilie. Ironically, however, it was Libussa who had been totally unfair to Emilie in the past, actually condemning Emilie, based on rumours her husband was spreading about her. According to Grosskurth (1986), Klein could not acknowledge any of this. In her eyes, her mother wore the white hat, and her sister the black. Melanie certainly did not move beyond the splitting of paranoid position here. If Grosskurth is correct, Klein twisted the truth in these late life accounts, just as Libussa had done so often in her letters: for example, when Libussa sought financial support from Arthur Klein, Melanie's husband.

The roots and dynamics of pathological mourning

Pathological mourning is preserved by the compulsion to idealise. However, it begins with an overwhelming or traumatic object loss. Also, it can be preserved and exacerbated by the continual assaults of narcissistic injury. The children of narcissistic parents feel such narcissistic injury most predominantly. In Klein's life, we can see patterns of defensive idealisation stemming from long before her mother's death. From these later patterns, we could speculate about disruptions at the critical developmental stage of separation–individuation (as defined by Mahler, 1967, 1971, 1979), in Klein's early pre-oedipal–toddler life, and related to her mother's ongoing attacks on Melanie's libidinal development.

What would Klein's mother have been like during the critical separation–individuation phases of development, as described by both Mahler (1979) and Masterson (1976, 1981, 1985, 2000)? Given Grosskurth's (1986) description of Klein's mother, taken from Libussa's own letters, I suspect that Libussa would have failed to facilitate Klein's early development in much the same way that most parents with narcissistic character disorder fail in that task. How available would Libussa have been for emotional refuelling once her toddler daughter, in her practising stage, set off on her own to find a world outside her mother? It is questionable. Would Melanie's mother, being busy running a shop in her home, have held her daughter when she returned to "home base"? In terms of the distinction between emotional holding and mere physical holding, as described by Winnicott (1986), did Libussa provide Melanie with an emotional holding and connection? Grosskurth (1986) states that Klein did hug her third child, Eric, who was not as dominated by his grandmother's usurpation of the mothering role as his older siblings, Melitta and Hans. But, even in relation to Eric, Klein acted more as a psychotherapist rather than a mother (Grosskurth, 1986). Would this kind of mothering by Melanie Klein not reveal the nature of her own mother's mothering with her?

When Melanie "checked back" to her mother during the practising period, or came over to her for refuelling, was Libussa responsive to her in terms of her daughter's central emotional needs, or was she only present in a perfunctory, merely physical way? Was Libussa more preoccupied with her own narcissistic concerns (possibly experiencing Melanie as abandoning her when she left her mother's orbit) and seeing Melanie as no longer a cuddly baby who wished primarily to be held and touched? Emotional abandonment during Libussa's own pre-oedipal toddler years would have left a profound mark on her capacity to be an adequate mother during this time. If Libussa was emotionally preoccupied somewhere else, would separation not begin to entail a primal loss for her daughter, Melanie? If so, such loss could significantly stamp Klein's later theories, particularly her theories concerning the traumatic pain of weaning (Klein, 1975). In fact, Klein speaks of separation–individuation in mere physical and instinctual terms, with the primal mother as the breast to be weaned from. In her writings, Klein focuses mainly on the primary act of weaning rather than the primal holding mother's capacity for symbiosis, or on the mother who could flexibly transform into a mother of separation as her infant turns into a toddler.

How could Klein's mother's emotional shortcomings during the practising period be exacerbated during the critical stages of rapprochement, when "communicative matching" of the mother with the toddler's developmental initiative is required (see Masterson, 1976, 1981, 1985)? How could someone like Libussa Reizes, who might have had her own narcissistic character disorder, have been able to connect with her daughter's rapprochement stage requirements? At rapprochement, the toddler experiences an internal developmental shift in his/her needs, from a practising stage thrust and desire to explore the world beyond the mother (often experienced as a "love affair with the world" — see Greenacre, 1957, p. 57; Mahler, 1971, p. 410) to a slightly disillusioned grandiosity, in which the need for the mother is once more powerfully felt. However, at rapprochement, the need is not experienced as a primal urge to emotionally merge with the mother and become one with her (as in the early infant holding and symbiotic periods), but as an urge to reconnect with mother as a separate being. During this period, the child wants to share his/her new-found and newly won experiences in the outer world (beyond mother's body and beyond the exclusive mother–infant orbit) with his/her mummy. This child brings to mummy things to show and share. He/she tells mummy things about his/her experience in this new stage of verbal expression, about what happened "out there". However, there can be a "rapprochement crisis" if mummy is not there to share with the child (Masterson, 1976, 1981, 1985, 2000). If this happens, the toddler feels the rapprochement as a damned-if-she-does-and-damned-if-she-doesn't dilemma between the developmental need to separate and the resurgent emotional need for mother's responsiveness. The toddler is sensitive to his/her mother's patholog-ical compulsion to have her child return to a cuddly symbiotic state with him/her (as with the borderline mother), or her mother's don't-bother-me rejection (as with the narcissistic mother). The child would then be compelled to identify with the mother's pathological or unavailable behaviour as a defence.

It is appropriate here to look into other examples of mothering that failed at the early stages of child's development. For example, in a biography of Virginia Woolf, Bond (1989) records Woolf's return to her mother at rapprochement only to find her mother totally preoccupied with her younger brother, Adrian. Bond (1989) thus illustrates how Woolf's mother failed to give her daughter the attention and emo-tional contact, as well as the mirroring and attunement, that Woolf craved and developmentally required. Bond (1989) traces the outlines of Woolf's pathology and mental illness from this critical develop-mental point, describing the critical trauma of developmental loss at this vitally important separation time, during which Woolf was robbed of a secure sense of self. She was only thirteen when she suffered the death of her mother. This radically compounded the earlier separation trauma, exacerbating a loss that could not be borne and subsequently led to psychotic symptoms. Compounding this situ-ation, Woolf suffered sexual abuse from her two half-brothers. De Salvo (1989), another Woolf biographer, describes the devastating imprint of this sexual abuse. Suicide attempts beginning after her mother's death and continuing until her successful suicidal act at the age of fifty-three marked the decline generated from the disrupted mothering during Woolf's separation stage. Given the suicidal impulse stemming from such a failing, it is possible that if Woolf had been a psychoanalyst, she might have also adhered (like Klein) to a belief in a "death instinct". Woolf's writing certainly exhibits the demon-lover theme (see Kavaler-Adler, 1996), a literary symptom frequently found in women writers, encased in a closed internal psychic symptom of pathological mourning rooted in the failures experienced in the separation stage. The demon-lover theme in the creative work of many of the women artists I have studied can be seen as a personified view of what Klein might have at first meant by the "death instinct". The death instinct can be the psychic pull of a split-off and eroticised aggressive component of the self (the undifferentiated mother-self) that is configured and enacted in the form of a split-off aggressive part of the psyche—as a demon lover. Klein at first spoke of such a split-off, hostile, aggressive energy projected into the mother, to avoid an implosion and explosion into annihilation of the delicate infant self. Klein herself had her own form of demon lover in her creative writing. This comparison of Virginia Woolf's and Melanie Klein's original thinking as a response to similar primal developmental trauma with a preoccupied mother is not so far-fetched.

How can a narcissistic mother respond to her toddler's need to have mother match the toddler's moves towards and away from her mother, both physically and emotionally? How can the narcissistic mother intuit any separate being's inner, true self, already present to a significant degree, so as to emotionally respond to that being, that is, her child? The mother's failure to do so is generally not related to free choice, but, rather, to the compulsive nature of her own character disorder. As Bach writes in his three books, *Narcissistic Phenomena and Therapeutic Process* (1985), *The Language of Perversion and the Language of Love* (1994), and *Getting From Here to There* (2005), those afflicted with the psychic structure of the narcissistic character are incapable of a psychic dialectic in which one can alternately focus on the experience of the other and on one's own feelings and reactions. The narcissist can either be totally preoccupied with his/her own concerns of the moment or can, in some cases, tune into the other at the expense of feeling in touch with his/her own self and own point of view. The narcissist experiences the other as an idealised extension of his/her self, and the effort of attuning one's self to that other as an investment. The narcissist then lives through the other for as long as the view of the idealised other can be maintained. However, when the other is a child in need of emotional attunement to the degree necessary for communicative matching during rapprochement, it is frequently impossible for the narcissistic parent to negotiate such attuned emotional matching, unless the child is the special star who shines forth as the idealised extension of the parent's own self. Such a parent generally responds very selectively to the child. The child's need for empathy in a separate emotional experience and a separate agenda from that of the parent's narcissistic agenda might be highly compromised and frustrated. This can be a traumatic experience for the child, especially if the mother has a rigid narcissistic character structure.

I suggest that this compromised response to the toddler's true self might be seen, from the perspective of Winnicott (1965), as the mother's failure to allow the omnipotent gesture of the child to at first predominate over her own. This might have well been the fate of Klein as a toddler, given her mother's personality that emerges from her letters to Melanie, as reported by Grosskurth (1986). Certainly, the behaviour of Melanie's mother during her adult years corroborates this. According to Grosskurth, Klein's mother treated her adult married daughter like a pampered child, granting her anything she wanted, but only as long as Melanie did everything according her mother's dictates, wishes, and agenda. At one point, Libussa required Klein to write a letter to her sister, Emilie, in the precise terms and language Libussa dictated, in which she condemns Emile—in the most contemptuous, self-righteous terms she can muster (i.e., manic)—for being an adulterer and a spendthrift. In actuality, Melanie's sister Emilie had been living in the most financially desperate and emotionally deprived state, constantly trying to economise, despite her husband's losses through compulsive gambling. Libussa Reizes' agenda also included plotting Melanie's trips away from home, using the pretext that Melanie needed to calm her nerves by relaxing in a hypothetical freedom from care at health spas. Libussa dictated when Melanie was to rendezvous with her husband, when she should separate from him, and how to address her letters home to herself, so that Libussa, and not Melanie's husband, would be privy to them. She directed Melanie to avoid all stimulation, as well—including the spiritual stimulation of piano music. She even wrote detailed instructions about what her daughter should wear (Grosskurth, 1986).

The perpetual self attack and the idealised mother

Klein's mother would not surrender her authority over her grown children. Libussa maintained the air of an all-knowing being in relation to her children. This is especially interesting in the light of Klein's theoretical emphasis on the resistance to taking in help in treatment by the analysand who maintains an air of omnipotence in the contemptuous and controlling attitude of the manic defence. Such manic defence, in Kleinian theory, is often interpreted as the patient's fantasied triumph over the transferential mother, whose knowledge is envied and, therefore, rejected. Spurning the knowledge of the all-knowing mother/analyst is a retaliatory strike, which will make the mother/analyst feel useless, as the patient hopes. This is all seen by Klein, particularly in "Envy and gratitude" (1957), as primal or oral envy, one most diagnostic, in Kernberg's (1975) view, of the narcissistic character disorder.

If Libussa was the original model for the parent envied as the source of all knowledge, Klein's theory would be seen to follow its psychodynamic course in terms of her own psyche in relation to that of her mother's. Furthermore, the psychic pressure upon Klein to preserve her mother's position of omnipotent knowledge would explain why Klein might have been unable to de-idealise her mother, and to come to terms with her mother as the highly complex, aggressive, and fallible human being that she actually was. If Klein, as her theory maintains, viewed her own transferential experience of aggression, she certainly could have seen that she was serving and preserving her mother's idealised image. She could have been serving the narcissism of her mother, who could not tolerate her children's normal developmental disillusionments with how they viewed their mother and how they constructed their internalised images of her.

In psychoanalysis and object relations clinical practice, we have come to appreciate the developmental necessity for tolerable disillusionments with the parents' projected image of omnipotence, and how these are necessary in order accept the disillusionment with our own omnipotence, or idealised self. The first theorist to inform us about this matter was Winnicott (1965, 1971b). Winnicott's critical view of development was further developed by Kohut (1971), particularly in his early work, *The Analysis of the Self*.

If I am correct, Klein's mother, Libussa, might be the typical narcissistic parent who cannot tolerate this de-idealisation and disillusionment process taking place in her children. When the disillusionment process is not allowed on a tolerable and (preferably) gradual basis, the child suffers traumatic and overwhelming disillusionment with both herself and others as a consequence. Much psychic truth must be evaded, in order to support the fiction of the parent as all-knowing and ideal. Then, the idealised object is used to fill the void created in the separation–individuation phases by the loss of necessary communication, contact, and object related connection (including mirroring) with the mother (see Winnicott's "Mirror role of mother and family in child development" in *Playing and Reality*, 1971b).

The idealised object is generally eroticised, particularly during the oedipal phase, in which eroticism emerges distinctly and profoundly. With pre-oedipal arrest and its pathological mourning state caused by a loss that is too traumatic to mourn, the child's turn towards the opposite sex parent in the oedipal stage will generally result in the two parents being merged into a combined idealised image (at least in one area of the psyche), and this idealised image will be eroticised. The dark side of both parents will be split off and the eroticised aspect will frequently be projected on to others, who become both muse and demon-lover figures (similar to Fairbairn's (1952) "exciting" and "rejecting" object). This process always has its critical turn from seductive tantalisation to that of an abusive and abandoning demon. Such a dark "shadow" (Jung) side of the personality can then be experienced as sucking one irresistibly and terrifyingly into a dark, death-like void, giving the personified air of an active instinctual death instinct, as Klein describes it. In contrast to Klein, Freud's (1920g) reduced concept of the death instinct was adjusted to the Hindu concept of reducing life's stimulation to zero and seeking an ego-less state of nirvana.

Filling the inner void with a fictitious idealised other, an all-knowing source of muse-like inspiration, is destined to result in the other eventually being perceived as a black and haunting demon. This is true for all, not just for the artist. In Fairbairn's (1952) words, this is the "bad object" held on to for its primary psychic connection. Also, as I state in describing the archetypical demon-lover figure in an object relations form, the demon lover arouses a sadomasochistic intensity (Kavaler-Adler, 1985–1989, 1992a,c, 1993a,b, 1995, 1998, 2000, 2003a, 2005b, 2009, 2010).

What form of internalisation produces the demon lover/bad object? All the consciously denied injuries and assaults of the narcissistic part of the parents come to constitute this negative internalisation. Fairbairn's (1952) concept of the "rejecting" object and its anti-libidinal alter ego (as an internal object created by the failings, intrusions, and abuses of the parent) is useful here. Alternatively, one might use Klein's (1974) own concept of the persecutory object, perceived as a one-dimensional and split-off form from the perspective of the paranoid–schizoid position. From the letters of her mother, as revealed by Grosskurth (1986), we can discern Klein's internal persecutory object, the haunting other, who lodges in her psychic structure, causing Klein's own impulses to initiate personified re-enactments against herself and against others, through her identification with the aggressor. Although Klein's conscious mind might have rejected all the memories of her mother's and her brother's envious and assaultative comments, she could not have escaped the unconscious impact of those comments. For example, Grosskurth reports Libussa's envious attack on Melanie when she and her husband are planning a vacation together in Italy. In Libussa's letters, she accuses her daughter of being "selfish" because Melanie did not think to invite her mother to accompany them to Genoa to see her father's grave (Grosskurth, 1986). To how many such assaults on her character was Melanie subjected on a daily basis? To be called selfish might seem mild compared to the kind of vicious and vindictive aspersions that Libussa cast upon the character of her daughter Emilie, whom she accused of a mercenary indulgence that put her family in jeopardy, and of an infidelity to her husband, with whom Libussa colluded in framing Emilie as her excommunicated enemy. "Let her toil," Libussa says, refusing Emilie financial help, while she splurges her son-in-law's money on Melanie's long health spa sojourns.

Surely, Melanie might at first glance be seen to have the better lot. Yet, what toll did Melanie pay when her mother's assaults on Emilie included having Melanie write a letter to her sister, proclaiming that Emilie's misdeeds had offended their mother, and that Emilie's amoral behaviour was keeping Melanie from seeing her sister? (Keep in mind that these supposed misdeeds were alleged by Emilie's husband.) Even more to the point, how much denial must Klein have had to employ to avoid seeing her mother's manipulative and self-serving behaviour in this instance, as well as in her mother's daily treatment of her children as self-objects or self-extensions? Inevitably, Klein's defensive idealisation of her mother and the effects of her mother's guilt-provoking narcissistic injuries and emotional blackmail would congeal together in her mind. This detrimental combination of denial, idealisation, and guilt, repressed within Klein's unconscious, could then be dissociated or split off into projections of personified persecutors that Klein later might have projected on to her own children. She might also have projected such feelings of persecution (internalised from her mother's behaviour) on to the students and analysts who expressed their less than flattering psychoanalytic views of the debates within the British Psychoanalytic Society, which would have been a closed system family re-enactment, indeed!

Libussa's treatment of her son, Emanuel, as well as Emanuel's treatment of Melanie, would also commingle in the dark, split-off side of Klein's mind. Emanuel's letters to Melanie are rife with envious comments on her prospective life with Arthur (Grosskurth, 1986). Suffering from terminal tuberculosis, Emanuel constantly compares his sister's life with the torment of his own, seeking to undermine her sense of security in her decision to marry Arthur. Although Emanuel first introduced the two, he warns her of the horrible fate she will encounter if she marries Arthur. Melanie, in her idealisation of her brother, later attributes his warnings to a depressive position level of empathic concern for her, given that she does meet with such disappointment when she marries. Grosskurth (1986), however, sees Emanuel's comments as coming from a more narcissistic position. He felt cut off from his own family, without any sense of security, having been sent off by Libussa to become a purposeless traveller for the rest of his life. Emanuel's envy, bitterness, and attitude of whining aggrievement can certainly be seen as symptomatic of his misery.

Libussa pretended her son was happy, having freely chosen to travel in Italy. Perhaps he idealised the Mediterranean, as he may have once idealised his mother. In his grandiose narcissistic pride, Emanuel saw himself as a world traveller, in the image of his hero, Lord Byron. Libussa took advantage of her son's romantic vision of the solo artist seeking inspiration in the Mediterranean atmosphere. Libussa, according to Grosskurth (1986), found it convenient for her son to be away, perpetually travelling. Emanuel's journeys may be seen as a reflection of his mother's own idealised image of herself as a great writer travelling the world. Nevertheless, in very practical terms, Emanuel's absences allowed Libussa to focus all her resources on marrying off her two daughters in a manner she considered beneficial and financially becoming.

In fact, although Libussa had doted on Emanuel when he was young and potentially brilliant, she makes short shrift of him when he does return home from his journeys. According to Grosskurth (1986), Libussa stuffs Emanuel with food when he returns, but neglects to offer any emotional reception (or holding). This probably reflects her overall manner of mothering. Libussa cooks and provides the perfunctory practical necessities of physical care, while failing to locate the emotional locus of her children's needs. The emotional deprivation and rage at being exiled from his family might have caused Emanuel to turn to drugs, alcohol, gambling, and prostitutes. These predilections could also explain Emanuel's active sadism towards any woman who became dependent on him, as attested to in his own writing, published posthumously by Melanie Klein.

I would conjecture, along the lines of Grosskurth's (1986) thinking, that Emanuel's vices probably resulted in his death occurring much earlier than it might have due to tuberculosis alone. Whatever the case might be, Grosskurth relates Libussa's reaction to Emanuel's death. Her narcissism is such that when her son's book is published, she seems more interested in Emanuel's artistic product, and in the fame she believes the publication and review of his work will bring, than she had ever shown in Emanuel's actual existence. In fact, Libussa's narcissistic character is revealed in one of her own letters. After reading the book, which she had prodded Melanie into publishing, Libussa (who was immune to the actual nature of the review) writes that her son's book had "silenced" all. Apparently, Libussa wished for the reflected glory Emanuel's worshipping audience might bestow on her. In her grandiose fantasy, Libussa took no note that the review was actually sceptical of the book's value and more critical of the author than not.

Libussa Reizes' attitudes and behaviours must have affected her daughter. Yet, Melanie Klein maintained her idealised image of her mother. In addition to Libussa's narcissism, she lacked any understanding of who her children actually were, or of the emotional injuries she inflicted on them. For Melanie, there was also the psychic exploitation she experienced as a projection screen for her mother's split-off, infant, inadequate self. From her childhood through the time of her marriage to Arthur Klein, Libussa Reizes cast her daughter in the role of an incompetent invalid, keeping Melanie ignorant of her own inherent strengths and talents. In addition, Libussa attacked whatever potential sources of pleasure Melanie might be attracted to, such as travelling, sex, motherhood, and playing the piano. When Melanie was pregnant with Melitta, Libussa asked Melanie to remove a painting of nymphs from her sight, presumably because sex must have been too upsetting for her eyes. She told Melanie to abstain from playing the piano. When Melanie cheerfully anticipated the pleasures of travelling with her husband, Libussa emotionally blackmailed her daughter into feeling guilty for not taking her mother with them.

Despite the dissociative mechanisms Klein employed to keep intact an idealised view of her mother, her mother's attitude and hostile messages affected her psyche. In her theoretical writings, she neglects the role of the parent in evoking a child's envy, as well as the parent's envy of the child. She focused exclusively on the envy of the child, characterising it as innate. Yet, Klein failed to see the spoiling envy of her own mother. Klein would later write of the child's envy spoiling the connection with the mother, and how the spoiling envy and damaged connection poisoned the child's internal world (Klein, 1957).

Fairbairn (1952) would later describe how the child blamed him- or herself to preserve the idealised innocence of the parent, a phenomenon that limns the unconscious defensive processes of Klein herself. Grosskurth's biographical research throws even greater light on how Klein's theories become a Rorschach of her need to protect her mother's image. As mentioned, in Klein's theory it is only the child who is seen as envying the mother, but there is no mention of how the internalised envy of the mother bears on the child's envy. Klein's theories also fail to acknowledge identification with the aggressor, a characterological defence prominent in the pathology of children raised by narcissistic mothers. Moreover, Klein's lifelong idealisation of her mother protected her from acknowledging how profoundly her thinking was influenced by the injury and object loss which were inflicted by her mother's emotional abuse and unavailability.

Despite the denial of her personal psychic situation, Klein intuitively understood the psychodynamics that drove her mother's behaviour. She spelled out her mother's defensive tactics in her theories, but assigned them to innate psychic fantasies in children. She even found the psychological significance of grief-stricken regret for the losses in love connections created by one's own aggression, provoked and exacerbated by the child's own innate unconscious hostility towards the mother. Certainly, the dependent position of the child can provoke intense frustration and trauma, leading to hostility towards the mother. However, the degree to which this dependent position becomes helpless (caused by the mother's character limitations in responding to the internal subjective world of the child and, thus, making dependency traumatic) is never fully acknowledged in Klein's theories. Klein only begins to offer some acknowledgment of this position in her thinking regarding the parents' critical effect on the child of the parents', and particularly the mother's, acceptance of the child's reparation for his or her aggression towards the parent (see Klein's "Envy and gratitude", 1957).

The absent father and idealised brother

All that Melanie Klein was subjected to as the daughter of Libussa might have been counterbalanced if her father had been emotionally available and involved with her, but this was not the case. Klein's father was a dentist whose business was failing, and he left his wife Libussa almost exclusively in charge of the children and of the family finances. She needed to earn an income by her own hand due to her husband's failing fortunes. Libussa kept her shop and home together, so that she was the one who spent the most time at home with the children. Libussa worked hard, which her daughter respected. Her husband seems to have been a distant figure on Klein's horizon, and more so for Melanie perhaps than for her older siblings.

Dr Klein was a judgemental and argumentative father to his son, Emanuel, Melanie's older brother. Grosskurth (1986) writes of the frequent political and intellectual debates between father and son. Dr Klein's availability to Melanie's older sister, Emilie, was apparently more positive. According to Libussa, Emilie was her father's favourite and, according to Grosskurth (1986), Libussa did not hesitate to torture Melanie with this fact in order to win her over as an ally in the family melodrama. Even more sadistic than Libussa's revelation to Melanie of her father's preference for Emilie was Libussa's disclosure that Melanie was an unwanted child altogether—implying that Melanie's father and mother had both rejected her before she entered the world. Grosskurth (1986) speculates that communicating this information to Melanie was a self-serving and cunning tactic, which Libussa employed to keep Melanie from becoming an adversary in Libussa's underground competition for her son Emanuel's affection.

Grosskurth (1986) reveals the dark lines of envy and jealousy of the family dynamics encircling Melanie Klein. Does it not then stand to reason that Klein (1957) had written the most profound paper on envy in psychoanalysis, following Freud's (1905d) more limited view of penis envy? Yet, when all the evidence provided by Grosskurth (1986) is added up, the irony still remains: Klein (1957) located the source of envy inside the psyche of the child, never touching on the unconscious hungry child harbouring the adult parent, causing Melanie's parent (Libussa) to be so calculating in her rivalries with her own daughter.

Whatever the truth in Libussa's claim that Melanie was an unwanted child, it seems obvious that such injudicious confidences would have alienated Melanie from her father, rather than bringing her closer to him. Unfortunately, Melanie knew her father mainly through Libussa's portrayals of him; otherwise, he was a detached parent who avoided any form of intimate contact. Melanie's need to admire and idealise a father figure might have been displaced on to her brother, Emanuel. The lack of the father's role in Klein's later psychoanalytic theory, so criticised by her daughter, seems to reflect Klein's denial of her father's impact upon her.

While denying her father's effect on her life, Melanie gazed upon her older brother as a glorious figure. Emanuel had been his younger sister's tutor and his intellectual views were engraved in Melanie's mind. Emanuel's romantic idealisation of art, for example, led to Melanie's idealisation of artistic striving, no doubt influencing her choice of a male lover when her marriage began to degenerate. This idealisation is also reflected in Klein's choice of psychoanalysis as a *zeitgeist* all-consuming art form, in which her clinical work was a phenomenological prelude to her "artistic" creation of a psychoanalytical theory. Like her brother, Klein often sacrificed interpersonal commitments to her devotion to her work as an art form. Ironically, she would become the victim of this same mode of sacrifice when she entered a relationship with an artist.

Melanie's brother had fed his own narcissism with the idealised glory he saw reflected in her eyes. When she was young, Emanuel was her most intimate source of male companionship. Emanuel was both her teacher and the one she depended on for emotional support. Ultimately, however, he might have become her nemesis. Melanie probably repressed her reactions to her brother as he grew increasingly envious, manipulative, and guilt provoking in his interaction with her during his years of illness and exile. Emanuel's journeys abroad initiated a life of dissipation, deteriorating from disease and his own suicidal impulses, no doubt a compulsive, retaliatory response aimed at his mother, who ignored him and yet exploited his image as her genius son. Emanuel's retaliation seems to have affected his attitude towards his sister Melanie as well. His letters to his sister were full of reproach for her successes as well as her prospects. According to Grosskurth (1986), these letters were extremely guilt provoking. As Emanuel's envy of his sister grew, he tried to destroy whatever peace of mind she might have salvaged from life lived in the shadow of Libussa, as well as from her own unexamined self-doubts.

Ernest Jones

Perhaps in Klein's later life, when she arrived at the status of being the favourite theorist and clinician of Ernest Jones, who served as president of the British Psychoanalytic Society for quite an extended era, Melanie was repeating the favourable side of her relationship with her brother, and it may have compensated for lack of favour with her father. This was all the more important because Klein had never been able to compete successfully with Anna Freud for the affections of Anna's father, Sigmund Freud. Just as Melanie's sister Emilie had been her father's favourite, so Anna Freud was her father's favourite child, as well as Melanie Klein's rival in the British Society.

Throughout the reign of Ernest Jones at the British Psychoanalytic Society, he supported Klein's articulation of her theoretical views. Jones never forgot Klein's efforts on his children's behalf. Klein was invited to London to treat Jones' children, which she did with great art and skill as she communicated with them, conceiving their unconscious parental images. She helped them to differentiate their internal world's parents from their external parents. In fact, Klein might never have gone to England (let alone established herself professionally in London for the rest of her lifetime) if Jones had not sent for her to treat his children.

Although Jones spent many years writing a biography of Freud, he remained a loyal follower of Klein, adhering to her version of the death instinct rather than that of Freud (Grosskurth, 1986). In turn,

Klein reciprocated with the greatest respect and admiration for Jones. When he died, Klein was grief stricken, demonstrating one of her rare mourning reactions, in which true loss and sadness predominate over aggression and manic–narcissistic triumph. Klein's reverence for Jones sustained her. In her professional relationship with Jones, Klein proved that she could be loyal to those loyal to her (just as she was unendingly loyal to her mother and to her mother's image).

Perhaps Jones could be seen as the positive father that Klein never had in her childhood. He supported her consistently, truly laboured to understand her views, and when Anna Freud's group became a threat to Klein in the British Psychoanalytic Society, he apparently played a supportive and even, perhaps, a protective role. After his death, Klein's thinking lived on in his family—his wife went into treatment with a Kleinian analyst (Grosskurth, 1986).

Oedipal trauma rather than oedipal romance

Leonard (1982, 1984), a Jungian analyst, has written about a "father–daughter wound" that develops in the psyche of a daughter who has an inadequate, absent, or malevolent father. Perhaps this term "father–daughter wound" can be applied to Klein, particularly when the need for a receptive father during the oedipal stage is crucial. Given the general absence of emotional connection with her father, it is very likely that Melanie Klein felt profoundly rejected during her oedipal phase of development, perhaps traumatically so. The only evidence of this is her behaviour in relation to men. Her sadistic behaviour towards one young man in her youth who was quite infatuated with her reveals a telling behavioural pattern in her background. Grosskurth (1986) reports that this young gentleman, named Wilsky, had attended school with her. When he learnt of her betrothal to Arthur Klein, his anguish was intense and evident. What is most significant, however, is the way in which Klein informed Wilsky of her engagement to marry. According to Grosskurth (1986), she relished the opportunity to stab Wilsky in the heart with the news and to inflict even more pain on a man she had already hurt by rejecting him. Klein's later life pattern of identifying with the aggressor seems already to be in evidence here. The aggressor she was identifying with was presumably her mother, as Melanie used Libussa's tactics to overcome her own feelings of exclusion, which she suffered when the closed circle of her father and sister kept her isolated. Grosskurth (1986) is unequivocal about Klein's sadism. Klein enjoyed seeing the intense suffering in the eyes of the adoring male who yearned for her in vain.

Why should Klein have enjoyed Wilsky's suffering so much? The most likely explanation is that Wilsky represented her internal hurt child. It is highly probable that her first childhood romantic yearnings for love were played out with her father, and that she felt spurned by him. Did she look longingly into her father's eyes? Did she feel a deep hunger for recognition of her feminine and sexual self, and was ignored by her father? Did she look for that gleam of fascination in her father's eyes and only receive a cold stare or a distant look? It is reasonable to assume that the answer to these questions is "yes". Klein's theory explains the retaliatory impulse that compulsively commits acts of sadism, which then causes the grief-stricken emotions leading to frequent and desperate attempts at reparation. How could Klein not have felt retaliatory against a father who eluded or snubbed her? Yet, her power to retaliate became so great when she grew into an appealing young woman, one who could arouse the longing of a vulnerable young man, which might have served symbolically as a displacement figure for her father. In Freud's (1927e) terms, she could have turned passive fate into active retaliation against a male displacement figure for her father.

Prior to her analysis and eventual entrance into the world of analysis, Klein wrote a short story that captures the retaliatory reversal of roles with her father. In the story, she relinquishes the manic defence stance of control, contempt, and triumph that she directed at Wilsky. She lets herself feel the acute pain behind her sadistic behaviour with Wilsky that had been repressed. The pain of Klein's own frustrated longing emerges in this story. Klein apparently used the creative process for self-reparation, finding in writing a way to express herself much earlier than her theoretical and clinical work (Grosskurth, 1986). The pivotal scene in the story takes place when a young man confronts Melanie's alter ego character in the dark, bewitching hours of the night. He looks longingly towards her. She instinctively averts her eyes and rejects his visceral overture, but suffers an acute sense of grief and regret by turning away. Klein reveals in this scene that the story's protagonist had missed an opportunity that she had been longing for, an opportunity for a form of fulfilment that she could not name, but which she knew she lacked. She sees her own repressed yearning in the young man's eyes, the yearning Klein probably felt towards an emotionally distant father. Much projective and introjective identification can be seen in this scene, as in the real event with Wilsky. The main character feels deep regret, taking quite a step into the depressive position. This moment of regret stands in stark contrast to the actual moment with Wilsky, in which Klein gratifies her defensive sense of power over her longings for her father by projecting them on to Wilsky. This defensive interaction with Wilsky temporarily excluded Klein's own heart, just as it excluded her childhood despair from being felt. Later, Klein's defences would yield to true psychic regret (Klein's (1975) "true self"), and her theories would manifest this experience. She becomes capable of writing about the depressive position and the growth that this position offers in facing psychic reality by tolerating the anguish of psychic pain, especially in the pain of regret.

In Klein's short story, her alter ego protagonist suffers even when she is in a position of control. Perhaps Klein was freer to own her feelings when portraying herself as an adult in control, as opposed to when (as a child) she suffered in a position of helpless dependence on emotionally absent parents. Although her childhood suffering might have had to be repressed, Klein's artistic nature allowed her to own, in her writing, the internal pain of frustrated romantic longings.

The absence of the father in Klein's theories

Given such a critical absence of the father in Klein's life, it is not surprising that her psychoanalytic theories, influenced by the vivid vibrations of her internal life (despite the filtering of such vibration through her astute clinical experience and observation) minimised the impact of the father on the child and on the psyche. Ironically, it was not only Glover (1945), but Klein's own daughter as well, who challenged her omission of the father's role altogether in her theories. Despite that, Klein did acknowledge the father as a main player in psychic life in her adherence to Freud and her wish to be considered a Freudian. Dr Wolfgang Pappenheim, who presented a case in one of Klein's seminars, attests that his presentation was greeted with a standard Freudian oedipal explanation of the case by Klein herself. Nevertheless, when it came to her theoretical ideas, the father played a minimal role. It is interesting to speculate whether this is due to Klein's focus on early pre-oedipal issues only (which, in Klein's day, excluded the father as a significant player), or is also due to Klein's disappointing relationship with her father. Her father failed to give her the inspiration she would have needed in order to give the father more importance in her theory. In Klein's theory, the father exists in the child's mind only as a part-object appendage of the mother, first as a phallic symbol, and, later on, as a whole creature. In the child's mind, the father continues to live inside the mother's body. Consequently, when treating children in play therapy, Klein would interpret how the chimney on the house (or the furniture within) represented the father in relation to the primal mother as the secure and all-encompassing house.

Father and mother are also a combined figure in Kleinian theory during her early oedipal phases, which predate the oedipal era of Freud. Although Klein might have acknowledged that the combined mother–father does differentiate itself out into separate mother and father objects during the more mature Freudian oedipal stage, this was never the thrust of her theory. Generally, her clinical examples, as well as theoretical thoughts, collapse experience back downward from Freud's oedipal stage to an earlier oral stage, where triangular oedipal jealousy collapses downward into a dyadic oral envy for the primal (breast) mother. Such thinking is extremely useful in reference to pre-oedipally arrested patients, whom we today call borderline patients, but misses the mark of defining intrapsychic conflict in those of higher level neurotic structures. Although Klein might still insert Freud's theory in the latter case, it is also likely that she might collapse the differentiated conflict and differentiated parents downward into oral dynamics in many cases. Klein's prejudice for believing in the long-ings for the early mother as the centre of all (with father dynamics being a content screen for the mother dynamics) might well be due as much to her own internalised history as to any issues of differential diagnosis of pre-oedipal dynamics.

The muse/demon lover

After her mother died, Klein remained locked in a marriage to a man who seemed unable to understand either her yearnings for an empathic listener or her desires for a sexual partner. She was ready to demonise her husband in the form of a displacement for all the frustration and traumatic disappointment that she had suffered in her compliant and regressed position in relation to her mother. Grosskurth (1986) believed that Klein transferred all her repressed rage towards her mother on to the figure of Arthur Klein, her husband. Grosskurth emphatically maintains that Libussa did everything possible to undermine Melanie's relationship to Arthur. The biographer gives ample evidence to support her beliefs, describing the interference of Libussa in all communications between Melanie and her husband. Grosskurth writes of Libussa's wish to take over as the wife of Arthur's household, welcoming Melanie's absences when Libussa shuffled her off to health spas. A poignant example is when Libussa gives a dinner party for Arthur's employer. Grosskurth notes that during a period when Libussa was not present in the Klein home, Melanie and Arthur recovered from their respective hysterical and pseudo-somatic ailments. Remarkably, the couple availed themselves of this period of reprieve to enjoy walks together, during which time Melanie is quoted as declaring her relationship with her husband amiable. Nevertheless, when Libussa returned, Arthur and Melanie Klein regressed to their neurotic symptoms, non-communication, and isolation from each other. At this point, it seems that the damage was truly done. Any opportunity for Arthur and Melanie to get to know each other in an intimate or friendly way was permanently lost. Consequently, in an atmosphere that lacks intimacy and the sexuality that might thrive from intimacy, sex became a severe bone of contention between Melanie and Arthur. This easily allowed Melanie to displace her rage with her mother on to Arthur. Arthur might have even become the masculinised demon of all Melanie Klein's negative mother and father projections. He became her personal fantasy demon, the internal psychic demon lover (demonic in withholding sexual intimacy), which contains her own split-off eroticism infused with the aggression of her rage.

CHAPTER TWO

Melanie Klein's creative writing revealing themes in her life and theorising

Through Grosskurth's (1986) research, we can see in Klein's own creative writing (produced after her mother's death) that the psychic themes, which were just outlined, manifest in a symbolic form. Grosskurth's conjectures follow, as do my own. Having constructed a psychic demon, Melanie Klein was most particularly in need of a psychic muse, a figure upon which to cast her fantasy mother ideal in conjunction with her yearned fantasy father, someone who might finally offer her erotic gratification, as well as inspiration for her creative writing. Klein's stories show the inspiration for her creative writing; they show both her need and her search. They also portray the binding guilt that imprisons her. It is such guilt that (when kept unconscious) kept her externally imprisoned in a detached and failing marriage, as well as internally imprisoned within a closed internal psychic system. In this closed psychic system, one that can be described by Fairbairn's (1952) theory of an anti-libidinal ego system in which self-sabotaging identifications dominate the whole personality, Klein is haunted by her mother's disowned parts. When Klein does finally burst (rather than evolve) out of her shell, her voice emerges in poetry, following her earlier prose stories with their stream of consciousness orientation (at the time of James Joyce). The denouement forecast in her short stories results in the demon-lover complex (see Kavaler-Adler, 1985–2013) that manifests in both literary and life themes of seduction and abandonment. Such themes harken back to both unresolved oedipal disappointment and to pre-oedipal entrapment, the latter being related to a mother who perhaps could not connect with her unless Melanie served as her self-extension or self-object. Such a father–mother figure is now seen as a lover, at the end of the symbiotic/oedipal "affair", precluding a relationship of two individuated selves.

Klein's short stories were written during the period of her marriage which followed her mother's death. They preceded her divorce and entrance into the world of psychoanalysis. Each story that Grosskurth (1986) depicts is revealing. One story is of a woman lying in a hospital bed who is visited by a man. The implication is that the female character has attempted suicide and that her attempt has been related to her wish for understanding from this man, who is her visitor. Grosskurth (1986) conveys her belief that this female, as are all Klein's female characters, is an alter ego expression for Klein's own self. In this particular tale, Klein is writing of her despair and of her suicidal thoughts when feeling entrapped and unrelated to. An analogy can also be made between Klein's male character and her own husband. For at that point in her marriage, no longer focused on compliance or rebellion in relation to her mother, Klein is ensconced by her longings for empathy from her rather detached, defended, and often rigid husband. Her disappointment at not receiving such empathy obviously has reached a traumatic level. Such disappointment (observed through neurotic symptoms during the time of her marriage) emerged as an internal world drama, subjectively revealed in her short stories during the time of the marriage, which she later escaped from through her work as a child psychoanalyst.

Such traumatic disappointment must, however, be judged in terms of earlier disappointments, particularly those Klein might have experienced back in the separation–individuation period of her pre-oedipal childhood years, as well as in later periods of striving for separation. It must also be seen in relation to the disappointment in her husband's response to her as a sexual being and sexual woman, and his obvious incapacity to love her at a psychological depth in their intimate relations, which, of course, must have also combined with her own failings to receive him. Oedipal despair, rather than oedipal disillusionment, combined with a prior trauma in the very formation of a primary and integrated self (resulting in splitting and defensive idealisation), would have contributed to the adult despair Klein then suffered in her marriage.

In her short stories, Klein begins to suffer consciously, but with no witness or listener (and with no mother or analyst) who could help her transform despair into mourning. She had nobody to help her to symbolise the meaning behind her rage, felt early on as despair. There is no tertiary party (such as a father in relation to mother and infant) to open transitional space for Klein's mourning process. The term "transitional space" is derived from Winnicott (1971a) to describe the psychological space first provided by the necessary gap, or "area of creation" (Balint, 1979), which exists in the sphere between mother and infant, and which then is internalised as psychic space, also manifesting as "analytic space", in the psychoanalytic "holding environment" (Winnicott, 1971a, 1986. Also, see Guntrip, 1968; Modell, 1976; Seinfeld, 1993). Kenneth Wright (1991) has expanded Winnicott's concept of transitional space between a mother and a child to that between the father and the mother–child dyad, speaking about the critical role of the father as a third, in allowing separation through a visual perspective outside the dyad. This transitional space between the "third" and the original primal dyad allows for the development of symbolic capacities, because this area of vision is not foreclosed by the operations on a concrete level of touching and doing. The third perspective of the father allows for differentiated representational forms that have the whole object dimensions of three-dimensionality. This can be seen in the literary characters of a novelist such as Charlotte Brontë (see Kavaler-Adler, 1990, 1993a, 2000, 2013), who does not suffer from pre-oedipal trauma, and who, therefore, can incorporate the father in her advanced, oedipal level psyche as the transitional space facilitated by separateness from the differentiated oedipal stage father. By contrast, there is a multitude of literary examples of pre-oedipally traumatised poets and novelists who have flat, two-dimensional, characters in their work, as can be seen in the work of Emily Brontë, Emily Dickinson, Edith Sitwell, and others (Gerin, 1971; Glendinning, 1981; Kavaler-Adler, 1986, 1988, 1989, 1991a, 1992c,d, 1993b; Salter & Harper, 1956; Sewall, 1974; Wolff, 1986). This includes Anna O's creativity, whose work I describe in the *Creative Mystique: From Red Shoes Frenzy to Love and Creativity* (Kavaler-Adler, 1996).

When the demon-lover theme appears with the psychological conflicts of a demon-lover complex, these two- (not three-) dimensional characters and villain–victim dramas (split idealised and bad part objects) appear continually in the author's/artist's creative work.

As best as I can deduce from Grosskurth's (1986) description of Klein's creative writing, it seems to depict the kind of two-dimensional character dynamics, which reflect an absence of a significant third as a separate perspective. Klein's short stories reflect an absence of the perspective of a separate and differentiated oedipal father. Therefore, they lack the father's outside view, which can provide an objective empathy for a daughter who has successfully reached the oedipal stage (without defensive splitting being perpetuated from an arrested pre-oedipal era). What we see instead, in Klein's creative work, are characters that appear often flat and two-dimensional. This offers the evidence of defensive splitting, seen in the object relations symptom of the demon-lover complex syndrome. The demon-lover complex is a literary symptom of psychic developmental arrest (Kavaler-Adler, 1993a, 1996). Klein's work, just like that of many of the women writers and artists I have written about who suffered from developmental arrest, lacks the third dimension of psychic and artistic inspiration. It lacks the metaphors and the "three-ness" (rather than "two-ness") of signifier and signified, as they correspond to the subjective agent or protagonist. Consequently, as readers, we find missing in Klein's creative writing (and perhaps in her case studies, where psychic fantasy can be portrayed as two-dimensional) the transitional space, where observing ego perception and reflection can be in dialogue with the subjective perception of the experiencing part of the self. This omission, or failure of evolution to transitional space and whole object thinking, obviates a developmental mourning process, a psychic process that can integrate the self and its psyche (see Kavaler-Adler, 1993a, 1996). A child's despair, brought on by character pathology in parents, can cause potential three-ness in psychic perception to collapse down into two-ness, manifesting in polarised dichotomies, rather than in interactions that depend on psychic integration and its psychic dialectic. Klein's fictional alter ego, her wife figure, illustrates a foreshortened mode of psychic despair. This results in the female characters in her stories reflecting her own belief that personal despair can only be resolved by the male-other (masculinised mother, or mother–father as muse/demon) fulfilling the female characters' wishes. This belief could easily lead to marital divorce, which it did in the case of Klein. Given Klein's background, particularly in relation to her father and brother, how could Klein actually know what a true response from a male character could be, let alone what a reparative response could be, which might engage her at her depth and bring her to emotional life? How could she know if (having the mother and father that she had) she had not sufficiently received emotional responsiveness from either parent? Yet, how she must have yearned for it from both parents. How she must have despaired of ever receiving such a receptive response, a response that would have been an acknowledgement of her unique being and personality. Not having had such response from her childhood parents, it seems quite understandable that there are thoughts of suicide in Klein's creative writing, especially when her marriage began to repeat the psychological deprivations of her upbringing.

In the bind of the rapprochement stage toddler who has a mother who fails at combining relatedness and separateness, the despair is a double-edged dichotomy of non-feasible alternatives. There is a threat of psychic annihilation, when the mother cannot sustain psychic connection during the child's moves to autonomy, which is extremely compounded when there is no related father present (which there was not for Klein). There is a psychic suicide in complying with the mother's need for merger, which disrupts developmental growth with the mourning and separation processes that promote the individuated path of the self. To stay with mother in a regressive merger feels both suffocating and entrapping. This experience can later be externalised on to relations with a spouse. The rage of retaliatory impulse, so atavistic, but also biologically built into us as animal beings, is persistently triggered and exacerbated. The frustrated and hostile reactions can be turned towards others and against ourselves. In the fantasy of suicide, however, seen in thoughts expressed in writing, Klein turns her retaliatory rage reactions away from the cold husband–mother–father, and towards herself. Nevertheless, even within this change in psychic direction lives the impulse to kill the other because the mother and her displacement figures are expressed as killing the dependent one. When Anne Sexton committed suicide, she psychically struck out at her mother's child (see Kavaler-Adler, 1996), a retaliatory strike resulting in her own death as the impulse's direction is turned inward. Klein's female character's suicidal impulse strikes out at her husband, for the man in the story is proclaimed to react by suffering karmically for his former indifference. As author, she weighs her own scales of justice and writes out her own karmic punishment, having the husband in one tale dissipate in his own despair after she has left him through suicide. But his actual reaction is less important than Klein's impulse to do him in, to seek a retaliation that does not yet foresee reparation. On one psychic level, with the personification of impulses, the demon lover lives inside the woman. Frequently the demon lover in the woman's internal world (seen in poetry and prose) leads the woman on a circular and entrapped pseudo journey. He leads her from the inspiration of the symbiotic muse mother to the eroticised sadism and psychic abandonment (mother–father), following the disappointment of the iterated mother–child disruption. Finally, the demon lover, in literary form, leads the woman to the land of death (Kavaler-Adler, 1993a, 1996). In the land of death, which is seen so vividly as the void of pre-oedipal trauma in the poetry of Emily Dickinson (Kavaler-Adler, 1991a; 1993a), a woman marries or merges with her internal demon lover (portrayed in fantasy as a seducer and murderer), as would a man merge with his form of demon lover. Both Klein, as author, and her female characters give up on ever receiving the symbolic level of empathic response they yearn for from a truly external other. Since, in childhood, Klein did not have a parent who could provide a response of a separate and self-integrated other (just as in the case of Emily Dickinson and Anne Sexton), she was forced to settle for the internalisation of a two-dimensional part object male with no subjective capacities for empathy, and who enacts unending persecution and torture.

Another short story of Klein's from this era is that of a triangle of part objects, rather than three-dimensional figures with subjective lives and responsive feeling states. It clearly appears as a preoedipal triangle, reflective psychically of developmental arrest. There is no oedipal stage era triangle, in her writing. There are no whole object figures who can have ambivalent and often competitive relations with one another, but who can truly desire each other as well. Given the way Grosskurth (1986) describes it, it is reminiscent of some of the poetry of Edith Sitwell, which I have studied (Kavaler-Adler, 1993a). In this tale there are three characters: the female protagonist and two characters called Spring and Night. Klein's fictional characters, Spring and Night, seem analogous to her mother and husband. However, they can also be compared to her mother and father, portrayed as archetypal forms. In this tale, Night is an amiable companion during the day for the female protagonist, who turns aversive and hostile at night. Spring, who feigns being an ally and a friend, is found out to be colluding with Night to entrap, seduce, and ensnare Klein's protagonist alter ego.

My own speculations about the symbolism of this tale are fairly simple. I assume that in as much as Night is Melanie Klein's husband, his company during the day is bearable because it does not require a demand for sex and for pregnancy as well. However, like the demon-lover figure that only appears at night in the poetry of such female artists as Emily Brontë and Emily Dickinson, "Night" appears, in Klein's short tale, as a vampire-like creature that metamorphosises during the mystical dark hours of the night through his unwelcome sexual advances. Emily Dickinson (1960) writes of "Peeping in parlors shut by day" (see Kavaler-Adler, 1993a). Emily Brontë (1908) writes of the wanderer who comes from regions of snow, night, and darkness, arousing an intensity of longing in the poetic subject as "visions" which appear and disappear, luring her into "desire". Emily Brontë's (1908) poem, "Night wind", portrays the atmosphere of night (alluding to death), as the dark demon lover who perpetually seduces and rapes young innocent women, such as the poet and her alter ego poetic subject (see Kavaler-Adler, 1993a). This would make sense in light of Grosskurth's (1986) report that on her wedding night, Melanie Klein was "shocked" by the first impact of the sex act as one that brought her nothing pleasurable, but only "disgust", which was probably a somatic conversion of her rage into a passive and yet inwardly aversive form. Klein herself is reported as questioning about the reasons of motherhood beginning with "disgust" (Grosskurth, 1986). To compound the effect of this first sexual experience, Klein conceived at this time, impregnated by a sexual act she felt to be aversive. She delivered Melitta nine months later, so that nauseating sex and pregnancy (and perhaps motherhood as well) were perennially commingled in her mind.

Brought up with the romantic myth of men and marriage in the Victorian era, sex as a reality was traumatic for Klein. Arthur Klein might have known as little about sex as she did. Consequently, within their marriage, Klein experienced her husband's sexual approach as an intrusive assault. The sex act, and the husband who committed it, could manifest in Klein's internal psychic fantasy world as the kind of greedy and envious baby that she wrote about in her later seminal paper "Envy and gratitude" (Klein, 1957). In sex within marriage, Klein may have experienced her husband as failing to take her, as the woman, into account. His appetite could have been experienced as destructive hostility, indifference to all the woman's own subjective yearnings and wishes. The romantic myth for the Victorian woman was that love in marriage was to fill up the woman with the idealised phallic male's power. As Kaplan (1991) writes about the Victorian romantic myth, it promised the woman that her deepest childhood wishes and needs would be fulfilled by the fantasy of joining through sex with an idealised male figure, since, in this era of patriarchy, feminine power residing in women was neglected. In fact, the myth falsely promised women that all the deprivations of their childhood would be healed, totally ameliorated by the glorious male figure. Such hopes on the woman's part could only be dramatically disappointed, especially when the undeveloped child in the man manifested in sexual demands that voiced a child's hunger in an insatiable male body that turns hunger to greed. But this Victorian myth of marital sex and romance was a demon-lover myth, one in which the female projected on to the male figure all her longings for an omnipotent parent, who would endlessly nurture her and penetrate her at once, as a combined mother–father figure with god-like endurance and dimensions. No wonder that muse always turned into a demon, for with the disappointment of the romantic promise of an omnipotent parent, the sexual act could only result in feelings of being betrayed and abandoned for the woman. This was all the more true, however, for those with early pre-oedipal abandonment trauma with the original mother. We can only guess, from the later behaviour of Klein's mother, that Klein experienced this. As Kaplan (1991) writes in *Female Perversions*, sex in marriage was a mystical vehicle for the woman's ultimate fulfilment, an unexplained paradox born out of stereotyped gender dichotomies that never added up. Sex in marriage was also to be the woman's cross to bear, dictating that she restrain herself into a forced compliance, rather than opening to an alive receptivity (Kaplan, 1991). Klein's compliance was reactive to culture, which demanded that a married woman satisfy the male as a way of reinforcing marriage as a social institution. Melanie Klein was enlisted as an agent of social conservatism. Grosskurth's (1986) research showed that Klein was brought up to believe in the idealisation of men, which started with idealising her brother.

Once Melanie Klein experienced the first thrust of sex in her marriage to an inexperienced and naïve young man (similar to Virginia Woolf and Leonard Woolf), who was (culturally) taught that women were repelled by the sexual act according to their nature, any romantic myth that might have formerly sustained her was shattered. Klein was also forced then to dread further pregnancies. She came to fear any further journeys into motherhood that would even more firmly tie her to her husband. In fact, Grosskurth (1986) reports that Libussa used the threat of pregnancy to keep Melanie away from her own marital home. Libussa wrote to Melanie that she would be happier at the health spa than returning to her husband, since the latter could result in another pregnancy. From Libussa's own words, in her letters, Grosskurth (1986) assumed that Libussa was aware that possible pregnancy would be a deterrent for Melanie. Such a deterrent could keep Melanie at bay, helping to perpetuate her mother's control, which also allowed Libussa to maintain control over Arthur Klein's financial assets as she hatched her schemes to divide and conquer between her daughter and her husband. Grosskurth describes Libussa using Arthur's pregnancy-threatening penis against Melanie. It is likely that in Libussa's own phallic (and manic, in Klein's terms) mode of unconscious defence, she did indeed wish to use Arthur's penis, as a symbol of the male patriarchal power, as well as a symbol of sexual gratification, under her own control. This could account for Melanie writing a short story in which her mother, as "Spring", colluded against her as an ally of "Night", the husband with unwanted sexual needs, which were unleashed at night.

A third story of Melanie Klein's reveals a great deal of the actual history of her life, especially prior to her psychoanalytic experience, when she found someone to listen to her for the first time. In this story, the female alter ego protagonist is passing her time in a health spa, in a state of depression, characterised by obsessive ruminations. She yearns to be at home with her children. She spends the time fantasising about how she might tell her husband of her loneliness, of her need for him, and of her disappointment in marriage. The husband comes to visit. She opens up to him and attempts an emotional communication, hoping that he can understand her pain. Instead of the desired response, her husband withdraws from her into a state of emotional isolation and indifference, failing to show concern or understanding. Rather than a suicidal reaction, Klein's female protagonist attempts to sustain herself by a stoical determination to do her duty as a Victorian wife, one who has no choice about her fate in marriage. She vows to herself that she will go home with her husband, to start again, attempting to be a faithful wife and mother. However, upon her husband's hiring of a male artist to paint her portrait, she yields to a love affair with the young male stranger who wants to capture her soul on the canvas. Finding sexual gratification in this erotic affair for the first time, the wife (in that tale) feels vengeance towards her husband, whereas in the past she used to feel guilt towards him. The protagonist experiences her betrayal of her husband as a justified act of retaliation against the man whom she sees as depriving of her right to life's fulfilment (Grosskurth, 1986). Formerly, she believed that she could only choose between the guilt of betrayal of marriage and the shame-inducing existence of the deprived and humiliated state of being a (Stepford-like) wife. Grosskurth (1986) indicates that the tale is thus ended in a form of manic triumph, where nothing internal is resolved, but action leads to the forbidden fulfilment, which she craved. The tale of the tale ended here. However, Grosskurth (1986) continues to inform us that there is also some poetry written by Klein which suggests that Klein did indeed engage in such a love affair, just as the protagonist of this story does. She also tells us that this affair seems to have ended when the male lover proclaims his first love to be his art, which he seems to idealise to the same degree as Melanie's brother had idealised his writing. Like the lover in this biography, Klein's brother never stayed with a woman. In fact, he devalued and humiliated each woman, and always returned to his art (Grosskurth, 1986). This might be compared to a toddler who is leaving the disappointing mother of separation to return to the fantasy symbiotic mother; so the present mother is the demonised one and the absent mother is the idealised symbiotic one. In this manner, the black and white dichotomy takes hold. The object, as well as the self, is split during a traumatic disruption in separation.

In Klein's love poetry, written after an affair with a male artist, the author seems to believe she has merged totally and ecstatically with her lover. She echoes the cry of Emily Brontë at the moment when that female poet believes she is merging with her omnipotent male (masculinised) muse-god. Brontë (1908) cries, "My outward sense is gone, my inward essence feels", and for one brief moment of creative ecstasy, she believes that she has merged with her muse for all eternity.

Klein writes of blood pulsing through her as her mouth merges with the voluptuous lips of her lover (Grosskurth, 1986). She feels that she is becoming one with her lover, as her heart, body, and mind is felt uniting with him, at least in her imagination. She goes beyond everything she could have experienced through sexuality with her husband, Arthur Klein. Consequently, Melanie speaks of the coming together with her lover as a miracle. She looks forward to the "miracle" being renewed with each merger in each act of lovemaking. She seems to have found the fulfilment of erotic desire and love that she has constantly yearned for and brooded about missing. Reading the poem, I am struck with the degree of twinship she experiences with her lover, for she and he are not just combined as one in the sexual act of lovemaking, but they also seem to mirror each other as twin-like beings, at least in so far as their desire for one another expresses itself. Kohut (1968) would probably see such a poem through the lens of diagnosing "twinship transference".

The poem does not show the end of the affair. If Grosskurth (1986) is right that it ended because Klein's lover felt he had to choose between her and his art, and chose his art, it appears that Klein suffered the demon-lover theme of seduction and abandonment. If Klein experienced this theme through a psyche arrested in the pre-oedipal separation period, this theme would become one of self- (soul) murder. The demon-lover theme becomes the demon-lover complex, as the female self is murdered, when the desired muse male is experienced as turning demonic through his rejection of the female, thus repeating the theme of pre-oedipal abandonment by the emotionally unavailable mother/father, on an unconscious level. On the oedipal level, as well, when oedipal dynamics are condensed and elaborated by the earlier trauma at the period of basic self-formation, disappointment can turn into psychic murder. With the earlier trauma affecting the oedipal conflicts, loss cannot be processed into a creative and symbolic sense of disillusionment. According to Grosskurth (1986), Melanie Klein seems to have offered total surrender to her relationship with her lover, offering her life as well as herself. However, there was one exception to this surrender. She would not relinquish being the mother of her four-year-old daughter Melitta, which consequently bound her to her husband and her marriage.

The end of the affair must have been traumatic. Yet, there was no writing that describes it. Perhaps, Klein became too depressed to write. Perhaps, she repressed her rage and pain, as she had in the past, to maintain the idealisation of her mother. Now, she idealised the lover, as she had idealised her mother, with the outcome of never mourning the loss of the fantasy ideal mother and never facing earlier disappointments with her actual mother. Klein might well have wished to preserve the idealisation of her lover, who probably was not only representing her mother, but also her idealised brother. Psychic determinism seems to be at play in Klein choosing an artist for her lover. I would suspect this, given Klein's childhood romantic view of her brother and her wish to sustain it. In repressing her rage and grief at the end of the affair, Klein might have perpetuated her unmourned loss with a lifelong retaliation of never again allowing a man to be important to her as an intimate partner, at least not important enough to jeopardise her total devotion to her art, her psychoanalytic practice, and her creative inspiration as a psychoanalytic theorist. Men in her profession became allies, such as Ernest Jones, or otherwise those to combat in her narcissistically invested theoretical discourse, such as Glover. With perhaps one brief exception mentioned by Grosskurth (1986), they did not become dates, let alone lovers. Freud probably remained a far off idealised object, until he and his daughter landed in England to escape the Nazis. Perhaps it seems his actual presence devalued him in her mind. Klein could then proceed to increasingly differentiate her own vision from Freud's.

After all this speculation on Klein's inner life and love life, Grosskurth (1986) throws us, eager readers of supposed (virtual) biographical truth, a distracting curve ball. She speculates that Klein's lover might, after all, not even have been a man, or, if a man, he could have mainly served as a displacement for her unacceptable and repressed homoerotic longings for her female friend and intimate companion, Klara Vago. Shades of Emily Dickinson's (1960) "Master letters" to a mystery lover strike me here. Among the biographies of Emily Dickinson, the poet now thought to be the greatest of all American poets, there is the study of the series of letters in which the object of Emily's admiration was a woman, although at first it was assumed to be a man (Cody, 1971). Cody supposes that Emily Dickinson might have been writing of her repressed longings for a female lover (probably her sister-in-law), from whom she might actually have had some initial response, whether a response of an erotic nature or not. There is one explicitly erotic and potently haunting poem of Dickinson that speaks of "mooring" herself "in thee". This raises an eyebrow, because, from the female point of view, one does not moor one's own body self in the male other. It is vice versa; only if the other were a woman could such a poetic phrase be taken as anatomical truth. So, it raises the question of the gender of the longed for other, which might have been the same as in the well-known "Master letters".

I cannot read Grosskurth's (1986) speculations about the gender of Klein's lover without thinking of this other biographical enigma. Yet, here, Grosskurth (1986) offers a compromise theory on the gender alternatives. She suggests that it could have been while looking at a portrait of her friend Klara on the wall of her own drawing-room that Klein was aroused by Klara, who represented an internal muse for the creative work of a short story fantasy, in which Klein wrote of a male artist as a lover. Grosskurth implies that as Melanie gazed at Klara's visage in a portrait on the wall, she was also taking in the artist who had put Klara on the canvas. According to Grosskurth, therefore, Klein is possibly displacing the unacceptable homoerotic feelings on to the male who is linked with the visage of her intimate friend and perhaps unconscious erotic love object. Another toss of the dice in biographical thought might be that Klein did actually have an affair with the male artist, but that she was displacing the erotic level of her love for Klara on to him, since he is linked to Klara through the portrait. Grosskurth indicates that there was a period in Klein's history, when still married, that she travelled on a vacation journey with Klara and stayed in an area where she might very well have encountered and entertained the male artist in question, while simultaneously enveloped in the atmosphere of her growing intimacy with Klara.

With Klara by her side, Klein might have very well dared what without her would be unthinkable. For, given Libussa's punitive condemnation of Melanie's sister, Emilie, at an earlier time, on the mere supposition (based on a rumour) on her part that Emilie might be having an extramarital affair, it is unlikely that Melanie would have been free to indulge herself in such a manner without experiencing similar severe condemnation from her internal mother, who constituted a punitive superego within her. Yet, with the addition of Klara's leverage voicing opinions contrary to those of her internal mother and unconscious superego, the deed might indeed have been done.

Perhaps, also, what might have seemed like a disappointing ending of the affair might have been less traumatic than expected if Klein still had Klara. Furthermore, the leap of liberation which Klein seems to have experienced in her soul, as her body opened to sensual touch at the psychic levels she had never known before, might actually have been sustained in a psychic atmosphere, in which Klara's influence as a formerly divorced woman pointed for her the way out of her imprisoning marriage. In such a case, the lover, in fact, might have been less of the muse turned to demon lover than the husband himself continued to be in her mind. Perhaps, this would account for the lack of post love affair poetry. By that point, Klein may have been busy preparing for separation from her husband. She was probably also entering into psychoanalysis and into the psychoanalytic community (first in Hungary, and then in Berlin), and was ultimately heading for a divorce.

Klara has another important role in Melanie Klein's history. During the period of their friendship, Melanie was exposed to the strong Catholic religious beliefs of Klara's family. This was possibly where Klein had unconsciously adopted aspects of those beliefs into her later psychoanalytic theorising. Grosskurth (1986) declares the probability of such an influence, citing Klein's theories of the death instinct as innate aggression (possibly associated with Catholics' "original sin"), the primal focus on the mother (as in "Immaculate Conception", or the mother-without-the-father), and her later theory of reparation (related to Catholics' beliefs in redemption/expiation). Given such precedents to Klein's psychoanalytic theories, Klara appears as a prominent muse in relation to Melanie Klein's later theorising. Any negative experience of Klara could split off Klein into her projected view of her husband. If Klein kept any anger at Klara out of consciousness (as she did in relation to her mother), she possibly used Klara as a steady model of female liberation. This would have allowed any ideas inherited from Klara or from her family's influence, including religious influence, to go underground until such ideas arose later in her conscious mind as psychoanalytic theories.

Side by side with such psychic splitting might be Klein's split-off consciousness of her own religious identity. Grosskurth (1986) cites a strange paradoxical dichotomy here. She states that Melanie Klein made an ultra-conscious and perhaps self-conscious statement in her later years to the effect that she had retained her pride in being of Jewish origin, while others had denied their past for social conformity, particularly during the Nazi time and Jewish persecution. She seems to have expressed at that time contempt for those who weakened into disavowing their past in order to comply with forces pressing in around them. One would think from this statement that Klein had been a stalwart Jew throughout the time of persecution, and certainly during her years before it. Yet, according to Grosskurth's extensive research, she found that, during a time in Klein's earlier married life, she and her nuclear family had actually converted to Unitarianism, and that she had agreed to have her three children (Melitta, Hans, and Eric) baptised, which they were. The conscious compromise resolution to this religious equivocation seems to have been a dismissal of religious belief and practice all together by Klein. Once Klein enrolled in her own psychoanalytic treatments with Ferenczi (in Hungary) and Abraham (in Berlin), she was prepared to disavow all spiritual beliefs that might be connected with religion, as if consciously disavowing her cultural Judaism (similar to Freud). Grosskurth (1986) describes that when Klein was doing psychoanalytic questioning of her son Eric (during his early years), just before his bedtime, she made an empathic display of citing the belief in God to be fairy-tale, along with the belief a child might have in monsters.

CHAPTER THREE

The phenomenological theory stands on its own: death instinct as demon lover

The demonic bad object as the price of
pre-oedipal stage arrest and idealisation

Those with defensive idealisation as a primary organising factor in their psyches inevitably split others into idealised and devalued figures. When the object is looked up to for creative inspiration, the idealised object becomes a muse figure, and the bad object becomes a demonic muse, or demon-lover figure. The demon lover evolves from early negative parent objects, combined with split-off or dissociated rage, and it is also the result of a split-off idealised image of the early parent. The idealised constellation of self and other exists in a polarised but isolated dimension of the psyche in relation to the bad object/demon-lover constellation. The rage associated with the demon lover is unneutralised; because it is sealed off in its dissociated state, as it remains unmodified by sustained internal love connections. The resulting visceral self-part (more than an impulse) combines with a negative parent representation, producing a powerful sadistic aggression that becomes personified as a demon. When eroticised, the personified demon turns to the unconscious psychic fantasy of a demon lover.

The despair that can reach suicidal dimensions in someone with such a closed-off psychic system becomes personified when projected on to an external other (such as the original parent) that traumatically disappoints, and, thus, turns from muse to demon. How many times did such a cycle of despair enact its drama upon the stage of Melanie Klein's internal world? This can never be determined. Given Klein's need to protect the idealised view of her mother, this cycle is likely to have occurred with each new disappointment and with each new splitting of the object. As Klein's husband became a personified demon, and in as much as she experienced him as a sexual intruder, he could become a demon lover who carried the image of the split-off bad mother in a masculinised and eroticised form. Also, at the point of abandonment by her artist lover, as discovered in Klein's writings by Grosskurth (1986), Klein might have transformed her lover into the split-off demon "other" in erotic form. But how did such psychic transmutation relate to Klein's creative process?

The women writers whom I have studied through careful examination of their written work, as well as their biographies, enacted their demon-lover themes and complexes in their literary work (Kavaler-Adler, 1985–2013). In those women artists, traumatised in the critical pre-oedipal years of self-formation and integration, the demon-lover theme emerges as a re-enactment of trauma and its sequence of despair. Such women yearn repeatedly for an idealised, masculinised, and God-like muse figure. This figure, based on the melding of individual-specific maternal and paternal impressions and visceral and symbolic components, inevitably turns into a rapacious and abandoning demon lover, leading each woman to the land of her death.

This land of death is often envisioned as a black void of internal despair, sealed-off rage, and the empty gap between mother and child, experienced traumatically as infinite, when the mother cannot sustain adequate emotional and psychic connection with her infant or toddler (see Masterson, 1976, 1981). In Emily Brontë's (1908) Poem No. 190, the land of death is cold and dark, with regions of snow, where she seeks the muse coming as a "wanderer". For Klein, I suspect that her land of death might be born from a psychic impression of the void as the limbo-land of psychic isolation in a health spa; a maximum security purgatory from which she could never escape and return to her mother or to her fantasised good family.

The demon-lover theme is, in itself, a theme of the suicidal despair. It becomes a demon-lover "complex", in which one is constantly possessed by her internalised demon, when a large or major part of her psychic life comes to reflect the primal enactment. This primal enactment operates in a closed internal system, without affect or awareness of present experience (Fairbairn, 1952).

To the degree that Melanie Klein was herself the victim of such internal psychic possession, due to her unconscious addiction to a muse/demon-lover figure, she would need to express its symptoms in her work, her art, as well as in her life. I propose that her tenacious and passionate attachment to the death instinct theory can be seen as a demon-lover complex. As with the women writers I have studied, Klein seems to have re-enacted her demon-lover complex within her creative work. Melanie Klein's creative work became the realm of her psychoanalytic theory making. She gestated theory in her mind and was constantly pregnant with it. As with the women writers and artists I have studied, the realm of Klein's art often spoke more vividly about the pre-oedipal trauma (with its demon-lover complex as a particular form of pathological mourning) than did her actual life.

The death instinct

Melanie Klein's attraction to the death instinct theory is curious. Although she acted at first as if she was just adopting such an idea from Freud (1915c, 1920g), her conceptualisation of the death instinct is of a quite different nature than Freud's. Klein's choice of the term "death instinct" could be of much more significance than any actual adherence to following Freud as a psychoanalytic theorist.

For Klein (1932), the death instinct is connected with a belief that we are all born with a reservoir of hostile aggression that is too much for any infant to tolerate without killing itself. She suggests this might cause the infant to rip and tear itself apart, as when borderline patients in a state of rage wish to rip and tear the other apart. Since such a presumed quantity of "death instinct" (impulse, energy, or substance) is too much to bear within one's own psychic domain, it must be deflected. For Klein, "outward" always means out of the id self and into the mother's body. Continuing in Klein's theory, when this so-called death instinct is deflected into the mother, the mother becomes a persecutor, as the infant (having imbued the mother with his/her own aggression) continually fears retaliation. In order to survive, the infant must split the internal mother into two parts, ideal and bad. In this way, the infant protects the belief in a good mother, who can be seen as presiding outside the realm of the bad mother. This metapsychological view of a finite amount of hostile aggressive instinct, which exists as a kind of malignant energy projected outward, differs significantly from Klein's clinical descriptions of the child blaming the mother for all the pain in life, beginning with birth and the very visceral level of pain of a stomach ache. As I understand Klein, she speaks phenomenologically of a baby in a primitive state of consciousness who assigns blame to the mother for every ache or pain in her body because mother is experienced as the omnipotent power in the universe. I believe this metapsychological view proposes that the infant's instinct energy is projected out on to the mother. Klein seems to imply here that the pain is not an internal interpersonal conflict phenomenon, but, rather, a concrete substance (death instinct). From this perspective, the psychological phenomenon becomes concretised, as if the visceral experience (e.g., in the stomach) was not a somatised psychic conflict, but, rather, an issue of the death instinct substance thrown back and forth between the mother and infant. It is questionable that such operation of projection comes from a primitive ego. For example, the conscious ego is not yet able to conceive of its own rage, let alone to conceive of it causing the other pain. Neither is the primitive ego able to cast the death instinct into the other, the mother, as if it were a basketball aimed at a hoop.

The mechanism of projection is a *psychic* mechanism, not a material entity subject to the laws of physics. Psychic operations relate to the manipulation and warding-off of affect states, such as retaliatory rage and anger. A phenomenological theory can define such operations in clinical terms. We need to understand circumstances, aversive psychic experiences, promoted by pathological repetitions in defence as having a relationship to an "other". Causation and motivation can then be understood in psychological terms. To label the projective mechanisms employed to manage aggression as a "death instinct" contributes nothing to our understanding of developmental strivings or the psychic causes. Yet, when Klein wished to go beyond a phenomenological theory to a metapsychological one, which would explain ultimate universal causes, she turns to the term "death instinct".

Some would say that this preoccupation with metapsychological theory was what had led Freud into trouble, especially since so little can be known about authentic infant experience. Both Klein and Freud have been most criticised when they reach beyond a theoretical model for that expressed in the treatment room to a metapsychological axiom of life. Freud's (1915c, 1920g) idea of a death instinct seems to have caused him to sometimes bypass the *in vivo* manifestations of sex and aggression seen in the treatment room, and particularly with regard to transference. In contrast to Freud's view, Klein's (1932) notion of a death instinct bypassed the clinical phenomena of retaliatory rage, as well as the urge towards reparation and sustained love.

A word on Freud's attempts to explain his late-life penchant for his form of the death instinct might be pertinent here. Klein did not think that any rationalisations in biology were necessary for her death instinct concept, while Freud did. Their different approaches to justifying the concept are, in themselves, revealing: Freud adhered to the nineteenth-century's empirical science approach, while Klein seems to have come more from a view of theory as art, which is particularly revealing when we understand that art (as a paradigm) was her dead and idealised brother's axiom of life. For instance, when Klein wrote out her free associations (prior to ever actually visiting a psychoanalyst), she chose the art paradigm of James Joyce's stream of consciousness. She never had scientific pretentions, although her work with children was admired by the anthropological scientist, Merleau-Ponty, who spoke of Klein as a "natural empirical phenomenologist" (Grosskurth, 1986, p. 447) in connection with her vivid attunement to the gestures and spoken attitudes of children.

Freud's (1915c, 1920g) death instinct theory became a theory of a yearning for nirvana. This is quite different from Klein's (1932) theory of aggression existing with an axiomatic drive compulsion. It is different also from a theory that proposes a compulsion towards hostility in the process of self-preservation, as Klein's (1932) theory of the death instinct would also have it. Freud's theory also differed from what Winnicott (1965, 1975) would do with a theory of aggression, following Klein and theorising that aggression was a core visceral motility that must be expressed for the true self to evolve. This is true, although Freud (1915c, 1920g) seems to have reserved the term "death instinct" for a primal yearning that, ultimately, is more libidinal than aggressive. Freud played with ideas of aggression being turned outward or inward. He consulted with Einstein (Grosskurth, 1986) about a possible explanation from physics for why aggression is turned outward as hostility or, alternately, inward as suicidal impulse. Ultimately, he adopted the Hindu idea of a primal spiritual yearning to merge with the universe in a state of nirvana as the philosophical grounds for his use of the term "death instinct" (Freud, 1915c, 1920g, 1940a). In so doing, he stepped closer to proposing a primary yearning that bypasses the aggressive impulse as a primary motivation. Although still basically wishing to be scientific, drawing on the biological idea of life as entropy, his philosophical turn to the idea of nirvana might have been an attempt to simplify a biological theory of aggression that had become too complex. However, Freud's attempt to simplify might have led down the road of reductionism. It is reductionist to simplify a whole theory of complex developmental levels of sexual motivation down to a theory of striving only for life, and then opposing it to a basic yearning towards death. To do so negates the complexities of visceral, impulsive, retaliatory, hostile, and symbolic modes of aggression and reduces them to striving towards death. Freud's (1920g) earlier theory was reductionist in its view of human motivation, always striving towards pleasure (the "pleasure principle"). When Freud began (in his late life) to see pleasure as some form of nirvana-like stasis, he totally polarised this idea of pleasure to his earlier concept of pleasure as excitement.

When the desire for pleasure, which was originally related to a biological drive, is transformed into a wish for a totally tranquil stasis, related to the Hindu idea of nirvana, human motivation towards excitement as being a source of energy, and, thus, of fulfilment, is lost. Thus, Freud's later-life attempt at simplification in theory takes him backwards, from the time when he discarded his original "pleasure principle", and beyond it to complex modes of eroticism and aggression. Yet, this is the route that Freud (1915c, 1920g, 1940a) took when he resorted to defining his late theory of psychic motivation in terms of a death instinct that operates on philosophical grounds as a striving towards the stasis of nirvana, even though he resorted to converting that philosophical level of thought into the realm of science by defining this striving towards nirvana as a biological movement of progressive decay, adopting the biologist's concept of entropy as his scientific explanation of the death instinct. The wish for nirvana might be likened to a libidinal desire, since it is most nearly relative to a merger wish, but the concept of entropy lacks even that dynamic of active striving. The theory of entropy submits the human being to a reactive state of mind that merely mirrors the biological body's decay.

Fortunately, Klein needed none of this to justify her attraction to the term "death instinct". Unconcerned with any presumption of science, Klein was quite content to separate from (or merely overlook) biology, despite her loyalty to the body-based human experience. She did not get tangled up in the need for scientific explanations that had led Freud into perplexing contradictions. Instead, she maintained her fascination with the volatility and passion of sadism, enabling her to return to a notion of the death instinct as an enigma of psychological motivation seen in manifestations of hostile aggression, which could possibly have innate motivation (King & Steiner, 1991). Ultimately, Klein brought a psychoanalytic theory of human motivation into the interpersonal realm, focusing on aggression not in terms of physio-logical or biological drive impulses, but as envy that can have psychic fantasy manifestations at an unconscious level, or through dissociated parts of the self that evolve through psychic fantasy. This was her statement in "Envy and gratitude", which she presented years before its publication in 1957 at a psychoanalytic conference and symposium, a symposium that caused Winnicott to abandon the Kleinian camp.

When Freud proposed his explanation of entropy as grounds for the theory of a death instinct, he met with an interesting response. According to Grosskurth (1986, p. 193),

> Most of Freud's colleagues were deeply disturbed by this fundamen-tal change in his thinking. Freud had hoped to convince them by drawing upon the second law of thermodynamics, but it was argued that the law of entropy operated only in a hypothetical closed system, not one to be found in nature, least of all in living beings. Nor could biology be brought in to buttress a primary aggressive instinct.

What is most interesting here in relation to Freud and Klein, both advocates of the death instinct, is the retort that the law of entropy operates only in a "hypothetical" closed system, which a human being is supposedly not, or, at least, is not in entirety. Klein was met with just such a retort from Sutherland (1989) to her idea of the death instinct (Grosskurth, 1986). He said that the death instinct phenom-ena, as described by Klein, are evidence of a closed psychic system, which could not be negotiated by any biologist (Grosskurth, 1986). In speaking of a hypothetical closed system, Sutherland (1989) implies a pathological psychological system. This is Fairbairn's sealed-off and split-off closed system, which melds together libidinal and anti-libidinal psychic structures and explains how these psychic structures continually enact their sadomasochistic dramas upon the stage of the internal world (Grosskurth, 1986). I find Sutherland's (1989) explanation, relating to Fairbairn's psychic structure, to be an adequate understanding of the suffocating experience related to the death instinct. It also explains the suicidal despair in those trapped in the closed system, originally created from pre-oedipal developmental disruption when the mother of infancy and toddlerhood has failed to maintain sufficient contact during the critical phases of self-development. In this view, such developmental disruption support of an "other" is needed to mourn the loss of the primary "other". In my view, this is a pathological mourning state in which the original traumatic disappointment is re-enacted repeatedly in a closed-off, internal world. This is an internal world in which the tantalising and rejecting part-objects relentlessly play out their dramas of seduction and abandonment, with their themes of torture, rape, and unrelenting psychic torment. The internal pressure demands an external expulsion of tension, similar to the idea of the deflection of a death instinct primal energy. The attachment to the primal scene of parental abuse and emotional neglect creates the experience of self-annihilation that resonates with a phenomenological sense of murder. This murder is either of the self or of the primal other invested with regressive and aggressive modes of attachment. The closed system of attachment to the aversive part object drama (two-dimensional objects, rather than three-dimensional ones) becomes a demon-lover drama, where annihilation terror anticipates death as a punishment for acts of retaliation towards the primary mother.

Death instinct as demon lover

Grosskurth (1986) reveals that Melanie Klein's mother, Libussa, combined the idea of love with that of relentless sadistic torture, to the point of murdering the psyche of the other. Libussa writes the following letter to Melanie and her husband Arthur, in reference to Melanie's older sister, Emilie:

We have done Emilie a grave injustice. Although she is guilty on the one hand because of her pleasure-seeking and because of her shallow character and her indolence, she has been, on the other hand, the victim of a person who is malicious to the point of cruelty. His behavior springs from a pathological jealousy that often works itself up into sheer madness. What he says and communicates are the delusions of his morbid fantasies. Thus he knows no limits, and he cannot distinguish between right and wrong, truth and slander—and with that he tortures his victim to death and ruins her reputation, mercilessly gloating over her torments, and the *reason for that is that he still loves her as intensely as in their first years of marriage.* (Grosskurth, 1986, p. 61, my italics)

Notwithstanding that Emilie is probably repeating with her husband what she had suffered at the hands of her mother, this is a statement by Libussa of her view of love as sadomasochistic torture and murder. The last two lines expose the horrific conclusion by Libussa that it is because Emilie's husband Leo loves Emilie so "intensely" that he is compelled to torture and abuse her, as well as to abandon her emotionally and financially. Perhaps, this exposes Libussa's underlying belief that love is always a state of possession, and that in order to not be possessed, one must possess and weaken the other. What could be a better description of the personified demon lover than this one offered by Libussa?

Libussa's view of the objective situation seems to bear the stamp of her own internal world, where perhaps she suffered early pre-oedipal trauma, which she, in turn, has inflicted on her children. Grosskurth (1986) indicates that Libussa herself might have played a significant role in pressuring Emilie's husband Leo into his mode of abusive action, which she calls love. She tells us that Libussa had engineered it so that Leo could take over her dead husband's old dental practice, even though he was reluctant to do so (Grosskurth, 1986). This might have played a part in his dissipation through compulsive gambling, all of which he blamed on his wife, who was continually pinching pennies to forestall starvation. It is ironic that even in the face of Emilie's tragedy, Libussa still plays her own demonic role in relation to her daughter, accusing her of "pleasure-seeking" and "indolence" and of having a "shallow character" (Grosskurth, 1986). She continues to demonise Emilie in order to maintain her malicious and envious alliance with Melanie, which has been based on mutual hostility towards Emilie. She is anxious that Melanie will be angry with her for any forgiveness she shows to her sister: "You will be beside yourself because I have changed my opinion of Emilie" (Grosskurth, 1986, p. 61).

Here is a paranoid–schizoid level alliance indeed. Anger between Melanie and her mother is continually avoided by the mutual ganging up against Emilie. In fact, Melanie is entrenched in using her sister defensively; she will not even yield her demonic view of Emilie as much as her mother does. Grosskurth (1986) concludes that Klein becomes her own illustration of a world in which nothing is seen objectively, but is always filtered through thick screens of distortion that are based on envy. I would account for such perpetual distortion on Melanie Klein's part differently than Grosskurth. I would not see Melanie's dynamics in terms of a screen of psychic fantasy that never allows for a realistic view of others and of the world, but, rather, as a reflection of Melanie's pathological mourning state. I see Melanie Klein as having been encased in an unresolved developmental arrest, explained in object relations' terms as a pathological mourning state, which could have resulted from Libussa's early possession and emotional abandonment of her, especially during the critical practising period, and in later stages of separation–individuation struggles. There could have been no mourning of the lost nurturing mother of infancy without an adequate and good enough mother being internalised in a symbolic form. I do not think such a good enough mother was established in Klein's psyche, although I do believe she began some mourning in her analysis with Abraham in Germany, and later mourning on her own when her son Hans died, which led to her writing one of her most insightful papers, "Mourning and its relation to manic-depressive states" (Klein, 1940). However, the mourning process was short-lived and, therefore, was not sufficient to help Klein beyond her developmental arrest to reach the whole and healthy psychic integration, even though she herself theorised about its possibility. Grosskurth (1986) writes:

> Why did Melanie adopt such an intransigently judgmental attitude towards her sister, unless she envied Emilie for seeming to have the fulfilled emotional life that she herself craved, as well as in the face of all her trouble—certain serenity? More fundamentally, she still retained the envy of a powerless baby sister. Melanie Klein was an

embodiment of her own later theories: the world is not an objective reality, but a phantasmagoria peopled with our own fears and desires. (p. 62)

If Libussa's internal blueprint of object relations is encapsulated in this view of Leo and Emilie, she must have transmitted it to both her daughters. It is a blueprint that defines love as demon lover possession, with its compulsion towards sadomasochism, leading to murder and death. Melanie Klein managed to turn her husband into a demon in her own mind when she experienced his sexual demands as an intrusion. She played out the role of a wife possessed until she broke free to a possible love affair and to a new life in psychoanalysis. Perhaps she also turned her lover into a demon within her mind when he, in turn, abandoned her.

It is easy to see how Klein replayed the script of the demon lover, who possessed her and/or abandoned her, as a reaction to her mother's view of love as a sadomasochistic torment. It is, perhaps, somewhat more difficult to imagine how this demon-lover personification then was transmuted (through sophisticated sublimating capacities?) into theory making, which was Klein's art, as the theory of the death instinct illustrates. This might account for Klein's reluctance to relinquish her theory of the death instinct, even when it undermined the value of her theory for many well-known theorists. Holding on to the theory of the death instinct was a way of holding on to her mother.

What is the price of the death instinct?

During the great "Freud–Klein" debates at the British Psychoanalytic Society, when Klein's followers, including Susan Isaacs, Joan Riviere, and Sylvia Payne, articulated their views of all main Kleinian theoretical concepts in front of Anna Freud and other Freudians, Klein was pressed to respond to the controversies about the death instinct (King & Steiner, 1991). According to Grosskurth (1986), it was at that time that Klein acknowledged that her other theories (those that I call her phenomenological theories, based on her vivid clinical experience) were not dependent on maintaining the death instinct theory. This is the only time I know of that she made such a statement, one that many who valued the clinical base of her theories would welcome. Such a statement could have made her question the whole death instinct concept. Perhaps Klein even began to differentiate it from other theories of aggression. She might have begun to distinguish a retaliatory impulse that could be innate and biological derivations of the death instinct. Such retaliatory impulse can be seen as being in the service of survival rather than death, and, thus, supporting an urge towards life, although it has deleterious effects on object relations.

At the time of the great debates, Klein made a point of emphasising the libidinal aspect of her theory, counterbalancing her former advocacy of a death instinct theory. She directed analysts such as Isaacs (who spoke for her) to emphasise that she considered the newborn infant to be preoccupied with wishes to return to the womb, and that these wishes were encoded in the unconscious through psychic fantasies. This merger wish, the wish of returning to the mother's womb, Klein referred to as a libidinal wish, but she also began to define this wish in relation to her death instinct theory. In doing so, she moved closer to Freud's view of the death instinct as a search for nirvana (bliss), rather than a hostile aggression deflected outward (Klein, 1957).

Klein also modified the dark sides of her theory by having Isaacs speak of the positive internalisation of the mother that can take place (when conditions are favourable) with an early benign superego structure that enhances the infant's positive strivings toward life. In speaking consistently of an infant-level superego formation, Klein was certainly contradicting the Freudians, who held on to Freud's theories of the superego not forming until the oedipal stage (King & Steiner, 1991). Klein's focus on the possible formation of a benign superego at this early time (in infancy) allowed her to forecast much of what Winnicott and later infant research would confirm. For it was here that she contradicted Freud's notion of an autoerotic stage in the infant, steadfastly developing a theory of object relations as the primary essence of life, as Fairbairn (1952) would do, in speaking of the striving towards the object from the beginning of life. Klein's spokeswoman asserted that Klein believed that the experience at the mother's breast results in an internal mother being maintained within the internal world psyche of the infant throughout all development (Grosskurth, 1986). The infant does not return to some hypothetical autoerotic state after contact with the mother, whether through holding and emotional care or through the time of breastfeeding. Thus, the imprint of mother and infant together during these times is maintained, which structures the internal world developmentally and also structures the personality of the individual that develops through this internal world. Nevertheless, Klein still maintained that such developmental internalisations required "a priori" (a prior) good mother fantasy. The innate predisposition to experience a good mother seems to come to life through the emotional bonding with the mother (according to Klein at the time of the Freud–Klein controversies), and is sustained as an internalisation of mother and infant together in nurturance and love. The bad mother experience of the mother becomes split-off from the good connection for the psychic survival of the infant, similar to the idea of any innate hostile aggression being deflected outward. This can only take place, however, because there is a core of primal good connection with the mother. Although, today, this may seem fundamental to us, after the studies by Mahler (1979), it was only late in Mahler's life that she began to modify her earlier theory, in which she had delineated the newborn infant as having an autoerotic stage prior to a symbiosis with the mother (Mahler, Pine, & Bergmann, 1975). This autoerotic stage originally confused her theory and undermined its object relations emphasis.

Nevertheless, the death instinct needed to be discussed, and among Klein's followers there were different interpretations that were aired during the debates with the Freudians. According to Grosskurth (1986), Sylvia Payne, at the time of the Klein–Freud controversies at the British Society, believed that the death instinct meant "the instinct to kill". At the same time, Joan Riviere interpreted it as the need for survival (on the part of the infant) and for "externalising" aggression.

Grosskurth (1986) writes that Hedwig Hoffer proposed that death instinct is a purely biological, and not a psychological, phenomenon. This was never the view of the Kleinians. The Kleinians defended the death instinct theory as useful in the clinical area. For example, in Heimann's (1950) view (while Heimann at that time was an avid Kleinian), this theory helped to better comprehend various difficult topics, like negative transference, projections, and symptoms of persecution (Grosskurth, 1986). Heimann would probably not have made such a statement if Klein had truly surrendered her theory. If my hypothesis is correct, Klein needed to hold on to this theory for her own intrapsychic and unconscious purposes. It was a way of staying connected to the demon-lover aspect of her mother, as she embraced Libussa within her internal world; hence, interpretations of the death instinct concept that would find justification in clinical phenomena were needed. There were many psychologists who admired Klein's views of early life as it transpires and evolves through non-linear psychic positions (the paranoid–schizoid and depressive positions), yet who could not digest this part of her theory when Klein retained the term "death instinct". They might have accepted, on the other hand, the point that the Kleinians made about the need not to under-rate aggression in favour of a purely libidinal theory, as was made during the British Psychoanalytic Society's debates (Grosskurth, 1986). Further, many of those dissenting from the death instinct theory would have almost surely agreed with the Kleinians when they presented their claim that they were counterbalancing Freud's focus on instinct as a pure drive-related phenomenon, with a theory empha-sising object relations being a part of the human psyche and internal world from birth (Grosskurth, 1986).

Some of the dissenters from the death instinct theory were well-known theorists, such as R. D. Laing, who studied with both Klein and Winnicott during the time when Laing (1990) wrote his best-known book, *The Divided Self*. Laing is reported by Grosskurth (1986) to have valued much of Kleinian theory, although he had an aversive reaction to Klein as a person and as a teacher. He was profoundly impressed by Klein's courage in exploring and theorising about the depths of the unconscious, when Anna Freud skirted above, on the psychic surface. He valued Klein's theories of primal modes of split-ting and the existential realities of the paranoid and depressive posi-tions. He was aware that the anthropologist Merleau-Ponty con-sidered Klein to be a monumental phenomenologist, particularly in her work with play therapy in children. Yet, Laing moved towards Winnicott and slighted Klein because he felt inhibited in her classes. Also, if Laing openly disagreed with her, Klein would claim he was envious of her as the good breast-mother or would direct him to return to analysis for more required sessions (Grosskurth, 1986). Whether or not this attitude was merely his paranoid position, one cannot say, but he seems to have benefited greatly from Klein's teach-ings. In fact, he valiantly supported her as one of the theorists that really mattered. When it came to the death instinct, however, he was a dissenter. He believed that the death instinct part of Klein's theory was a "minus" (Grosskurth, 1986), subtracting from the major contribution she had made to understanding unconscious phenomena, psychic defence, and object relations. Laing admired Klein for the "depth of sensibility" in her writings, and her firm stand against those who neglected psychic dynamics, "undeterred by scorn and contempt" Grosskurth, 1986, p. 447).

Grosskurth (1986) speaks of Laing's respect for Klein as a theorist:

> As for understanding of the unconscious, "If it hadn't come from her, I don't know where it would come from." She above anybody else was "a witness to psychic reality which most people denied." . . . She was "a natural empirical phenomenologist" in the sense that she considered what children were actually saying or doing—although she would not have known what phenomenology was. Laing describes her as "someone of caliber, not trivial!" (p. 447)

Michael Balint was another dissenter on the basis of the death instinct. He was an old friend of Klein. He had been in analysis with Ferenczi in Budapest at the same time as Klein, having witnessed her exit a session with tears in her eyes (Grosskurth, 1986). Having proposed his own theory of primal love in several books, including the *Basic Fault* (1979), it is obvious why Balint would not be sympathetic to seeing all babies (not just traumatised ones) as living primarily in the paranoid–schizoid position. Given this notion, it is even more obvious why he would object to the idea that babies are born with a built-in death instinct. Grosskurth (1986) wrote that Balint understood the term phantasy, but he could not agree with Klein's "*undue emphasis on the role of hate, frustration and aggression* in the infant" (Grosskurth, 1986, p. 319).

Bowlby had been an analysand of Klein and had begun his psychoanalytical career as a Kleinian. He eventually corroborated Klein's theories on mourning and reparation in animal research. He is particularly connected to Klein theoretically in his view of object loss being the primal human reason for suffering (Bowlby, 1969, 1980). However, in studying animals, he found *attachment to be the primary human motivation*, which corresponds to the need for mourning of object loss. Bowlby did not focus on aggression as primary, although he did find the need for reparation in animals, as well as in humans, to be a profound innate need, which would imply that he acknowledged aggression, if only through the frustration of attachment, as an ongoing reality in all of us. In the Great Debates, he spoke of a frustration–aggression hypothesis being more parsimonious as a theory than aggression as an instinct. When it came to the death instinct, Bowlby's comments at the British Psychoanalytic Society's meetings were quite insightful and helpful. He maintained that the dynamics of the death instinct, which were discussed at the meeting, might actually be related to the life instinct (or, I might add, to a desperate need to survive). Some of the Kleinians presented the death instinct as any frustration experienced in the state of the infant resulting in a terrifying fear of death (annihilation anxiety). He seemed to have pointed out that the terror of death is not a death instinct, but, rather, an instinct to live. He might have observed in animals how such terror resulted in a desperate need to cling to the other. Grosskurth (1986) writes, "Dr. Bowlby was not convinced. It could be argued, he replied, that the reason the organism cannot bear the idea of dying is due to a strong life instinct" (p. 333).

Segal is reported by Grosskurth (1986) to have spoken of the death instinct as a response to the terrifying shock of birth, and the wish to recede from the world as a response to such a shock. Such a view, reported from the time of the British Psychoanalytic Society's Debates, might not have been Segal's view later on, but it does seem to reflect the ambiguous point to which Bowlby responded. To be afraid of life does not mean that we have an instinct to move away from it into a state of death, but, rather, indicates a wish to survive. To return to the womb is also a return to an object relationship, the one only of the most primitive nature. Balint (1979) writes about this most primal form of relationship with the other (even if only in a non-verbal atmosphere) in *The Basic Fault*.

Furthermore, the external mother modifies the shock of birth and the terror of infant dependency. If the external mother is inadequate to do this, the wish to return to the womb could become a permanent state of mind. This might also be true, however, if the infant is born with a profound terror that is more than the ordinary fear of an infant. Innate factors cannot be disqualified when we look at developmental issues, although there is usually an overall interaction. Klein over-emphasised the innate components of trauma and conflict, but her acknowledgment of these components was important when we consider exaggerated levels of psychic fantasy. Other object relations theorists often dismiss these components due to the obvious pathological effects of the parents' personalities. If the possibility of reincarnation is considered in our theory (soul and personality integration, or dissociation looked at by the Jungians), the psychological endowment of the newborn infant becomes even more important.

Certainly, the kinds of fantasies that have accompanied active suicides, such as that of Virginia Woolf (Kavaler-Adler, 1996), include oceanic wishes related to wishes to return to the maternal womb. In Woolf's case, it was the wish to sink into the ocean to be at peace and rest. Her mother seems to have had similar thoughts, as she lived out a compulsive life, which masked her own pathological mourning state. To fear life, or to wish to be relieved of its burdens and anxieties, however, is still not an "instinct" or drive towards death. When Woolf dreamed of suicide, she wished to return to a good primal mother, which is often associated with the ocean. This was true as well in the case of Anne Sexton, who wrapped herself in her mother's fur coat when she entered an automobile to asphyxiate herself with gas fumes (Kavaler-Adler, 1996; McClatchy, 1978); Sylvia Plath, prior to her suicide, had a fantasy of joining her dead father in a glorified state (Kavaler-Adler, 1993a). The wish to enter death as if it is a psychic space is an object relations wish that has been too frustrated within the dimensions of this life to allow hope in this world.

Paradoxically, the wish to join the object is essentially a wish towards life. It is a wish towards a spiritual life and towards a state of tranquil being (like Freud's nirvana wish), although a life of ambivalent and frustrating corporal existence can ultimately obviate it. Klein and the Kleinians are most eloquent when they speak of the infant terror of life, of feared persecution (and punishment) by a split-off, persecutory mother, and of the yearning towards the idealised good-breast mother. When this is reduced to a death instinct *vs.* a life instinct, the whole rich and ambivalent state of existence is negated. However, when we translate the yearning to return to the womb into a longing for a muse–god father–mother, combined with an intense and perverse wish to cling to the dark side of the father–mother, which, in its primal instinctual form, is personified as the "demon lover," the death instinct appears as a shorthand phrase for a complex ambivalent striving towards fantasy objects.

Sutherland was another dissenter on the death instinct (Grosskurth, 1986). He agreed with Fairbairn (1952) that our primal trust as human beings is towards others, no matter how terrifying, absent, or abusive those others turn out to be. When we fantasise or perceive those others to be out in the world, we move towards life and reality (Sutherland, 1989).

Winnicott's response to the death instinct

Winnicott was a Kleinian theorist. As those who are familiar with the work of both Klein and Winnicott are quite aware, Winnicott was in a continual dialogue with Kleinian theory in practically all of his own papers. Klein became a foil upon which Winnicott could launch his increasingly distinct and partially polarised views. While Klein (1932) wrote about the internal good mother, Winnicott (1960a) wrote about the external "good enough" mother. While Klein (1957) wrote about depressive anxieties of hurting or killing the one that one needs and loves, with a resulting remorse and regret focused on the other, Winnicott (1965) wrote about "the capacity for concern". While Klein (1975) wrote about internal world space, Winnicott (1971a) wrote about transitional and potential space. While Klein (1975) wrote about innate aggression, Winnicott (1947) wrote about hate (in "Hate in the counter-transference"). While Klein (1975) wrote about the sustaining of authentic and loving object connection, through remorse and reparation, Winnicott (1960b) wrote about the true self being allowed to emerge into object relations from within. While Klein (1957) wrote about interpreting impulses and fantasies of retaliatory rage often based on envy, in order to promote the capacity to love through consciousness of one's hate and its meaning, Winnicott (1971b, 1975) wrote about the analyst's non-interpretative survival of a primal rage, without retaliation or abandonment on the part of the analyst.

Up to a certain juncture, Winnicott was able to remain within Klein's world in the British Psychoanalytic Society's realm. According to Grosskurth (1986), Winnicott greatly admired Klein (while also wishing to contest all her theories with his own). Apparently, Klein tolerated him through benign neglect and with a modicum of recognition for his theoretical contribution exemplified by her acknowledging footnote in "Envy and gratitude" (Klein, 1957). Grosskurth (1986) reports John Padel's comments on Klein's interaction with Winnicott: "Klein was the ballerina to whom Winnicott was constantly offering something, which she rejected with a toss of her head as if to say that she had it already" (p. 400). In one such scene, Winnicott is reported to have challenged Klein with the proposal of a theoretical amendment. He supplicates Klein with his request to change the title of the depressive position to that of the "position of concern". According to this anecdote, reported by Grosskurth (1986), Klein responds with characteristic indignant pride and self-aggrandisement as she tells him that "she had waited twenty years for Dr. Winnicott to accept . . . [the depressive position] . . . and she was willing to wait another twenty for him to accept the paranoid schizoid position" (p. 400). Such admonishment might have been tolerable up to a point for Winnicott, but when Klein's group insisted that he rewrite an article he wrote in order to conform to basic Kleinian concepts, if he wanted to have it published in an honorary journal on Klein's work, he refused and left the meeting disheartened. Afterwards he tells his wife, "Apparently Mrs. Klein no longer considers me a Kleinian" (Grosskurth, 1986, p. 398). Winnicott responded in his own dialectic to Klein, and only later, when Klein (1957) first presented her paper, "Envy and gratitude", did Winnicott completely break with Klein on theoretical grounds. According to Grosskurth, Winnicott "held his head in his hands, muttering, 'Oh no, she can't do this!'" (p. 414). Grosskurth further reports that, as per Heimann, "this paper marked the irrevocable theoretical break between them" (p. 414).

It is interesting to speculate why Winnicott reacted in this way to Klein's (1957) "Envy and gratitude" paper. This paper focused on the sadistic fantasies in the transference of psychoanalytic patients, theorising that these fantasies are unconsciously part of everyone's psychic disposition towards the primal mother, upon whom they are completely dependent during the early stages of life. The role of the real mother is more or less irrelevant in "Envy and gratitude" (Klein, 1957). The paper focuses on intrapsychic life as expressing ubiquitous modes of aggression towards the one who is loved ambivalently, due to the extremely frustrating state of dependence. However, the theory extends beyond aggression as consequent to frustration and disappointment when it posits a primal (a priori) form of psychic fantasy compelled not only by an aggressive drive, but by a distinct aggressive manifestation of oral hunger for the mother as well. This oral hunger manifests as a primal object related envy (as opposed to an oedipal stage jealousy).

Klein returns to themes of retaliatory aggression in this paper. However, she sees this retaliatory aggression as reactive to a truly aversive external mother. In contrast to Winnicott, who refers to a "too omnipotent mother" as a real mother not "good enough" at maintaining the psychic container of a safe "holding environment", Klein views the child's retaliation as a response to his/her own fantasy of the mother being "too good" and, therefore, having too much, thus stirring up the child's envy. The real mother's role can be a modifying one in relation to the effects of the fantasy scenario, which operates on an unconscious level, but she is not seen as causing the retaliatory reaction of aggression in the child. Thus, according to Klein, nobody can escape the dynamic of unconscious envy and all its self-sabotaging consequences. Klein's resolution of psychic development with mental health theorises that unconscious envy can be neutralised through love, if the dynamics of this envy are brought to consciousness. This, then, becomes a main goal of transference analysis in psychoanalytic treatment.

Obviously, Klein is working at odds here with Winnicott's own work on the impact of the real mother, and on the modifying of aggression in the infant through the real mother's capacity to hold the infant and to psychically contain the infant who is in a state of need and fear. Winnicott works forward to the idea of the analyst as providing the functions of the holding mother, so that interpretation is de-emphasised, and survival of a patient's aggression, at least during the stages of protosymbolic modes of aggression, is emphasised—particularly in work with the borderline patients, or "false self" patients, as per Winnicott. All this follows a different emphasis than Klein's focus on an interpretation of sadistic "phantasies", which have reached the symbolic stage of a patient's dream associations and free associations.

Even more at odds with Klein's "Envy and gratitude" is Winnicott's view that aggression, no matter how sadistic, hostile, and murderous it might seem on the surface, can be transformed into a healthy form of assertive motility, if a patient can express it with the full affective intensity in which the unconscious needs to express itself. He arrives at this by working with borderline and schizoid patients who were pre-symbolic, that is, operating in the paranoid–schizoid position. Therefore, for Winnicott, the focus on the sadistic wish, which assumes that the analysand has a symbolic transference to a differentiated analyst, is counterproductive. Winnicott would view such interpretation as merely leaving the patient with such an overwhelming sense of badness that the guilt would remain unconscious, since it could not be transformed into the sublimated sense of "concern" through bringing a symbolised unconscious experience to consciousness. Analysis of the contrasts between Klein's and Winnicott's respective theories, particularly in relation to Klein's paper "Envy and gratitude" (1957) and Winnicott's "The use of an object and relating through identifications" (1968), indicates that they are partially divided in response to the kind of patients that they look at. Klein was doing a lot of training analysis with psychoanalysts in training, who had symbolic capacities and, thus, the capacities to use interpretations, as this can be seen in her clinical examples in "Envy and gratitude". Winnicott was focusing his theory on severely disturbed character disorder patients with critically arresting trauma in the first three years of development. Nevertheless, Klein and Winnicott also expressed different biases in their beliefs about aggression. Klein's focus on the innate aspects of aggression (which she implicitly and explicitly relates to Freud's concept of drives) contrasts with Winnicott's developmental focus. This conflict is highlighted when Klein's explicit belief in a death instinct provides a background for her paper "Envy and gratitude", where she emphasises unconscious experience as manifestations of innate hostile aggression. This hostile aggression is further depicted as a death instinct, despite momentary acknowledgements of the real mother, the real analyst, and of development in relation to these real life figures. Winnicott reacted to this background of theorising on the death instinct, causing him to neglect that "Envy and gratitude" is a profound *clinical* paper, which stands on its own, without being reduced to a de-personified and biologically based death instinct.

The mere fact that Klein uses the object related concepts of "envy" and "gratitude" makes her clinical observations personal and interpersonal. She brings blocks to love and intimacy into focus. Yet, in her commitment to psychoanalysis, she also stays with the internal world and its level of psychic fantasy as freeing the individual from unconscious dynamics. Winnicott might have appreciated all this, as would have many others, if Klein had not thrown in her metapsychology of the death instinct that slants the clinical phenomena so profoundly away from the character of the parents and their influence on development (as in Freud's (1917e) "shadow of the object" falling upon the ego). Klein's clinical work and theory are well-grounded, but her own metapsychological statements, so tied to her wishes to identify with her internal mother and to please Freud in his view as a drive theorist, obscure this from the reader's view.

Klein places her own clinical observations in jeopardy by excluding the profound impact of the real mother from the time of earliest development, only acknowledging the mother as a psychological factor at the time of the oedipal stage (Freud's oedipal, not her earlier oedipal). She also jeopardises the importance of her clinical findings by her emphasis on destructive aggression being inchoate within us all, not acknowledging the major differences in the capacity to use and integrate aggression based on the interaction with the real mother and real parents. Klein's need to hold on to all her original theories, without explicit modification of her metapsychology, even as her clinical and phenomenological theory grows, seems to have caused an emotional reaction in other theorists, such as Winnicott, as with its consequent conceptual response. Klein contrasts with Freud in this way, as he revised his theory of aggression three times. Perhaps, as Klein moved into new areas of the study of love and the primal need for reparation, Winnicott would have hoped that her original belief in humans as subject to a death instinct, irrespective of their parents' degree of psychic pathology, would be inadvertently modified, if not relinquished. If so, upon hearing her revitalised interest in innate hostile aggression in "Envy and gratitude", he might have suffered a particularly personal as well as theoretical mode of disappointment (especially because Klein was his earliest mentor, with all subsequent implications for his transference to her).

For Klein (1957), however, "Envy and gratitude" might have been a way of reinforcing the idealisation of her mother, while simultaneously attempting to differentiate that idealised view from her mother's dark side. Klein seems to have generalised her idealised view of her mother to all mothers, while focusing on the child's insatiable hunger, which she sees as turning vicious through the envy it induces. Klein spoke of her adult analysands as envious children grown up, without acknowledging the real deprivations and assaults from the mother that could have incited retaliatory impulses. With the theory of innate aggression, and of the death instinct, she protects the image of the mother, just as Fairbairn (1952) describes frustrated and traumatised children protecting the image of the mother. Although this is not true for modern Kleinians, Klein's original clinical theory was contaminated by her metapsychology of the death instinct, despite her astute clinical observations, and the real mother remains free of fault. She appears as aggressive only in reaction to the child's aggression, rather than the other way around. The child's demonic view of the mother is seen as a distortion based on the child's own hostile aggression. This aggression arises from an innately insatiable hunger, without any view of real deprivation of contact and connection with the mother that would lead to the child's aggression and retaliatory motives. In fact, in Kleinian theory, the mother can be seen as "too good", thus inciting envy and unconscious aggression in the child. This stands in stark contrast to Winnicott's "good enough mother". By having rich psychic gifts in her body and breasts, according to the view of the infant and child, the real mother becomes "too good". The mother, therefore, becomes the innocent victim of the child's hunger. This hunger is manifested as a sadistic rage that "weaponises" the child's body parts. (Here, Klein's theory is based on her experience and observation of children's fantasy and play during the "play therapy" she conducted.)

Klein views the child as seeking retaliation against the mother for her mere tantalising presence, which arouses unbearable and intolerable hunger. In the child's fantasy, the mother is always withholding from him/her, because she is seen as having the whole wealth of creation inside her body. Although this might be true on the level of psychic fantasy, making the world a place where complaints proliferate and gratitude is scarce, Klein makes no distinctions between the retaliatory agenda of a traumatically deprived child (one continually deprived of contact and connection with the mother) and the average child of frustrated desire, which was one of Freud's concerns. Neither does she discern the child's retaliatory impulses as a result of identification with the parent's retaliatory impulses, rather than as merely innate or the product of a death instinct.

Klein protects the image of her own mother in her theory as she speaks of the child's view of a fantasy mother dominating the child's perceptions, generalising this view to mothers in general. Winnicott, whose mother was more depressed than Klein's mother, studies the strengths and weaknesses of the real mother. Instead of focusing on the child's hatred, Winnicott focuses on the hatred in both the mother and the analyst. In the paper, "Hate in the counter-transference" (Winnicott,

1947), Winnicott analyses the lyrics at the end of the first stanza of the lullaby "Rock-a-bye baby" ("When the bough breaks, the cradle will fall, and down will come baby, cradle and all") and discovers the universal mother as a creature who harbours secret wishes to murder her child. In the same paper, he similarly views the analyst's object hatred of the pre-oedipally traumatised character disorder patient.

Only with recent developments in American object relations theory and developmental research can we look more critically at both Klein's and Winnicott's views. Through the work of Margaret Mahler, James Masterson, Jeffrey Seinfeld, and Althea Horner, we see the role of developmental stages in the interaction of infant and mother, child and mother. These stages overlap with Freud's libidinal oral, anal, phallic, and oedipal drive stages, and reveal an interesting psychic dialectical relationship with them.

Retaliatory aggression is not a death instinct

In "Envy and gratitude", Klein demonstrates her clinical approach to helping her analysands become conscious of their hidden, covert, and disguised expressions of hostility in the transference with the analyst. She followed Abraham, her own analyst, in being attuned to this negative transference, and saw its vivid manifestations in the comments, associations, fantasies, and dream fantasies of her patients. She noted the devaluing tendencies of some of her analysands, without noting any differential diagnostic distinctions that would help us see if such devaluation was more prominent in narcissistic patients than in others. For Klein, behind the fantasy of the aggressive behaviour in her analysands is the implied drive impulse. While "Envy and gratitude" is quite clinical, it does not focus on a metapsychology of drives *per se*, although she mentions the death instinct as a fact at the beginning of the paper. Klein implies that all hostile fantasy is directly attributable to the death instinct, which places psychic fantasy itself within the drive and its impulse motivation, as opposed to placing it in an internal world based on identifications with parental figures. None the less, there is room for questions about this hypothesis. Is this drive impulse, which is part of an object related state illustrated through psychic fantasy (unlike Freud's pure biological impulse of the primal hunger), or one primarily related to a retaliatory intention towards the object for whom one hungers? Is the drive impulse a retaliatory attack on an internal parent fantasy, which is partially based on the internalisation of a real mother, or is it merely a response to a pure fantasy mother, which already has libidinal and aggressive drive impulse built into it?

Klein's theory actually allows for both options. Although we step away from clinical phenomena to implied motive, and although we conjecture a drive impulse, we need not see this drive impulse as being in any way related to a death instinct. Libidinal hunger, in Klein's theory, always turns destructive, because it has a tendency to invoke envy. Klein does, however, distinguish between conscious and unconscious envy. It is the unconscious envy that results in an irrational belief that if one cannot have what the other has, the object must be destroyed in order to eliminate its tantalisation. When the infant's mind is possessed by unconscious envy and cannot distinguish (as those more developed, and in the depressive position, can) that you hurt yourself if you hurt the hand that feeds you, the infant supposedly turns to hostile impulse and attack. In relation to Klein's thinking, the infant's or child's mind cannot foresee that destroying the very essence of the nourishment offered, through devaluation as well as visceral attack, will inevitably lead to emotional starvation and to a perpetuation of the feeling that one is the "have not" while the other is the "have". Klein attempts to bring such understanding about the unconscious infant self by interpreting the unconscious hostile impulse to the adult mind of the analysand. She interprets the impulse by interpreting the psychic fantasy attached to that impulse, which is often semi-enacted in the transference, or is articulated in dreams and associations as transference fantasy. If Klein succeeds in her clinical approach, the analysand enters more deeply into a depressive position state of mind, as illustrated in "Envy and gratitude" (Klein, 1957). Once the depressive position has been entered, the analysand can feel love, need, and concern towards the other (always partially a displacement for the original mother), rather than remaining stuck in a polarised comparison with the other as the "have not" in relation to the "have". Consequently (and here is Klein's genius), the analysand can then become increasingly more comfortable taking from the other, on a conscious basis, without unconscious agendas, manipulative motives, and, thus, without dominance by persecutory terrors related to retaliatory agendas.

In Klein, the basic aggressive impulse is only modified by a consciousness that is dependent upon a growing capacity for object related concern. This involves a desire to develop basic "other"-related capacities for love, in the form of intimacy and in the passionate desire for mutuality within that intimate love. In Klein, this mature and mutual love also intermingles with, and is expressed through, gratitude. This movement into the depressive position evolves a growing capacity for love that need not be erotic love, although it can encompass erotic love. Ultimately, there is no theoretical need for a death instinct that must be overcome by a hunger for life. The hunger to love and the passion to interact with another in the immediate moment, so that an environment and sensation of love is created, is enough.

The hunger and desire for the mother expresses a life instinct, which brings the disturbing realisation that dependence on the mother includes frustrations and retaliatory rage reactions. Retaliatory rage may be experienced as a murderous wish. Yet, this has little to do with death, either for the mother or for the infant, latent in the unconscious of the adult analysand's mind. I might want to destroy the other to destroy what it has that tantalises me, over-stimulates me, overwhelms me, and eludes me. Yet, I do not really want the other to be dead. As Winnicott (1969) implies in his paper "The use of the object and relating through interpretations", and in *Playing and Reality* (Winnicott, 1971b), the infant perceives the mother as omnipotent, immortal, timeless, and eternal. Therefore, my wish to murder her had nothing to do with believing that she will ever or could ever die. Consequently, as long as she cannot die, killing her will not result in my death. To the degree that the primal mother is infinite and God-like, the child's attachment to her shields her from death. I would propose that this can be seen as a possible infant state of mind prior to the object relations consciousness of Klein's depressive position, and prior to the conscious struggle with life's limits and mortality. Such a depressive position awareness of death, however, has nothing to do with a death instinct.

I believe that Klein's focus on aggression, crystallised in "Envy and gratitude" (Klein, 1957), is best understood in its clinical form as an impulse to attack the other. I also believe that such an attack is experienced as retaliation due to the fantasy of the infinite richness of the other as the source of life and its nourishment. For example, I might feel compelled to retaliate against another just because the virtue of her existence seduces me. Then the real active seductions of the mother might add much fuel to my impulse to retaliate against the mother. In this way, I can create the illusion of having power over the all-powerful mother, and, ultimately (if I am unconsciously at the infant oral level), the illusion of being able to eat her all up.

The oral level of the aggressive manifestation is highlighted in the Isaacs' (1943) paper, "The nature and function of phantasy", during the era of the great debates. She gives the following example of psychic fantasy as it is born in a preverbal and oral form. King and Steiner (1991) describe how Isaacs spoke of a little boy of two who, when he was younger, would scream each time that he viewed ducks, and then had night terrors. It was only at two that he could put the terror that made him scream at night into words, saying, "White rabbit biting my toes" (King & Steiner, 1991, p. 313). The oral and envious wish towards the mother of the primary infant era is projected through a scream, turning the other, as represented by the ducks, into a persecutor. The scream expresses fear, defence, and aggression. It might have a hostile impulse that is retaliatory, one aimed at entirely consuming the mother, in addition to the hungry libidinal wish projected. However, it is certainly a sign of a need and desire to live, not to die. One screams at that what is feared, to defend against projected attack at an oral level, as well as to retaliate. Nevertheless, all this is part of a deep need to live, to survive, and to respond to the other, to whom one is intimately tied in an object relationship which began at birth.

Klein contributed greatly by extending Freud's focus on libidinal stages to a focus emphasising aggression and object relations. The Kleinians, during the British Society debates, were quite explicit about this (King & Steiner, 1991). Klein was particularly vivid in her descriptions of psychic fantasies of attack and retaliation against the other (who is perceived as persecutory), as they appear in clinical phenomena. Her contribution is compromised when her deep insight into the instinctual nature of retaliation is reduced to a death instinct. Whether one believes in innate aggression, or that it is merely a reaction to frustration (as Bowlby and Fairbairn maintained), the impulse to retaliate can be seen as having predispositions in the psyche (Masterson, 1979). However, Winnicott (1968) writes in his paper on "object usage" that the infant (or patient) wishes the other to survive the attack, even if the wish is profoundly murderous. One wishes to be able to fantasise murder without the ramifications of real-world death and retaliation. Consequently, to leap theoretically from Klein's vivid phenomenological theory on retaliatory aggression to that of a death instinct is unnecessary and probably fallacious. We could postulate, however, that if Klein herself had an internal world drama in a closed-off psychic area of re-enactment from childhood (see Fairbairn, 1952), she could well have turned her internal demon-lover mother into a theory of death instinct. She could have then clung to her death instinct theory as the metapsychological underpinning of her clinical phenomenology. In this way, Klein could have unconsciously been aiming to immortalise her mother, who seems to have also represented her own idealised self. By shaping her mother into a theory, Klein could have magically believed her mother would live forever. This would indeed have been Klein's "manic reparation". It is truly distinct from Klein's "true reparation", which would have involved confronting the extent of her mother's faults, problems, and weaknesses.

CHAPTER FOUR

Explicating and utilising the phenomenological theory

W innicott (1965, 1975) wrote about the formation of a "true self" in a human being who begins life in a dyadic relationship with a mother, who hopefully can offer "primary maternal preoccupation" to facilitate her infant's developmental growth into the state of having a "self". In dialectic with this, Klein offers us a phenomenological theory that can be fleshed out in developmental terms, but which also offers us the poignancy of a theorist who has lived very close to the existential nature of human suffering. In fact, Klein's phenomenology looks at moral growth through the lens of a human heart that bears its imprint on psychic experience.

Klein's phenomenological theory is one of two primary psychic state positions, each having its own unique constellation of defences, modes of object relations, and psychic structure. In *The Matrix of the Mind*, Ogden (1986) has done an admirable job of offering clinical examples for the different mental experience of the two positions. Prior to his work, Segal (1964) gave clinical examples in *An Introduction to Melanie Klein*. My own books, *The Compulsion to Create: Women Writers and Their Demon Lovers* (Kavaler-Adler, 1993a), *The Creative Mystique: From Red Shoes Frenzy to Love and Creativity* (Kavaler-Adler, 1996), and *Mourning, Spirituality and Psychic Change: A New*

Object Relations View of Psychoanalysis (Kavaler-Adler, 2003b), also offer such clinical examples. Here, I wish to merely make some fundamental observations about the importance of Klein's *psychic position* theory and its independence from a metapsychology based on the death instinct.

Although Ogden (1986) maintained that we all have oscillations back and forth between the paranoid–schizoid position and the depressive position, there are distinct movements in developmental growth that make us all increasingly capable of inhabiting the depressive position and working through its cycles and labyrinths. The clinical movements from one position to the other become critical in a moment-to-moment, alternating process when working with borderline level character disorder patients. The depressive position psyche is a position of increasing psychic integration. It is a position in which one can tolerate the grief of object loss and tolerate the disruptions and disappointments in object connection. Through the mourning of such loss in the depressive position, we find an avenue to self-integration and to symbolic forms of interpersonal connection, including interpersonal love and its components of emotional and erotic intimacy. In the borderline character, however, traumatic disruption of mother–child bonding during the varying phases of separation–individuation creates a dissociative process that manifests as the dynamics of the paranoid–schizoid position. This view, based on Mahler's (1979) research, and the work of Masterson (1976, 1981, 1985, 2000) and Rinsley (1982, 1989) at the Menninger clinic, differs in terms of its developmental timetable from that of Klein. Klein proposes that the paranoid–schizoid position is a natural early developmental phenomenon that transforms at six months of life to the depressive position. Although Klein might be right that we all have a primary mode of developmental splitting (which involves a polarised view of the self and of the internal mother as "all good" or "all bad"), the pathological splitting that appears in the defensive processes of the character disorders (narcissistic, borderline, and schizoid) need not be present from birth. I concur with Seinfeld (1990) that much of what Klein describes as the dysfunctional aspects of the paranoid–schizoid position could, in fact, be related to critical pre-oedipal trauma in which the primary self cannot stay cohesive when separation comes about with an inadequate mother. Therefore, the objections of Balint (1965, 1979), Bowlby (1969, 1980), Winnicott (1971b), and others to the idea of an infant first existing in a primarily paranoid state, while joining in an alliance with the idealised part of the mother to ward off the anticipated persecutory part of her, might be quite justified. Winnicott's mother–infant dialectic allows for the experience of communication in both the mother and infant from the beginning of life. This is supported by infant research on mother–infant *in vivo* interactions (Beebe & Lachmann, 1988; Beebe & Stern, 1977; Stern, 1985).

Unlike Klein, modern theorists, including neo-Kleinians, influenced by both clinical work and developmental research, have emphasised the critical role of the real mother from the beginning of life. Given this view, early infancy can be seen much less as an ongoing persecutory state than Klein proposed. Klein might have been not only adultomorphising the infant state, based on her work with adult patients and children that were at least two years old, but she also might actually have been theorising from a position of projection and generalisation in relation to her own unconscious antagonism with her mother. Nevertheless, when we look at common psychic fantasies from childhood that persist in the unconscious, we find Klein's belief that the child perpetually wished to blame the mother for all hurts, disappointments, frustrations, and narcissistic injuries strongly persuasive, whether these were related to an interaction with the mother or not. This tendency to externalise blame can be seen as part of the paranoid–schizoid position state of mind. However, as Klein (1946, 1975) acknowledged when she wrote about the normal child's capacity to form an alliance with the idealised mother or the idealised, "all good breast", the paranoid antagonism with the mother is not an ongoing state. It is only in pathological cases that this paranoid attitude of the paranoid position becomes a perpetual state of mind. See the case of Phillip in *Mourning, Spirituality and Psychic Change* (Kavaler-Adler, 2003b) to view the fantasy level of infant paranoia in a depressive position level patient, who can symbolise the paranoid state and the externalised blame that comes with infant helplessness.

Borderline/narcissistic pathology and the paranoid–schizoid position

On a clinical level, in borderline patients who have suffered critical trauma during the separation–individuation period, or who suffer ongoing abuse and attack, the splitting and paranoia of the paranoid–schizoid position appears prominent and perpetual. In understanding these patients, Klein's view of the paranoid–schizoid position and the projective identification enactments that result from the splitting and dissociation of this primitive position becomes helpful. From this clinical perspective, it becomes unnecessary to refer to the death instinct, which Klein added to the clinical observations in her metapsychological discussions. There is no need to add in the death instinct to understand a toddler caught in a bind, in which developmental needs for individuation are opposed by a mother who (because of her own borderline condition) cannot let go of a more merged and symbiotic way of relating. The child will be forced to split off the experience and image of an intolerably "bad" mother, as well as the deprived, angry, and helpless perception of the self in relation with that mother. There is no need for the "death instinct" metapsychology to understand that the conscious ego becomes depleted and enraged as a consequence of this splitting off and clings to the hope of finding an idealised mother to repair the situation.

It is a matter of developmental object relations interactions and internalisations. Winnicott described the real mother's impact, although he focused on the "good-enough mother" rather than the pathological mother. Yet, it is clear that the schizoid form of depression of Winnicott's mother massively affected his own character development. His personal musings in his poetry illustrate how Winnicott always felt he had to enliven a dead mother: "To enliven her was my living" (as quoted by Phillips, 1988, p. 29). We can contrast this to how Melanie Klein seems to have always felt she had to defend herself against the persecutory intrusions and guilt-provoking accusations of her narcissistic mother.

With an inadequate mother at the separation–individuation phases of development, the toddler (because of his extreme dependence on her) feels torn apart by the conflicting impulses to move towards and away from the mother. To protect the self, the toddler splits off the mother into "good" and "bad" parts (Masterson, 1976, 1981, 1985). Once this splitting-off of the mother is done, the bad mother (who threatens death because the self cannot grow in relation to her) becomes a pervasive fantasy, as well as a reality. Then the toddler's terror of her control and manipulation cause the heightening of paranoia and retaliatory impulses.

Grosskurth's biography of Klein indicates that Melanie Klein's mother exerted the kind of control and manipulation that could induce the child's helplessness in the face of losing any adequate sense of self. This can be seen when Melanie's mother infantilised her by sending her off to vegetate in health spas, rather than allow her to struggle with the responsibilities of early adult life. Split-off retaliatory impulses can cause the child to perceive his/her own aggression as coming from the other, and can sometimes make the other's aggression appear to be coming from the self. Through projective identification, any "other" present with the borderline child or adult (including the other of the therapist) will experience the impact of the borderline person's provocation to be and feel like a sadist, as the sadistic control and aggression of the mother and the angry self is continually re-enacted. By provoking the other's sadism, the borderline employs his unneutralised aggression (combined with the internal bad mother's imprint), to convey an aversive visceral-level experience to the "other". Perhaps Klein had first-hand knowledge of these dynamics from her own childhood and, hence, was sensitive to seeing them in her clinical work. Klein addressed just such a phenomenon when she described the paranoid–schizoid position and its primitive defences: splitting, projective identification, primitive denial, introjective identification, and spoiling devaluation, in which any sense of good in the object is destroyed. When the capacity to tolerate ambivalence is lacking (along with the lack of observing one's own ego reflection) the object is perceived as "all bad" or "all good". Then hate and its manifestations of anger will not be tolerated along with love for the same object. This signifies a paranoid–schizoid state of mind, along with the many significant lacks in ego functioning, which result from splitting and its continual disruption of the self and its psychic development. One significant lack in ego functioning that keeps the borderline character in the state of a reactive being is described by Ogden (1986, 1994) as the inability to be an "interpreting subject". Without the depressive position level of symbolic functioning, the person sees the world as black and white, as made up of victim–aggressor relations (see also the "demon-lover complex" in Kavaler-Adler, 1986, 1988, 1989, 1993a, 1996). Rather than perceiving and interpreting all that is around him or her, such an individual reacts and blames. There is no sense of processing one's own experience in this position because mental processing of experience is a symbolic process.

This understanding of psychic structure is not dependent on any theory of life and death instinct metapsychology. As Kernberg's (1975) diagnostic views have articulated, ego structure is either healthy or a pathological conglomeration of self and other object relations structures within an internal world. The formation of the ego can be understood as the exigencies of life in relation to the real mother from prenatal life to birth. However, the formation of the ego also reflects the psychic fantasy from a hypothetical primal self that has libidinal and aggressive urges. These urges need not be reduced to life and death instincts. A primal realm of unconscious self-experience also need not be called an id. However, psychic fantasy at a conscious level portrays an experience of internal dynamic objects. This experience can be felt through visceral sensations, through emotional affects, or through a sense of internal voices or thoughts and feelings that "speak to us". Our sense of being a self, and of having an identity or personality, is always joined with these internal objects on an affect level, and operates as a phenomenal psychic gestalt. It is this phenomenal psychic gestalt that comes so alive in the vivid visceral and visual image world of Melanie Klein. It is a world that cannot rise or fall on the basis of change in metapsychology, whether it is towards or away from the idea of a death instinct. Whatever we experience at the conscious level is a mixture of dynamics of self and other. Between self and other we have affective links that make visualising our hearts, our hearts' connections to others, and blocks to those connections so meaningful.

With this thinking in mind, Klein's theories become more consonant with those of Winnicott, who always viewed pathology as a result of failings in development, although he, like Klein, knew that much aggression could be innate (Winnicott, 1945). In their clinical observations, both Klein and Winnicott noted how severe character pathology related back to the early life experience with the actual mother. Klein attributed a great deal more to the power of the internal world's psychic fantasy mother, particularly in the more malignant forms of the fantasy mother, but she always viewed the actual "good" mother as being needed for compensation against an internal persecutory mother. In this way, Klein accounted for the mother's developmental impact. Winnicott went along with Klein's distinction between an idealised fantasy mother and an actually experienced "good" external mother by coining the term "good enough mother". He then focused on descriptions of mother–child bonding, some of which related to a mother whose "impinging" interfered with "good enough" mothering. In fact, according to Winnicott, when impingement reaches a traumatic level, character pathology manifests, which he referred to as "false self" pathology (Winnicott, 1960b, 1965). So, there are overlaps between Klein's and Winnicott's theories, in developmental terms, but their theories contrast and form a dialectic: Klein's persecutory mother is seen as an internal world fantasy, while Winnicott's impinging mother (or "too omnipotent" mother) is seen as an actual part of the external mother.

The depressive position

When we reach Klein's depressive position, we no longer feel blocks to connections, primarily in the form of splitting, which cut off connections to others and to ourselves. In the depressive position, we do not experience externalised impulses combined with early affect links to internal objects as projections of haunting ghosts and aversive or intrusive monsters from without. We begin to feel our own monstrous longings and fears, our own powerful and conflicting urges towards and away from connections with others. We become aware of our own tendencies to cut off feeling our connections and our presence with others when pain and aggression threaten to overwhelm us or merely threaten to make us uncomfortable. The depressive position is a psychic place of longing, compassion, and regret. It is a position of mourning loss, of disappointment, and of guilt-laden remorse that can turn grief and love into concern and reparation. It is a place of tenderness, or of the deep and subtle pain of hurting when conscious of hurting the one you love. The depressive position is also a place in which retaliatory impulses are contained and relinquished, and a place that shelters many different shades of pain.

Depressive position pain is affectively felt and, therefore, it can bring meaning through conscious suffering. Such conscious and existential suffering always has meaning in relation to the other, as well as in relation to carrying the burden of conscious struggle between parts of one's own self; parts that can speak and create a dialogue, if they are held and sustained together in one's awareness. For Winnicott, the critical route to self-integration and to the ownership of one's own internal experience (including motivations and impulses) is the process of progressive internalisation of a "good enough" external mother figure. One example of this is Winnicott's (1958) article "The capacity to be alone", in which one becomes able to tolerate and fully enjoy being alone through the developmental process of internalising the "good enough" mother, a mother who can be with her child in a tranquil state of presence and attunement, rather than impinging with any of her own needs, demands, or emotions. Through this internalisation process, Winnicott (1963), in a related paper titled "The development of the capacity for concern", proposes that the child can develop authentic concern, that is, empathy, for the mother, and learn to tolerate and contain guilt, although concern requires a mother to validate the good qualities of the child, not just to be there in a tranquil state of being. Winnicott's journey to such thinking about the capacity for concern definitely overlaps Klein's thinking about feeling for oneself and about the subjectivity of the other, that is, the growth of empathy in the depressive position. In fact, Winnicott even suggested to Klein that she call her depressive position a position of concern (Grosskurth, 1986).

Klein's incomplete mourning

Klein foresaw this place, but she only outlined certain basic aspects of its psychic organisation. Like Moses looking forward into a promised land that he could not enter, Klein did not stay there long enough to see the broader dimensions of the psychic world she had discovered and called the "depressive position". I believe, after reading Grosskurth's extensively researched biography (1986), that this was a consequence of her own developmental trauma, and to the continuing exacerbation of this trauma through her dependent reactions to a characterologically disturbed mother. I propose that a regressive pathological tie to her mother had promoted an arrested psychic state of pathological mourning, and this prevented Klein from proceeding with the "developmental mourning" of the depressive position (see examples in Kavaler-Adler, 1992a, 1993a, 1996, 2003b, 2004, 2006a,b,c, 2007). I propose that Klein did not have a psychoanalyst long enough, or one with enough awareness of the mourning process, to help her proceed far enough with her developmental grief and mourning. She did not have the transitional object she needed to internalise a better internal object. Klein did experience the first intimations of her own developmental mourning and its connection to her internal world and internal mother object when she began to mourn the death of Hans, her adult son, when she wrote a description of Mrs A in "Mourning and its relation to manic-depressive states" (Klein, 1940). I believe that she was capable of this mourning through Mrs A's role as a temporary transitional object, which, of course, is also dependent on her having had sufficient infant good mothering from her mother in order to use another as a transitional object.

Mourning, compassion, and symbolisation

The clinical cases I have presented in my earlier books and articles, such as *Mourning, Spirituality, and Psychic Change: A New Object Relations View of Psychoanalysis* (Kavaler-Adler, 2003b), give a broader perspective on the depressive position than anything I can describe in more abstract terms. Each mourning process is unique, and yet shares certain developmental progressions that can be related to psychic structure formation and integration. Each clinical mourning process illustrates that what might feel like self-destructive compulsions in the self (and which might even feel, at the level of deepest despair, like some instinct to die) can be transformed through consciously suffering the pain and grief of loss, disappointment, guilt, and regret. A fully conscious regret, just like a fully conscious object loss, can be a turning point towards self-integration and developmentally progressive psychic change. Conscious experience of these self and affect states can result in a transformation of self-feeling that expands and enlivens one's capacities to maintain loving connections with others with whom one can then also promote intimacy. Such conscious experience of self- and object-related affect states also reinforces one's capacities for creativity through such loving connections (Bion's (1959) "links") as they are internalised.

Melanie Klein seems to have understood much of this. She understood that love and creativity come from the same psychic object relations avenues, and that opening channels to loving connections energises them both. Since intimacy in love and inspiration in creative work both come from the same form of psychic energy (and from the same form of psychic structure, based on internal self and object connections), they can also be blocked in the same way. That is the mourning process that Klein discovered within herself. She noticed that this process could be opened up from unconscious blocks and resistances by making conscious hostile aggressive fantasies towards primal love objects. This conscious processing of aggression became part of the mourning process that opens the mutual avenues leading to love and creativity. I address this dynamic in my theory of the "love–creativity dialectic" in *The Creative Mystique* (Kavaler-Adler, 1996).

Klein's original conception of the depressive position led to all of this, even though her original understanding of this position was related to tolerating an ambivalent love. When love and hate towards the same object can be felt consciously, one has reached the depressive position level of this ambivalent love. This means that one can become angry at the loved other without spoiling the other's image in one's mind, without deserting it, without devaluing it, and without throwing it away. Even primal envy can be tolerated in consciousness within the depressive position state of mind, since it can be symbolised through words and, thus, can be conceptualised and communicated, rather than being acted out in a destructive assault or in a mental annihilation of the external/internal other. Klein realised that when aggression can be contained and symbolised, it could be modified by love for the object, whether that aggression is thought of as innate or as reactive to frustration and/or narcissistic injury. If the impulse to retaliate can be conceptualised, and the feelings of rage can be felt, rage can transform into compassion and concern, since the primary bond of love with the object is sustained. Klein counted on love as a modifying force.

Klein knew, however, that love can transform hate and modify hurt and loss only if it survives, which love cannot do unless one is in the depressive position state of mind. It is in the depressive position that one experiences how the good in the other can be sustained in one's heart as well as in one's mind. Within the paranoid–schizoid position, by contrast, any hurt, disappointment, or injury immediately cancels out the good in the other. This creates a spoiling operation that promotes and perpetuates emptiness in the self, where once the object connection was felt with love. The self is weakened each time retaliatory rage causes hatred to wipe out love and the goodness of the object. In the depressive position, however, the self is sustained, strengthened, and even deepened as its capacity to modify conscious rage with love develops for the object, as well as for others in general. Sustaining love results in compassion and concern. Yet, this results without the denial of retaliatory impulses, as they manifest in visceral sensations and visual fantasies. The hate can be felt and conceptualised. It is not repressed or split off on to another. Persecution is, thus, lessened rather than increased as the owning of one's hate allows for its neutralisation through compassion and love. Concern develops as guilt over one's own hate can be contained rather than being acted out as an aggressive assault on the other. This all follows from Klein's original tenet that the depressive position is a position of tolerating hate and love for the same object. If we accept Grosskurth's (1986) biographical view, however, it is just this tenet that Klein herself could not live up to. If Klein denied the degree of pain, loss, and frustration that her mother caused, with the result that she defended against that repressed and dissociated "identification with the aggressor", it appears that Klein did not modify her hate through love (because she denied that her hate for her primal mother existed). Significantly, Klein seems to have become acutely aware of the hate in others, and perhaps this was in part due to Klein's own repressed hatred, which could easily arouse her sensitivity to hate in the other.

Consciously, Klein denies her own hate towards her mother and brother, except when she explicitly and bravely identifies it in the case of Mrs A in "Mourning and its relation to manic-depressive states" (Klein, 1940). It is in this paper that Klein begins the mourning process that she never completes, one she so developmentally and psychically needed. When Klein is not identifying hate and owning it as she did in "Mourning and its relation to manic-depressive states", she is vulnerable to projection, as well as to the enacted rivalries that were rife in her own professional group and context. Keeping her hate unconscious seems to have resulted in it being split off and projected on to those considered her enemies in the psychoanalytic camp. The description of this is vivid in Grosskurth (1986), particularly when she looks at the great debates and at the overall politics of the British Psychoanalytic Society at that time. Splitting off from her hatred related to early traumatic disruptions, whether in dissociation or in later repression, Klein could have created an internal world of sealed off animosity for herself. Such sealed off animosity could, in turn, be felt on an affective level to have the explosive impulse energy of a death instinct. Consequently, Klein relates to Freud's concept of the death instinct in purely psychological, rather than biological, terms.

Klein's journey in "Love, guilt, and reparation" with references to Winnicott

Although Klein wrote her preliminary study on "Envy and gratitude" in 1924, she did not publish it (in more developed thinking) until 1957. Meanwhile, her thoughts moved away from the instinctual aspects of aggression into the object relations areas of what she might classify as part of a basic life force or life instinct. In 1937, Klein published her major work, "Love, guilt and reparation". This was three years prior to her exploration of the mourning process as an incipient developmental process in "Mourning and its relation to manic-depressive states". The triad of love, guilt, and reparation was a profound examination of the reparative motif of hope that evolved and transformed itself throughout the lifecycle of human interpersonal relations.

If "Love, guilt and reparation" were followed only by "Mourning and its relation to manic-depressive states" and not by the culminating note on innate aggression in "Envy and gratitude", Winnicott, as well as others, might have remained Kleinians. Significantly, Winnicott's interest in the human capacity for concern following a period of infantile ruthlessness is certainly resonant with Klein's (1975) theoretical endeavours in *Love, Guilt and Reparation*. The primal craving for attachment, which ultimately achieves the existential moral level of concern for the other, is related to by Melanie Klein through the metaphor and motif of what I would call the "reparative gesture". Its impulse is primary and its motive of attachment profound, and is one of depth. Children and animals alike demonstrate it. All of us yearn for the forgiveness of our retaliatory attacks through the initiation of reparative gestures, following the transformation of guilt into remorse and regret.

The striving for reparation with any displacement figure representing the primal mother is, for Klein, as passionate as any sexual act, and it sometimes includes a sexual act. Klein's deep libidinal core of longing for her own mother, as well as its colouration through oedipal desire for her father, are seen in "Love, guilt and reparation", an article of spiritual faith. Klein is perhaps the only theorist to deal with the ingredients of true tenderness. This article also reflects Klein's generative interest in the subject of creativity:

> The baby's impulses and feelings are accompanied by a kind of mental activity which I take to be the most primitive one: that is phantasy-building or more colloquially, imaginative thinking . . . Such primitive phantasizing is the earliest form of the capacity which later develops into the more elaborate workings of the imagination. (Klein, 1975, p. 308)

One form of creativity employs aggression, as Winnicott (1965) would also point out in his paper on object survival, in response to Klein's views. In "Love, guilt and reparation", Klein (1975) writes, "In his aggressive phantasies he wishes to bite up and to tear up his mother and her breasts, and to destroy her also in other ways" (Klein, 1975, p. 308). This is a vivid description of what borderline patients express quite readily in the clinical situation. In others, such fantasies may remain unconscious until repression in analysis is lifted over time. But for Klein, the raw gutsy quality of inner life, with all its violent body-based forms of murder, is the fuel for creative development, as the symbolic gifts of the depressive position evolve. Klein, as a woman, knew that birth is violent, and she never excluded violence from the most generative form of pregnancy of the mind. She would very well understand Virginia Woolf's experience of the word flow in her conscious mental space as being an erotic flow that is felt as a form of uterine eroticism, with pregnancy resolving through the creative act (see Kavaler-Adler, 1996).

In "Love, guilt and reparation", Klein (1975) updates psychoanalysis by challenging the belief that the oedipal lust of a child is only directed in a gender stereotyped way towards the opposite sex parents. In this paper, Klein is quite explicit that the little girl also has erotic desires towards her mother and wishes to win her away from her father, and that the little girl also wishes to express love for the father. Klein does not reduce this phenomenon to a linear stage pre- and sub-category such as the Freudian notion of the negative oedipal stage. She maintains, as always, the complex multi-textural determination of psychic events, emphasising again psychic positions and attitudes as opposed to developmental stages. This is both a weakness and a strength in her theory. Klein even allows room for the superiority of the homosexual connection, particularly in women, where the mother is the desired object:

> Nevertheless sexual phantasies and desires towards her mother do remain active in the little girl's mind. Under the influence of those she wants to take her father's place in connection with her mother, and in certain cases *these desires and phantasies may develop more strongly even than those towards the father*. (Klein, 1975, p. 310, my italics)

In a footnote, Klein explains that aggressive dynamics are always concurrent with the loving side of human affairs. However, on the loving side, we have faith in a deep innate compassion, which can thrive when guilt and narcissistic defence systems are not too powerful. Here reparative strivings emerge:

> Even in the small child one can observe a concern for the loved one, which is, as one might think, merely a sign of dependence upon a friendly and helpful person. Side by side with the destructive impulses in the unconscious mind both of the child and of the adult, there exists a profound urge to make sacrifices, in order to help and to put right loved people who in phantasy have been harmed or destroyed. In the depths of the mind, the urge to make people happy is linked up with a strong feeling of responsibility and concern for them, which manifests itself in genuine sympathy with other people and in the ability to understand them, as they are and as they feel. (Klein, 1975, p. 311)

In contrast to Winnicott (1963), Klein (1975) sees concern as an innate capacity, disregarding developmental milestones. It is her depressive position that develops the true capacity for concern. In her view of sacrifice, however, an altruistic element enters the picture. Such an altruistic psychic element could become an unconscious burden, especially in those who have not entered the depressive position sufficiently to accept the limits of life and mortality.

In her paper on negative therapeutic reaction, Riviere (1936) converted Klein's words on sympathy and sacrifice from infancy into essential cause of a negative therapeutic reaction. In writing of the intransigent nature of a negative therapeutic reaction in a manic-depressive patient, Riviere (1936) writes of the unconscious terror of any psychic change towards integration and health, mostly due to her patient's unconscious belief that in order to get better she has to become responsible for repairing hundreds of others who exist in a purgatorial state of pain in the patient's internal psychic world. I believe that Riviere (1936) is actually describing a paranoid–schizoid experience of omnipotence and primitive guilt, which is quite different from the depressive position state of mind, in which concern for a separate individual is felt. The others in Riviere's patient's world seem to be part objects, and the compulsion towards self-sacrifice seems to almost be some form of self-mutilation. Nevertheless, even within the depressive position, the sense of obligation within the mourning process can be quite burdensome. This is illustrated by one of my male patients who felt he was doing the grief work for seven generations of relatives every time he sobbed out his own grief on the couch. Klein does not see the capacity for concern as a threat, but, rather, as an asset. Discussing it, she moves into her theory of empathy (without using that particular term), through the theme of reparation.

> To be genuinely considerate implies that we can put ourselves in the place of other people: we identified ourselves with them. Now this capacity for identification with another person is a most important element in human relationships in general, and is also a condition for real and strong feeling of love. We are only able to disregard or to some extent sacrifice our own feelings and desires, and thus for a time to put the other person's interests and emotions first, if we have the capacity to identify ourselves with the loved person. Since in being identified with other people we share, as it were, the help or satisfaction afforded to them by ourselves, we regain in one way, what we have sacrificed to another. (Klein, 1975, p. 311)

Klein continues on the resolution of guilt through reparation:

> Our grievances against our parents for having frustrated us together with the feelings of hate and revenge to which these have given rise (in us, and again, the feelings of guilt and despair arising out of this hate and revenge because we have injured the parents whom at the same time we loved) – all these, in phantasy, we may undo in retrospect (taking away some of the grounds for hatred) by playing at the same time the parts of loving parents and loving children. At the same time, in our unconscious phantasy we make good the injuries which we did in phantasy, and for which we still unconsciously feel very

guilty. This "making reparation" is, in my view, a fundamental element in love and in all human relationships; I shall therefore refer to it frequently in what follows. (1975, p. 313)

Klein's thoughts here can be seen to be leading up to the topic of mourning, which emerges three years later in "Mourning and its relation to manic-depressive states" (Klein, 1940). I say this because separation involves making good through a necessary acknowledgement of loss as a conscious regret towards the loved other. One acknowledges the aggression only at the point of mourning the loss. Otherwise, retaliatory impulses would overcome reparative urges and strivings. For Klein, reparation is a mourning process. This can be seen *in vivo* within my "mourning regrets" groups, which I conducted for over fifteen years. In her own life, however, I think that Klein had failed to repair her retaliatory attacks on her mother by being a good mother because idealising her mother kept Klein even more in the position of a displaced retaliatory rage. She displaced the rage at her mother through attacks on her children. For example, Grosskurth (1986) reports how Klein (as a parent) criticised her son, Eric, after she insisted on supervising her child's analyst. Grosskurth (1986) also reports that Klein battled with colleagues who were seen as theoretical opponents, some of whom were truly antagonistic to her, such as Edward Glover. Klein identified with her mother as an aggressor. In keeping with Klein's biographer's view, the aggressive mother was the real mother of Klein's childhood whom she internalised, not merely a fantasy mother as Klein herself might have advocated. Klein's internal mother, as well as the pre-oedipal attachment to that mother that Klein internalised, also involved a primary identification that formed a blueprint within Klein's psychic structure. In other words, in keeping with Grosskurth (1986), Klein can be seen to have formed an internal bad mother/bad self structure reminiscent of Fairbairn's (1952) form of anti-libidinal ego structure.

Failing to have faced her rage at her own mother sufficiently when she played the role of a good mother, to whatever extent she did so, Klein might have only been promoting a defensive compensation, rather than a truly reparative experience. To be truly reparative, in line with her own ideas, Klein would have had to have mourned her mother more fully—which would include facing her mother's envy and possessiveness—as a way of facing the source of her rage.

Consequently, Klein could have mourned losses that she created in retaliatory attacks against her mother, but to have done so she might have needed a psychoanalyst on a much more long-term basis than she had when she entered treatment with Abraham, a psychoanalyst, who, like Abraham, could have allowed the negative transference to emerge focused on him.

In speaking of the heterosexual love and marriage between a man and woman, Klein brings an important factor into the mutuality of a true and complex love relationship. She never neglects the dark side, although she apologises for being too schematic at times (as in a footnote, Klein, 1975, p. 313). She emphasises the sharing of grief as well as the sharing of pleasure in a full relationship, knowing that one cannot exist without the other:

> This implies a deep attachment, a capacity for maternal sacrifice, a sharing – *in grief as well as in pleasure*, in interests as well as in sexual enjoyment. A relationship of this nature affords the widest scope for the most varied manifestations of love. (Klein, 1975, p. 313, my italics)

In the above extract, Klein is quite intuitively aware that love can only thrive when both partners in a relationship can tolerate grief. They can share it and, through this sharing, allow a natural mourning of life's "necessary" and extraordinary losses to emerge. Klein would be well aware that in any couple, if one partner defended against grief with a manic defence, the other partner would suffer from depression as well as from the unnecessary burden of the necessity to grieve on one's own (in order to repair the self through mourning). When one partner is stuck in depression or is overloaded with the responsibility of mourning losses that affect both members of the couple, there can be no adequate reparation of the couple. This prevents any renewal of love and mutuality from coming about within the couple. There will, thus, have to be an impasse between the members of the couple with modes of defence structure being reinforced on both sides.

Klein does not, however, deal with the threat of incest. She claims that a man can find a good mother in a wife, perhaps even better than his own original mother, without suffering guilt. Here, Klein is weak theoretically (while Freud would be strong here). She writes. "The man has now, as it were, this mother for his own, with relatively little feeling of guilt" (Klein, 1975, p. 313). Klein also neglects to account for all the problems that stem from adults trying to recreate their childhood and compensate for it in adulthood, with the impossibility of internalising that which was lacking in childhood in a fully defended adult psychic structure, without the deconstruction of that structure and the painful mourning process that goes with it. Even with such deconstruction in analysis, the compensating internalisation in adulthood is never what it would have been if formed in childhood. Consequently, Klein's poetic view in this paper begins to sound somewhat naïve.

Klein writes of the happy and gratifying sexual relationship in a marriage that she never had herself. From Grosskurth's (1986) research on Klein's life and correspondence, it appears that she turned her own retaliatory rage towards her husband, displacing it from her mother. Perhaps Klein could easily blame her husband and protect her mother from her wrath because of the idealisation of a husband's power that she expresses in "Love, guilt and reparation". In this paper, Klein idealises a husband's power to heal his wife. Klein writes of a good husband while rejecting her own husband, whom she experienced as the bad object, going back to a split-off bad mother. Despite any degree of defensive idealisation of a husband, Klein's theoretical points are still important in terms of the potential reparative nature of external interpersonal relations, providing that one is not sealed off in a closed system due to pathological mourning (with its splitting and repression):

> All these unconscious phantasies influence greatly the woman's feelings towards her husband. If he loves her and also gratifies her sexually, her unconscious sadistic phantasies will lose in strength. But since these are not entirely put out of action . . . they lead to a stimulation of phantasies of a restoring nature; thus once more the drive to make reparation is brought into action. Sexual gratification affords her not only pleasure, but reassurance and support against the fears and feelings of guilt which were the result of her early sadistic wishes. This reassurance enhances sexual gratification and gives rise in the woman to feelings of gratitude, tenderness and increased love. Just because there is somewhere in the depths of her mind a feeling that her genital is dangerous and could injure her husband's genital – which is a derivative of her aggressive phantasies towards her father – one part of the satisfaction she obtains comes from the fact that she is capable of giving her husband pleasure and she is capable of giving her husband pleasure and happiness, and that her genital thus proves to be good. (Klein, 1975, p. 314)

There is no other psychoanalytic theorist who so poignantly deals with these difficult and complex emotional states of tenderness and gratitude. In her writings on "Love, guilt and reparation", Klein (1975) acknowledges the impact of real parents and real objects in a significant way. For example, Klein writes,

> The emotional attitude and the sexuality of a man in his relation to his wife are of course also influenced by his past. The frustration by his mother of his genital desires in his childhood aroused phantasies in which his penis became an instrument which could give pain and cause injury to her. (1975, p. 315)

As Klein grew into her theory on reparation, I find her to be increasingly focused on the influence of the real object, the real primal parental object (mother), as opposed to focusing primarily on hypothetical "a priori" fantasy objects. Looking over the time span of her theoretical work, as described by Segal (1964) in her *Introduction to Melanie Klein*, as well as my own experience of reading the text of her critical paper "Envy and gratitude" (Klein, 1957), it is clear that Klein's focus on the real object began at the point when she spoke of the importance of the mother receiving reparative gifts. I use the term "reparative gestures", related to Winnicott's (1965) omnipotent "gestures", as expressed by the child and/or character disorder patient. Segal (1964) stated that the child within the mind of the adult psychoanalytic patient will decline into depression and paranoia if the transference mother does not welcome any reparative offering. Klein (1957) shows a similar dynamic in her own original work in "Envy and gratitude". She gives the example of a patient's dream in which a ball is thrown up towards a couple and is not caught or received by the couple. In her interpretation, the ball represents a reparative gift that is not received, with the consequence of depression descending upon the one who has offered the reparative gift.

Envy and gratitude: Klein's relationship with Winnicott, where only opposition was seen

In the fuller version of "Envy and gratitude", Klein (1957) returns to her preoccupation with a primal aggressive force within us.

Nevertheless, it is important to note her relatively new open-mindedness to the idea of internalisation as a developmental and clinical process that emerges at the very end of this more finished paper. Klein speaks of the "good enough" (Winnicott's term) clinical experience in which the analyst is internalised as a good object, which she distinctly distinguishes from an idealised object, which is a psychic fantasy object. This internalisation depends on the analyst using her role as an interpreter of repressed experience adequately to help relieve the analysand's distress of an overwhelming psychic condition in the face of hunger and its related mode of oral aggression, unconscious envy. Klein does not account for the mere psychic presence of the analyst, as Winnicott does in his concept of the "holding environment", but she does see a state of benign goodness in relatedness being internalised by the analysand, especially when the analyst relieves anxiety and depression through the astute and apt offering of psychoanalytic interpretations. By accounting for internalisation within the clinical treatment room and its interpretative interaction, Klein acknowledges the avenue for developing an increasingly benign influence on the analysand's psyche (as long as the analysand remains open to taking in help, knowledge, understanding, and concern) and is not trapped in a closed psychic system, like the anti-libidinal ego system based on layers of dissociation, as described by Fairbairn (1952).

Although Klein focuses mainly on internalisation as a by-product of psychoanalytic interpretation (emphasising that the analyst must be experienced as a good object rather than an idealised one) in order for the interpretations of the analyst to be used, she also opens the door to a broader view of internalisation that Winnicott developed. For it follows that if a good analyst can be internalised through interpretations, then the actual experience of being with the analyst, of relating to him/her, the experience of the presence and containment of the analyst (Winnicott's "holding environment" and Bion's "container") can also be internalised through psychic digestion (converting Bion's "beta" into "alpha" elements, or the proto-symbolic into symbolic psychic elements). Once Klein allows for this entry into the developmental process within the clinical process, her ideas on envy become more easily associated with a retaliatory impulse of revenge. Although instinctual origins might be noted in relation to such a retaliatory impulse, and although Klein might neglect the critical identification with the real parent in an identification with the aggressor, there is no mention in this later thinking of the "death instinct" as an abstract and idiosyncratic malignant force. Destructive envy, as opposed to envy with admiration and concern, can be associated with primal developmental ruptures and developmental arrest, rather than with a form of retaliatory aggression that is assumed to be innate. When there is a primal rupture in mother–child bonding during the pre-oedipal stages of self-formation (called a "basic fault" by Balint, 1979), a closed system is created. It is this closed system that can be experienced as a "death instinct". Actually, Klein's clinical material (as well as her theoretical views on infants) reflects more of a fear of death or "terror", rather than a death instinct. In his article, "Some notes on the origin of despair and its relationship to destructive envy", Alexander (1997) addressed the developmental failings that precede a personality configuration exhibiting destructive envy as a primal motivation. Alexander (1997) wrote that Melanie Klein accepted Freud's idea of the death instinct as an "inborn force", which causes "fear of annihilation". Persecutory anxiety, which originates as a reaction to this fear of annihilation, converts into child's own aggression. Klein (1957) wrote about primary hostility as an inborn impulse to possess the breast, a source of "all good". If containment of primitive fears is not adequate, survival anxieties, hostility, and despair are overwhelming. Alexander (1997) notes Klein's theoretical move towards issues of "inadequate containment" and towards a closed system due to trauma in the primal dyad that results in pathology (similar to Fairbairn, 1952), indicating secondary, rather than innate (or primary), forms of envy. Such theoretical direction moves Klein towards rather than away from Winnicott.

Related to this developmental perspective, Alexander (1997) disputes the notion that destructive envy (which he distinguishes from envy mixed in with admiration) is related to primal aggression in the form of a death instinct. Instead, he sees destructive envy as being the result of a closed narcissistic system caused by core self-disruption through developmental arrest, which is also experienced as self-annihilation. Thus, Alexander (1997) is in keeping with Winnicott's (1971a,b) view of the mother–infant dyad as primary, as opposed to an innate death instinct. Alexander (1997) also does not eliminate Klein's theory of core retaliatory aggression, which is also accounted for in Winnicott's developmental writings. In interpreting Klein's moves forward in her theoretical writings, Alexander (1997) focuses on the idea of retaliatory aggression, rather than on either innate death instinct aggression or on a mere benign form of "reactive aggression". In speaking, then, of a predisposition to "retaliatory aggression" in relation to a broader form of reactive aggression, Alexander is focusing on the full developmental imprint of the mother–infant dyad as Winnicott might see it. To expand on these views, Alexander cites the seminal paper of Socarides (1966), "On vengeance—the desire to get even", which describes an urge to "get even". Alexander interprets this impulse and motivation as being clearly distinguished from the concept of an innate death instinct, again consonant with Winnicott's developmental vision. Whether fantasy or fact (but more probably fact of some nature), Socarides implies that deep down, these patients are operating from a sense of having been victims of emotional abuse and from a belief of being quite entitled to retaliate in kind. On the micro level, however, this vengeful action takes the form of ridding the psyche of feelings that were once, and continue to be, too painful to bear. Therefore, this vengeful action constitutes an attack on the mind, particularly that aspect of mind responsible for conscious awareness; thus, the close relationship between vengeance and the mechanism of projective identification as a means of ridding the psyche of unwanted mental pain can be seen. Furthermore, since projective identification operates as an omnipotent mental mechanism, its excessive use can further the unconscious belief that emotions are to be used as weapons of power, and, thus, provide the very means by which one can "get even". This view leads directly into Joseph's (1989) interpretation of the death instinct as an eradication of all feeling parts from the personality through an unrelenting compulsion towards projective identification. Joseph, in my opinion, would represent a neo-Kleinian view better if she were to adopt Alexander's (1997) and Socarides' (1966) developmental view of retaliatory aggression and its potential turn against the self as self-annihilation. This again would be more consonant with Winnicott's ideas. From Alexander's and Socarides' perspectives, retaliatory aggression would be an inward provocation from a core developmental arrest. The retaliation can be seen as "getting even", or a response to the subjective feeling of annihilation anxiety.

Alexander (1997) follows his former comments on Socarides' (1966) "vengeance" with the view of a "negative personality" as growing out of actual developmental failing at the primal "basic fault" level by stating that vengeance is directed towards "linking process" and those emotions that "link objects" (p. 428). He explains that vengeance destroys or "omnipotently" controls relationships, internal or external, through the means of projective identification, while envy "constitutes the motive for the attack" (p. 428). In this state of vengeance, however, one has given up on, and ultimately lost contact with, the existence of possibilities, that is, the chance for new growth and constructive change. These people, therefore, are incapable of thinking in terms of the "glass being half full" and instead remain peculiarly limited to a pessimistic view in their confinement to the process of "getting even". Since the subject is unable to advance, envy is further stimulated by, and directed against, those who can. In the clinical setting, the emerging self, with its capacity to value the advantages of work accomplished by the analytic couple, will be resented, and hope, in particular, envied. In turn, progress of this kind will bring about a negative therapeutic reaction, mostly because of the weaker "healthy" connections being "overwhelmed". Greed will also become quite active, since any possibility of "better" has been rendered inoperative, and only efforts in the direction of "more and more" will be able to preside. Boris (1990) has shown how greed may overpower the possibility for gratitude by way of (projective) "identification with a vengeance", operating out of envy to deny the analyst a separate existence and thereby prevent the possibility of his being experienced as a true source of goodness. A fourth emotion that operates in the realm of the negative side, which also resides in vengeance, envy, and greed, is that of a deep-seated, extremely begrudging attitude. This impulse is directed against any sense of goodwill and accomplishment, and maintained in conscious awareness, thus, available to the mind to facilitate further advance (Alexander, 1997).

When these destructive efforts can be laid bare, enabling the patient to recognise the advantages that mental growth provides, then it will be possible to demonstrate the nature and action of the internal conflict (Bion, 1962), that is, that the difficulty lies within one's own personality and is not based in a problem between patient and analyst. Until this is accomplished, there can be no possibility of the envy being experienced as "ego dystonic" and, thus, the analysand will continue to function in an "impenitent" manner and in the state of entitlement, attempting to justify his/her grievances, often in a perverse manner, at the expense of the analysis—an important issue previously noted by both Spillius (1993) and Alexander (1997). It is these emotions, spearheaded by hostile envy, which bring about a negative therapeutic reaction, a response that is operative due to the split between the frail but healthy and dominant side (Alexander, 1997).

To make meaningful use of the theory in clinical work, a dialectical contrast between Klein's emphasis and Winnicott's emphasis is always needed. The deconstruction of the death instinct metapsychology involves a new look at envy, its relation to retaliatory aggression, and its projective identification manoeuvres. Alexander's (1997) contribution, related to the primal split at the pre-oedipal level of the psyche, is one that confirms my own clinical experience, with patients who live predominantly in the paranoid–schizoid position. We can also substitute Balint's "basic fault" terminology and Mahler's "separation–individuation" terminology for the more Freudian "pre-oedipal" term, which, unfortunately, biases developmental thinking towards the oedipal level. When we see a vengeful form of envy as the perpetuation of a primal split and developmental arrest at the primal level, we can more clearly understand the sadistic anti-libidinal side of the personality that is antagonistic to love and connection. Then we can see how a psyche with a sealed off (due to primal splitting) psyche structure creates a perpetual closed system drama that manifests as a demon lover scenario. The analyst becomes cast in the role of the demon lover, that is, in the role of the bad object, the "other" who pressures the analysand toward self-sabotage, object possession, and death.

This self-sabotage can be seen as a manifestation of the internal bad object situation without proposing a death instinct. However, Klein and many of her followers have proposed the death instinct as an abstract cause of the powerful self-sabotage, often seen in treatment as a form of negative therapeutic reaction. As I have described, I believe there are biographic psychic reasons, based on Klein's own internal object world and the original maternal object disruptions internalised in her internal world, that explain Klein's metapsychological view of psychic causation. Klein seemed to maintain a profound attachment to the sadistically aggressive mother of her childhood and young adulthood through identification with her mother's sadomasochistic view of love. I propose that Klein clung to her childhood's mother, a bad object mother, as all traumatised children do (as described by Fairbairn, 1952). I am suggesting that Klein clung to this mother through an identification involving a powerful affective tie, one that was enacted in her intellectual theory regarding the death instinct. Klein's aggressive defence of her theories had aspects of both healthy sublimation at a symbolic level and a pathological re-enactment of identification with the aggressor. I propose that the aggressor she identified with was a real internalised mother who became combined with Klein's own hunger and aggression to form a psychic fantasy mother, and to form a metapsychological theory based on wedding herself to that psychic fantasy mother. This marriage to metapsychological theory of the death instinct is not necessary to Klein's developmental and clinical theory of the paranoid–schizoid and depressive positions, as we will see in the clinical cases. Klein seems to have played a part in driving Winnicott away from any association with the Kleinian group in the British Psychoanalytic Society. If, however, we relinquish the death instinct metapsychology, as I have been proposing in this chapter, Klein's clinical and developmental theorising becomes more interactive with Winnicott's views about the mother–infant dyad and its transitional space. We can then promote a rich and powerful psychic dialectic view that provides us with access our own clinical work. If we do not cling to the "death instinct" metapsychology, as Melanie Klein might have as a consequence of her own unresolved intrapsychic object splitting related to her mental negotiation of her mother's trenchant impact, we are free to benefit from a Klein–Winnicott dialectic without reducing it to polarisation.

CHAPTER FIVE

Developmental evolution within the theory of Melanie Klein

M elanie Klein's phenomenology of the paranoid–schizoid and depressive positions is a developmental as well as a clinical theory. It is, however, a too limited developmental theory, as strictly defined by Klein's writings, and many clinician-theorists, including myself, are attempting to significantly expand Klein's phenomenology of developmental usefulness (Alexander, 1997; Ogden, 1986). To extend the developmental aspects of Klein's phenomenological psychic states, which are dynamic in their dialectic of regressive and progressive psychic motions, her death instinct metapsychology must be, at least partially, eschewed. The concept of primal trauma, similar to Balint's (1979) "basic fault", can be accepted as a foundation for pathology as opposed to the notion of pure psychic conflict that is exclusively related to instinctual impulse.

For Klein, movements from the paranoid–schizoid to the depressive position state of mind are fundamental to primary developmental growth in self-integration, as well as the driving force of a continuing psychic evolution in an individual's way of thinking that takes place over the course of a lifetime. As long as primal trauma does not disrupt this natural developmental change, there is a vital shift in a self- and world perception that occurs in each of us in our primary years. This shift in psychic perspective becomes a progressive realignment of our emotional blueprint, as it effects our interpretation of our experience in the external world. The shift from the para-noid–schizoid to the depressive position is a progressive develop-mental shift due to the ability in the depressive position to tolerate all psychic parts of oneself, both loving and hating parts, so that an ambivalent state of good-enough love for the other as a whole (with good and bad parts) can be tolerated. Prior to the depressive position, the disowning of one's hate for a loved object places one in the dilemma of cutting off from any desired and needed object at the point of anger and disappointment. Wandering from one person to another, following each disappointment in love and in the idealised perfection of the "other" results in a fragmentation of experience that leaves us to exist in a fragmented self-state. Without primary sustained relationship in one's life, nothing is sustained.

Melanie Klein spoke of the six-month-old infant travelling psychi-cally from the paranoid–schizoid position to the depressive position. She seemed to be assigning the change to the six-month period, in relation to her concept of weaning from breastfeeding (and breast holding) as the primal era of separation. Today, particularly with advances in infant research, we know that eighteen months to thirty-six months (the time of practising and rapprochement) is a critical era of separation, although the infant seems to have certain distinct and interactive self-states, even in the first few months of life, as Stern's (1985) work has informed us. Klein spoke of the newborn infant as an automatic deflector of overwhelming hostile aggression, which she, unfortunately, called death instinct energy in her metapsychology. Perhaps Klein's theoretical fantasy about this infant self-state, long before our major infant research, was in part a projection of her own overwhelmed psychic state, having grown up with an extremely aggressive, narcissistic, and envious mother. Based on Grosskurth's (1986) biography of Melanie Klein, cited here in earlier chapters, we have seen how Klein's mother reveals her true self in her letters to her daughter. Her mother's aggression imploding upon her, and the impact of her own frustrated developmental strivings (due to her mother's use of her daughter as an extension of herself) could have engendered Klein's defensive psychology, which she imagined in the newborn infant. This is a state of persecution and terror in which one's own aggression is felt as a continuing attack or threat from others outside the self. Klein's infant aligns with an idealised breast mother to ward off the persecutors.

In my amended view of Klein's defensive psychology state, the persecutors might often be based on psychic fantasy experience of the separation mother, who, unlike the breast mother, can be experienced as cold, if she opposes her child's need for autonomy and separateness. To protect the mother as a good object, the child must view the mother as ideal. All frustrations from the mother, from one's own body, and from the world, which would be experienced by the infant as caused by the mother, are split off and experienced as the persecutory attacks of a "bad" mother, an alien "other", who is not felt to be part of the ideal mother. This "bad" mother must be defended against by an alliance with the good mother, who in fantasy is perfect or ideal (with the proto-symbolic sensation preceding the cognitive symbolisation of fantasy). In such a state, where the other is perceived as all good or all bad, the reality of the other, the self, and the world can never be accurately perceived. Klein (1957) proposed a developmental leap at the age of six months from this experience of the world to a radically different one, as this leap is one made continuously throughout life. From this psychological transition, as more and more of experience is viewed from a sense of self-agency that is based in the capacity to own one's aggression, and which connects us to an internal psychic truth, we can tolerate ambivalent perceptions, which much more accurately grasp the reality of the world and of oneself. The leap is, as already described, one of leaving behind a state of loving one object (part object, good mother–breast mother) and hating another (another part object view of the mother, seen as the bad mother). Entering the depressive position, the infant (or toddler in my new schema), embraces the whole mother and tolerates loving and hating the same object. The infant tolerates the "good enough love" for an imperfect mother. Then, we come to accept an intimate relationship, where others are felt in depth, with all their strengths and weaknesses.

In this way, the infant can re-own aggression in itself, which was split off in the era when no hate for mummy could be tolerated. This allows for the development of self-agency, and a relief from the position of persecution in which one is automatically a helpless victim, unless backed up by the omnipotent good breast mother. However, it also brings psychic conflict to the front stage for the infant/toddler (and for the adult he or she eventually becomes), who enters the depressive position, where ambivalence is felt. Such conflict involves love *vs.* hate for the other, and good *vs.* bad experiences of oneself. Conflicts also arise between sexual longings and aggressive impulses, between sadistic impulses and dependent longings, between masculine and feminine strivings, etc. (see Bach, 2005, related to the two sides of psyche that can be split off or integrated in the form of a linked and cohesive psychic dialectic). The pay-off for an ability to tolerate and process psychic conflict is the growth of new developmental capacities. This was not explicitly addressed by Klein. Unlike her arch-rival, Anna Freud, Klein was more focused on the unconscious, as it emerged through psychic phantasy and transference fantasy, than on the development of the ego. In other words, she was focused on psychic contents rather than on psychic process. Nevertheless, all these developments in the ego are implied by the depressive position's capacity to negotiate ambivalence, tolerate one's own aggression, and transform that aggression into healthy self-assertion and ego function. Once guilt and loss can be felt and mourned in the depressive position, ego developments continue beyond that internalised from the parents. Some of the ego capacities that develop in the depressive position are the observing ego, the capacity for self-reflection, and the capacity for self-agency, self-assertion, and differentiation. This involves what I describe as a "developmental mourning" process that begins in the first separation–individuation years, overlapping the two-year-old's anal period, when parental limits and parental responsiveness profoundly influence "good enough" self-integration rather than the developmental arrest, which promotes character disorders. To the above list of ego capacities, I add prime growth in the form of psychic dialectic between one's own subjectivity and the subjectivity of the other (see Bach, 1985), and between love and anger, rage and renewed love. Psychic dialectic evolves in terms of what I have described as a "love–creativity dialectic" (Kavaler-Adler, 1996) between an inner world connection to internal objects for artistic creativity and creative work, and an external world connection for intimacy, love, and communication in the realm of the interpersonal world.

Further, there is developmental growth in two powerful forms of processing experience, both referred to by Ogden (1986, 1994) as the emergence of becoming an "interpreting subject" and an "historical subject". Becoming an interpreting subject means becoming conscious of one's own interpretations that convert experience into new meaning, particularly through the influence of psychic fantasy and psychic blueprints of what one has perceived in the past. Without being an interpreting subject, one is always a victim, and reactive to what others impose on him/her, as Winnicott's (1965) infant impinged on, with a violation of the need for its own initiating gesture. When one realises being an interpreting subject, he/she sees creating one's own experience, no matter what the objective reality is. Then, objective reality is filtered through one's own perception, shaped by his/her ongoing belief systems, which incorporate psychic fantasy and psychic blueprints from the childhood experience. Throughout life, one creates new forms of psychic fantasy (e.g., dreams) through merging the primal internalised blueprint of self and other relations with the newly experienced reality. However, the formation of new psychic structure with its psychic fantasy content, joined with the facile capacity to retrieve memories and to form unconsciously linked "free associations", depends on the experiencing self remaining open to connection through relationships in the world. Primal trauma in the first three years of life will promote split off and sealed off areas of the core self instead. Then, relationships will be sadomasochistic rather than composed of mutual and responsive interactions, as they will be stunted by compulsive projections and enactments through projective identification.

To become a historical subject means knowing that there is a sequence of cause and effect experiences of time, which cannot be altered by mere wish fulfilments. One can wish that something disturbing to him/her never happened, but once one becomes a historical subject (e.g., in the depressive position), he/she cannot deny what happened. Neither can one pretend that he/she can start life over again without experiencing the effects of the past experience. One cannot wish away the past and start anew, and is stuck with life as it evolves. One cannot just eliminate from consciousness the knowledge of doing something, seeing something, saying something, and that this something might have caused feeling shame, guilt, or regret. In this situation, conscious acceptance of what reality is allows a choice to change one's ways of being in the future. Denial (in a paranoid–schizoid subject) creates a continuing vicious cycle of repeated behaviour, which the subject refuses to accept as happening. Such an individual denies all psychic conflict, believing that he or she can start again without ever having to feel the ambivalence and the frustration of disappointment that come with the historical subject's awareness that what is done, is done. This denial prohibits any learning or growth in psychic awareness and for future change.

Extending Klein's developmental view of the depressive position

Klein wrote of the growth of self-integration through the depressive position, growth through tolerance for ambivalence. She also wrote about the conscious experiencing of one's own hostile aggression, when guilty of assaulting connections with another who (on an unconscious level of primal relation) represents the primary love object. Such aggression is self-destructive, undermining the limits and connections with both one's own loving capacity and with external others upon whom one projects the original primal mother. Facing consciousness of the relationship, destructive aggression creates conflicts between hate and love for one unique other, who is perceived as both vulnerable and desirable. These are developmental struggles. Nevertheless, the reasons why one person could master the challenges of the depressive position while another cannot remains vague and abstract in Klein's metapsychological theory. However, in her clinical theory, as well as in her clinical work, Klein did consider the contributions of the real parents to the patient's capacity to overcome these challenges. From Klein's perspective, it is merely a toss of the dice that determines whether a person is born with more hate than love or more love than hate: in a word, luck. Klein further obscures this mystery by calling feelings of hate, based on primal anger and hostile aggressive impulses, an implosion of the "death instinct" energy. Without including real life object relations in this fateful equation of hate *vs.* love or love *vs.* hate, the psychoanalytic clinician is left without any comprehension of why one individual can tolerate guilt in their relations with others and another individual cannot.

According to an article by Safan-Gerard (1998), Melanie Klein (and Kleinians in general) saw those who cannot tolerate guilt and the consequent concern and regard for others (which could come from the toleration of guilt) as having suffered from the experience of guilt too early in childhood. What is shockingly absent from this explanation is that a child who is impinged upon (by guilt) too early in life is a child unprotected from emotional assault and blame by the parents, and initially by the mother. Winnicott (1945, 1947), in contrast to Klein, did speak of the mother who impinges with her own needs before the child has expressed his own needs and desires through his own initi-ating or "omnipotent gesture". Winnicott does not speak, however, of the specific impingement of guilt by the parent, either through a lack of understanding of the child's need for understanding and forgive-ness or through the parents' active aggressive assault by repeatedly blaming and condemning a child for its behaviour. The worst assault happens when parents condemn the mere mode of being of the child, while projecting on to him/her their own parents' projections on to them.

A good example of this combination of neglect, assaultative accu-sation, and abuse can be seen in the case of Anne Sexton, as I formu-lated it from biographical sources in *The Creative Mystique* (Kavaler-Adler, 1996). (See also Kavaler-Adler, 1989; McClatchy, 1978; Middle-brook, 1991; Sexton, 1981.) When Sexton's elder daughter filled a toy truck with her own faeces, as any child might at the age of four or five, Sexton threw her against a wall. Sexton's assault on her daughter landed her in a mental hospital and resulted in her children being removed from her care for an extended period of time. Yet, how often do we find instead that the parent is not controlled in any way that might prevent such behaviour? In fact, if the assault solely verbal, the parent is generally not held accountable at all. In a case such as Sex-ton's, the child's perception that she has somehow betrayed the parent is internalised, thereafter resonating in her psyche throughout the rest of her life as a self-abusive blame, as a condemning internal voice telling her that she is bad. With such internal assault, any minor crit-icism may become intolerable, let alone a realistic confronting of one's aggression towards others, and particularly towards a loved one. By not including the real parents' behaviour in the scenario of those who seem incapable of tolerating guilt, and using it to understand and repair love relations with an attitude of concern through reparative gestures, Klein leaves us with a solipsistic expression of one sole being who is presumed to be cursed by the universe with the inheritance of more hate than love. However Klein (1957) does begin to give some tribute to the parent in "Envy and gratitude", where she speaks about the significance of a parent receiving the child's reparations, or what I call "reparative gestures". However, this is an extremely limited view of the parent's role. It places the parent in a reactive position to the child's aggression rather than in a responsible position as an agent who actually incites the child's aggression. With Klein's (1975) view of guilt as an innate energetic phenomenon (which she demonises in the form of the vampire-like death instinct energy), a developmental view of the depressive position is obviated. As Fairbairn (1952) would put it, how can there be a developmental view of self-agency in the face of existential guilt when the parents' initial input to the adult's childhood development is dismissed or remains radically unaccounted for?

Alexander (1997), a Kleinian with one foot in developmental research, helps to deliver us from this dilemma. He brings all breakdowns in depressive position capacities for ambivalence, enacted as hostile aggression, back into the axiomatic roots of the mother–infant dyad. It is when this dyad of developmental origins breaks down that hostile aggression becomes a perseverative assault. If the break, often called a rupture, occurs before a core cohesive self that can relate to the world develops, parts of the self can become so split off and sealed off from the true self (which is open to the world), that a "constructed self" (or a "false self") is mentally contrived to encounter others (see Horner, 2005). The result is a perseverating aggression, which becomes a malevolent force undermining the relationship. In its most extreme form, this force becomes what the Kleinian Rosenfeld (1971, 1987) has called an internal "Mafia". I would add that with a milder break in the mother–infant dyad system during the separation–individuation era, as described by Mahler (1967), Masterson (1976, 1981, 1985, 2000), and Horner (1984, 2005), one main split will result in the self. The split results from the parents' failure to maintain adequate, attuned, emotional contact with a child who is individuating and separating itself out from the primal mother. This split would result in a "bad self" and a "bad other" constellation, which is projected out in the borderline character (higher level), which takes over the self-identity in the schizoid character (lower level), and which also resides behind the defensive grandiose self-structure in the narcissistic character. Destructive envy can be seen to have its origins in this "bad self"-and-"bad other" constellation, or in the "inadequate self"-and-"contemptuous other" constellation of the narcissist. This is an explanation that contrasts with Klein's off-handed one, which makes envy and destructive spoiling aggression (in general) a mere automatic reaction to an innate state of hate dominating one from birth and emerging as a demonic death instinct energy.

In keeping with Balint's (1979) "basic fault", and following from Alexander's (1997) criteria for a failure of development of the depressive position capacities, the "two-party system" breakdown rescues us from Klein's metapsychological obscurities, while allowing us to retain the brilliant clinical phenomenology that evolves from her understanding of the depressive position struggles. When Alexander (1997) refers to a two-party system, he refrains from assigning blame to either the mother as a primal parent or to the child. Like Balint's (1979) term "basic fault", Alexander's (1997) two-party system implies that something has gone amiss between two active agents, parent and child, and proposes that the disruption of the two-party connection has devastating consequences, especially when the disruption is a primal one, related back to the function of a dyad that has been essential for the developmental growth of the infant. However, the disruption or collision in the parent–child system is not reduced to any standard explanation. The infant could be ill and the mother unable to accommodate sufficiently. The mother and infant could be a poor match to begin with (we have no matchmakers for mothers and infants). The infant might want to be breastfed, while the mother is unable to do so, due either to life's conditions or to the mother's disinclination. This is a developmental view of the depressive position that bypasses a moralising theory in which blame *must* be assigned. With developmental growth through a two-party mother–child connection, the child is able to free him- or herself from being seen by self and others as "bad", as well as of calling the parent "bad" or defective. This depressive position view of one's own breakdown is related to a critical developmental truth about the fundamental role of the mother–infant dyad in all psychological development, a truth most vociferously promulgated by Winnicott. The two-party system breakdown explanation does not even use the word "fault" as Michael Balint does, as a metaphor for a fault-line in geographical formations. Yet, it still leaves room for holding the parent/mother highly responsible for her infant, and for her child's capacities to deal with all vicissitudes of development. The parent's characterological problems become of ultimate concern here. The perpetual disruption of the two-party system is generally a direct consequence of a parent's character pathology. Such character pathology interferes with the child's need for both contact and connection, and for freedom to initiate its own separate sphere of autonomous functioning, demonstrated by infant research (Beebe & Lachman, 1988; Beebe & Stern, 1977). According to such infant research, mutual regulation and self-regulation are both required for the infant's development and the infant needs attunement by the mother.

The possible conclusion is that Melanie Klein might have been psychologically (not intellectually) incapable of arriving at the fundamental theory of a two-party system because of her need to deny the character pathology of her own mother. For Melanie, to look at her mother's true being might have been like looking into the face of Medusa. According to Grosskurth's (1986) research, Klein had idealised her mother to protect herself from seeing her mother's failings and the aggressive modes of intrusion and assault that sprang out from these failings—intrusions and assaults that plagued Melanie Klein's adult life. Perhaps, Klein could not bear to face the truth, but she could displace her mother's attitudes and behaviours on to others. It is well known that Klein was constantly battling with psychoanalysts in the British Psychoanalytic Society, and that she was highly critical of her own children, even to the point of supervising her son Eric's therapy (see Kahr, 1996). Grosskurth (1986) also notes that Klein displaced her mother's controlling hostility on to her husband. Klein could try to own her own aggressive impulses and thoughts towards her mother, which would be accompanied by the remorse of the depressive position, but without facing the truth of her mother's envious and undermining behaviour (as it has been described by Grosskurth, 1986), Klein might have been compelled toward self-blame, as Fairbairn (1952) had theorised. Klein's need to protect the image of her mother might have cost her the ultimate theory that she sought. She avoided facing the reality of having been brought up by a psychologically ill mother, one with a narcissistic pathology, which must have resulted from unresolved trauma in her own life. Klein failed to face the sadistic part of her mother, as well as the inadequate part of her, and this could have housed an internal emptiness (see Seinfeld, 1991, on the "empty core" phenomenon). Klein displaced her mother's manipulative and enviously spoiling operations on to her own daughter, and then her daughter might actually have grown into that role, too. To face the true character of her mother would have meant facing the reality of her mother's internal emptiness. It would have meant facing her mother's psychologically sealed-off state, which could have led to an insatiable emotional starvation, manifesting as envy and manipulative emotional blackmail.

In spite of this, Klein managed to encounter the critical need for the mourning process in which aggression was acknowledged, particularly in terms of murderous impulses towards the lost primal love object that became displaced on to others throughout life. In spite of her avoidant view of her own mother, she reached a theory of the real mother being profoundly important in the child's capacity for development, in terms of the mother's capacity to receive or reject reparation for her child. Should Klein have extended this interactive capacity of the mother to a two-party system, as did Winnicott (1965, 1975) and Alexander (1997), she would have encountered the truth of the primal trauma underlying all character pathologies. Existing beyond (or in addition to) neurotic conflicts over the repression of raw biological impulses of aggression or sexuality, such primal trauma does turn this conflict into split-off self-parts, to avoid the demon energy, which Klein called the death instinct. Furthermore, it allows for an understanding of the terrors of primal object loss, and its accompanying annihilation anxiety. Primal trauma is at the core of warded-off experience, which underlies pre-oedipal character pathology (as in Bollas's (1987) "unthought known"). I propose that Klein herself was operating out of anxiety over loss when she avoided awareness of her mother's dark side. She might have avoided separation by identifying with the aggressor, thus, in many ways, becoming like her mother. In her own unconscious functioning, Klein was too immersed in this identification dynamic to see it from a depressive position, and without this, she was unable to symbolise the dynamic into a theory. She touched on the depressive position as a psychic state, where both loss and guilt over aggression can be faced; however, she focused more on the split-off or repressed aggression than on the loss itself.

To extend Klein's theory, along with Alexander's (1997) idea of a two-party breakdown, I would broaden it to include defence against loss in the depressive position, and to a theory of defence against trauma. Unlike Klein (but in keeping with Alexander, 1997), I propose that it is the trauma (so often brought on by a parent's pathology) that causes the two-party system to break down. The breakdown then becomes a powerful mode of parental betrayal, committed by a mother compelled to it by her own terrors of primal object loss. This emphasis on loss brings us back to Klein's theory of mourning. We can look at Klein's approach and avoidance process in relation to this theory as she herself begins a personal mourning process over the death of her son, Hans. Yet, her mourning process becomes arrested, perhaps as her own terrors of primal object loss (annihilation and abandonment anxiety) compel her to avoid the truth about her mother. Facing the truth requires the capacity to mourn both one's sense of betrayal as well as one's own regret. Part of this developmental mourning process is feeling the consequences of one's own injuries to others, even when we are compulsively repeating the traumatising behaviour and betrayal of our parents, while identifying with the aggressor, to avoid loss of the mother.

Klein is the first psychoanalytic theorist to follow up on Freud's (1917e) views in "Mourning and melancholia" with a view on mourning that extends beyond bereavement, to mourning as a potentially life-long developmental process, one that manifests as a critical clinical process within psychoanalytic treatment. Klein stops short, however, of putting her ideas into effect in the clinical realm, as attested to by Claire Winnicott, Winnicott's second wife, from the time of her training analysis with Melanie Klein (Kahr, 1996). Claire Winnicott told Donald Winnicott, her husband, that tears were not welcomed on Klein's couch (Kahr, 1996). Further, Klein dismissed Claire's feelings towards her mother with a concrete statement, reducing the symbolic to the concrete: "There's no use talking about your mother. She's dead, and there's nothing you can do about it" (Grosskurth, 1986, p. 59). Rather than encouraging Claire Winnicott to express all her feelings towards her mother, which could have resulted in an overall mourning process that engaged the rage and complaint needed to grieve over loss, Klein suppressed Claire Winnicott's reactions. This may have been compulsive on Klein's part, particularly if she had to keep her own feelings toward her own mother repressed. Claire's feelings, as Klein's analysand, could have threatened to trigger Melanie Klein's own breaking through the bounds of repression. If Kahr's (1996) report is accurate, not only were Klein's words intended to suppress Claire Winnicott's mourning process, but her mode of action in the treatment sessions was as well. Claire Winnicott described with outrage to her husband how Mrs Klein would carry on with long interpretations of Claire's dreams, "serving the dream" up to her, rather than allowing the psychic space for Claire to freely associate and explore the meaning of her own dream for herself (Grosskurth, 1986). It might be reasonably argued that this was a symptom of Klein's own compulsive and defensive reaction to her own narcissistic mother, who interpreted all of her daughter's motives, and who monopolised all the narrative space for herself by avoiding listening to, or engaging in, a dialogue or conversation with the other. Perhaps Klein's own unresolved unconscious denied rage at her mother motivated her to suppress the outrage of Claire Winnicott's anger at her mother. According to Grosskurth (1986) and Kahr (1996), Klein prevented her patient from getting past her anger and becoming conscious of her longing for her mother, as well as her wish to forgive through the compassion of grief in the state of mourning. Also, instead of Claire facing her rage at her mother through the transference mode of displacing it on to Klein, Klein's dominating control of Claire's sessions made Klein the actual target of outrage. Thus, I would suppose that Claire Winnicott could not reach the grief about losing her mother. Mourning was forestalled, and even when tears were forthcoming, Klein discouraged them (Kahr, 1996).

Klein's view of reparation as developmental theory

Despite Melanie Klein's deficiencies in her own mourning process, she was the psychoanalytic theorist who discovered how intricately aggression was a part of the mourning process and of the experience of object loss. Klein always addressed psychic loss as being accompanied by aggression that creates guilt. So, in Klein's theory, guilt and loss continually cohabit the space of the theory of the depressive position. She has taught us that to repress the sadistic fantasies towards the lost love object creates manic and vicious paranoid defence cycles that do not cease until the defences can be brought to consciousness. Once consciousness of these defences is achieved, the unconscious rage and grief behind them can be brought to consciousness. For Klein, these beliefs found validation in her clinical work, as well as in the clinical work of others. We find it in our clinical work today. In Klein's view, once sadistic impulses, sadistic fantasies, and memories of actual sadistic actions are brought to consciousness, one feels a primal need to repair the love connection with the object of these sadistic passions. The attempt to repair takes place both within the internal world of internalised/fantasised love objects, as well as in the external world with the other who has offended in thought and/or deed. Klein's view of reparation as a primary psychic process brought her later theory into the realm of interpersonal relations more than any other part of her theory. The need to make reparation towards the love object was the need to make actual behavioural gestures of reparation towards the other. This was not something that could be done in the mind alone. Further, Klein distinguished between true reparation, which involves recognition of the psychic truth of one's own aggression towards the other (which, in fantasy, is always a displacement figure for the primal love object, mother), resulting in feelings of remorse, sadness, and manic reparation: these feelings form the basis of a defensive belief that all—by some miraculous quick fix—can be totally as before. (Drugs are often used to promote just such an illusion.) True reparation includes awareness that reparation is never perfect. In other words, the consequences of one's aggression still leave their mark. True reparation is also slow, often requiring repetition, because remorse is a human experience that exposes one to vulnerability and, therefore, cannot be sustained without working with the defensive processes that shield us from it. Neither does forgiveness come immediately or quickly to human beings. Any mode of reparative apology or gesture towards the offended one most probably will only result in moments of forgiveness, interludes of forgiveness, in between retaliatory and revengeful feelings that one has naturally aroused, as a human being. Manic reparation, on the other hand, is an attempt to magically and immediately fix one's hurtful aggression towards the other, by forcing the other to forgive and forget, as if nothing has happened (see Kavaler-Adler, 1993a). It always involves denial and, like an antidepressant, it covers over the disturbance, so that one does not have to face the psychic truth. In her book, *Introduction to Melanie Klein*, Segal (1964) gives a beautiful example of the difference between manic and true reparation, which I have further described and elaborated, in relation to an adult patient, in *The Compulsion to Create* (Kavaler-Adler, 1993a).

Klein's focus on psychic and interpersonal reparation has been called the most innovative and original of her psychoanalytic theories, particularly by Joan Riviere, who used this theory extensively in her own writing and clinical work. Riviere used Klein's theory of reparation to understand the unconscious pressures lying behind the

negative therapeutic reactions in manic depression and other seriously disturbed patients (Riviere, 1936). This part of Klein's theory is
so deep and profound that it is, in my opinion, worthy of expansion,
particularly in its mode of clinical usefulness, as aggression within
loss is now understood as a retaliatory and survival impulse, rather
than as an abstract death instinct. Klein's focus on reparation was seen
by Winnicott as an invitation to talk about a "position of concern" in
meetings of the British Psychoanalytic Society (see King & Steiner,
1991). Winnicott might have hoped to modify the name of the depressive position in the direction of psychic health and developmental
growth, rather than using the term "depressive" position, which is
prone to being confused with symptoms of pathology, rather than
being appropriately viewed as strivings towards relating to separate
others, and to promoting healthy internalisations that promote psychic health.

Winnicott was rebuffed by Klein. The rebuff seems as if it was an
instinctive and impulsive territorial response on her part that under-
cut her openness as a theorist. Caper (1988), in a more recent commentary on Kleinian theory, suggests that the depressive position might
more aptly be called a mourning position. This is a theory and title I
would be in agreement with, and which is congenial with my own
theory of "developmental mourning" (Kavaler-Adler, 1985, 2007). I
want to propose, however, a more specific aspect of an overall theory
of mourning, following my own theory of "developmental mourning"
(Kavaler-Adler, 1993a, 1996). In keeping with Klein's idea of psychic
positions, I will outline here a position of psychic regret that would be
part of a depressive position or a mourning position, one which interacts with Klein's most profound contributions on the theory of true
and manic reparation. I will examine true and false regret using clinical examples in order to determine to what degree the capacity to
consciously face the experience of regret—at any one powerful
moment within an overall experience of remorse—allows for critical
openings to psychic change and development.

Although Klein began to move in an interpersonal direction with
her reparation theory, I intend to change that direction by moving her
reparation theory into the intrapsychic realm. I believe that the pro-
fundity and deep human and existential anguish of regret is a self-
contained experience, prior to any communication to another. It is an
internal emotional experience, viscerally felt in the heart and gut, and

it often leads to deep body crying and sobbing. The interpersonal experience exists at first in the internal psycho-physical domain, when consciousness emerges from memory or intrapsychic repression, opening up into memory. What can become interpersonal through a choice to communicate regret is an intersubjective experience in the internal psychic realm for, in a true moment of regret, one empathises with the other whom one has offended. This empathy requires that, at the moment of regret, one heightens the subjectivity of the other in one's consciousness so that one feels the keen and acute affects of grief, longing, loss, love, and compassion for the other whom one has offended. In a true moment of regret, the experience of these emotions is heightened to a transformational level. True behaviour change can grow from such moments, moments that are not easily forgotten, but only as long as the former compulsions that might have resulted in the offence or betrayal of the other can be understood in terms of the underlying psychic need that led to the offence. Also, the possible repetition of a parental betrayal or offence that compelled an identifying repetition needs to be understood as symptomatic of trauma that is not mourned. In my view, the emotional release into grief at the moment of regret is the critical sign of authenticity in reparation. The two-party system of connection is repaired in one moment. Such reparation can occur within a moment of gratitude, as is shown in "The conflict and process theory of Melanie Klein" (Kavaler-Adler, 1992c). Regret renews love, through the path of affect-laden and grief-modifying guilt, into yearnings for reconnection.

Regret has to do with the sense of betrayal of oneself or of the other. Often, the betrayal one feels guilty about is a betrayal compulsively repeated from the past. One repeats the betrayal to avoid the loss of the original parent who was too limited to acknowledge and also to grieve the regret of the betrayal. To face the truth of a parent's betrayal seems unthinkable. One resorts to disavowal of the traumatising events and of the traumatising part of the parent, which then is identified with as in "identification with the aggressor" (A. Freud, 1936), or as in introjective identification, in Klein's terminology. In this way, the traumatic object relationship becomes the "unthought known", sealed off in its repetition with the split-off parts of the self (libidinal and anti-libidinal or dependent and anti-dependent). This is the betrayal that never stops. To preserve the tie to the once needed primal parent of betrayal, the truth of the parent's betrayal must be evaded. However, repression of the truth, or dissociation from the internal experience of the traumatising truth (splitting off), which, in Bollas's (1987) terms, creates "the unthought known" experience dominating the dissociated part of the psyche, similar to Bion's (1957) "attacks on linking", causes a disruption of the psychic continuity of connections that allow the flow of love and creativity as mental processes. This is true because there is no love or creation without existing spontaneously in the present, and symbolising that present experience in communication. Being present is obviated by alienation from one's inner truth and the affect experience of its origins.

Psychoanalytic object relations treatment can allow for the critical mourning and separation process that can free the self from this endless and destructive repetition. Through mourning that evolves in its own developmental course, one can reach the capacity for moments of regret. True remorse can ensue, which transforms formerly troubled relationships into opportunities for reparation and love. The moment of regret requires a certain degree of developmental separation and individuation, as described by Mahler, Pine, and Bergmann (1975). However, with mourning allowing this separation process to proceed on an affective level, the adult psyche can build on what Mahler has called "low keyedness" in the healthy toddler at the point of separation. Loss must be felt, and grief over this loss is intermingled with guilt, as one's own agency in creating such love in relation to another loss through misdeeds of one's own aggression is faced. To tolerate guilt mixed with loss, as Klein has characterised the affective task of the depressive position, one must be separate enough to not intrapsychically turn guilt into a renewed attack on the self, or on the other as an internal object within the self, or upon the actual external other. One must have a built-in internal holding environment through good-enough other (object relations) internalisations—regardless of whether such internalisations were formed with the mother in infancy, or much later in psychoanalytic treatment.

This view of Klein's depressive position is more congruent with Winnicott's views than earlier depressive position Kleinian theories in which the contents of psychic fantasies were considered more important than the process of the mind that transforms through developmental evolution within a depressive position psyche. Extending the phenomenology of the depressive position into its developmental process easily leads to the theories of Winnicott: all have a developmental emphasis. In the following chapters, I present clinical examples of the developmental function of mirroring, transitional objects, and transitional space. I also examine Winnicott's view of solitude and its relation to self-development. The true self, mirroring, and transitional space all interact with Klein's phenomenological theory of the developmental evolution within the depressive position.

CHAPTER SIX

Developmental evolution within the works of Donald W. Winnicott: psychic and transitional space

According to Rodman (2004), Winnicott's biographer, Anna Freud wrote to Winnicott that his "transitional object" concept had taken the world by storm. The transitional object is an external other that serves a mothering role in facilitating development. The transitional object is not a symbolic representative of the primal holding mother (the symbiotic or chthonic mother), but is the symbolic representative of Winnicott's transitional phase mother, equivalent to the mother of separation in the American separation–individuation stage parlance of Mahler (1971). The transitional object represents the mother who is more separate from the child than the early infant-holding mother (the mother of the primal "unity"), and is symbolic of a mother who is affectively present and attuned to the child. However, unlike the early holding mother who, through the reverie of psychic fantasy, has merged with her helpless and totally dependent infant, the transitional object mother does not symbolically fuse with the child and, ideally, she imposes no personal or narcissistic demands on the child. By being more separate from the child than the holding mother, the transitional object mother can relate to the child's developmental needs through words and vision without having concrete sensual body contact (see Wright, 1991). Whoever occupies the role of the transitional object operates symbolically as the transitional phase mother, if the real mother of that phase of development is inadequate. Thus, in Winnicott's thinking, the transitional object is a functional role assumed by psychoanalytic psychotherapists.

Winnicott's transitional stage of development refers to that which Mahler (1975) has called separation–individuation. It is in a period of development that is pre-oedipal. During the transitional stage, the child is no longer an infant and no longer needs to have a mother's physical holding. Supposedly psychic fantasies of fusion and emotional symbiosis have already been internalised. However, this finding from Mahler's infant research (Mahler, Pine, & Bergmann, 1975) was not articulated specifically by Winnicott, who spoke of a general need for emotional holding by the mother. In the "transitional stage", the child needs to be separate enough to feel a differentiating identity and autonomy, while still having an external mother or mother substitute present and sustaining connections. For example, a teddy bear can represent the soft, warm, cuddly holding of the mother. With such concrete objects having symbolic significance for the child during the transitional stage, the child is partially separate from the mother. However, she/he is not separate enough to sustain an internal connection with the mother for more than short periods of time. The mother's literal presence is still needed throughout all of Mahler's phases of separation–individuation, which overlaps with Winnicott's transitional stage. Without the mother's "good enough" presence during the transitional stage of development, the symbolic image of a good enough, or present enough mother, cannot be internalised. Consequently, core self-structure would be missing in the personality of the growing child without a transitional object that represents the mother being present.

Furthermore, without such symbolic internalisation of the mother during this transitional stage, there can be no further development into the independent interactions of the oedipal stage. For example, there can be no conscious experiencing of psychic conflict between parts of the self, such as a superego *vs.* impulses, or between masculine and feminine sides of the self. Without the adequate internalisation of the "good object" (Klein) or the "good enough object" (Winnicott), parts of the self—particularly instinctual parts related to aggression and sexual impulses—become split off, dissociated, and projected out into others. To control such impulses inside oneself, one must have an internal self-image that is bonded to a mothering object-image. It is this bond, and only this bond, that allows inner space to be felt as alive, and for an internal world within the self to be felt. Consequently, psychic space depends on the internalisation of the mother, and not only on the internalisation of the holding other in the symbiotic phase of infancy. Psychic space depends on the internalisation of the transitional stage mother, called a "mother of separation" by American object relations theorists such as Masterson (1976, 1981) and psychoanalytic theorists such as Bach (1985).

In order for this transitional stage mother to be internalised, the mother's presence during all the phases of this period—that is, during all the phases of separation–individuation—must be "good enough" in terms of the transitional object being available to the child. Backing up the transitional object, the actual mother must be fully alive and emotionally present, without withdrawing, or abandoning, or impinging on the child. If mother is physically absent, the transitional object (in the form of a teddy bear or blanket) can temporarily represent her. For this to occur, the mother at this phase must be separate enough within her own self. If she clings to the infant for her own unfulfilled infant needs, the child will feel encroached upon. If she withdraws to avoid consciousness of her own regressive infant needs, the child will feel that she is abandoning him. So, the external mother is critical during the transitional phase, even though she can be physically absent on a temporary basis, if she is represented by an object that has some mothering functions and qualities, such as the cuddly quality of a teddy bear. The mother, however, also needs to be separate enough to be absent at times from a child who is now a toddler and not an infant in her arms. It is no longer the time to be "fobbed off with a good feed", in Winnicott's terms. The two-year-old child, as well as the adult false-self patient (Winnicott's term for a patient with a character disorder), is no longer an infant. The critical symbiotic phases of early infancy have passed. Consequently, the transitional stage of development requires the challenge of separation. In this way, psychological development can proceed in terms of internalising the symbolic representation of the good enough mother and of good enough maternal responsiveness (not just physical feeding). In the transitional stage, the mother needs to be literally absent enough as well as present enough. When the actual mother is absent, it is the transitional object, picked for its soft maternal qualities, that can meet the child's need for attachment. Through the internalisation of the mother that takes place in the life stage of literal physical holding, the transitional object is experienced as nurturing.

Unlike the literal mother, the transitional stage object can be controlled by the toddler in terms of the toddler's needs. It can be controlled as the actual mother cannot be. The transitional object never walks away and leaves. Mother does. The transitional object fills in for the mother, who is always leaving. This allows the child the illusion of control over mother and over mother's meeting of his/her needs. If the mother is only away for a short time, this illusion can be sustained, offering the toddler a sense of security when emotional need for the mother is present without physical hunger. Metaphorically speaking, the breastfeeding mother can retire while her psychic and emotional holding aspects are still present for the child through the memory of her mother that is provided by the warm, cuddly quality of a blanket or teddy bear that represents her. To the degree that the transitional object does allow a psychological gap between the mother and toddler to be felt, but without the traumatic void of an intolerable absence, the child will internalise a warm and supportive symbolism in relation to mothering. However, when the gap becomes a perpetual void due to abandonment trauma related to a mother's too prolonged absence (either physical or emotional), psychotherapeutic treatment will later be necessary to allow a "good enough" maternal representation to be internalised in symbolic form in the psyche. If this kind of psychotherapeutic help is needed, the analyst must be able to be the transitional object in human form, providing a presence like that of the teddy bear or blanket, but the analyst must also be able to endure the patient's rage at the intolerable absence suffered. If the psychotherapist/ psychoanalyst can sustain a transitional object presence, the foreclosed psychic space and foreclosed transitional space from the early traumatic disruption in mother–child bonding—and its internalisation— can open up as it does in normal or "good enough" development.

All this was Winnicott's discovery. Klein, by contrast, saw the mother as always good and, thus, compensatory for split-off aggressive images of a persecutory mother emanating from the child's internal world. Although Klein's early theory included the concept of an actual linear progression from the paranoid–schizoid position to the depressive position in earliest infancy, in her later view development takes place in a series of regressive and progressive movements: backwards from the depressive position to the paranoid–schizoid position, and then forward from the paranoid–schizoid position to the depressive position. As proposed earlier, this transition seems more related to the two-year-old transitional stage period of Winnicott than to the first six months of life.

Given the role of the external mother in Winnicott's transitional phase, his thinking is often seen as an extension of Klein's theory. Winnicott's theory, however, is simultaneously, and somewhat paradoxically, outside of Klein's theories. There is the issue of internal psychic space opening when the transitional phase mother is internalised, or later when the psychoanalyst—in the role of this transitional phase mother—is internalised. There is also the issue of the "transitional space" between mother and toddler that allows this to happen. For the child's symbolic internalisation of the mother, there needs to be a space between the self and the other. If the mother remains a holding mother past the developmental time when this is appropriate, and if she clings to this position in the transitional stage, the mother will not be internalised as a symbolic image, since the internalisation of the natural experience requires separation, which would allow connection through vision (see Wright, 1991) and beginning verbal communication, rather than through touching or doing. As a consequence, the emotional bonding with the mother will be too regressive. Physical holding will be perpetually sought, interfering with the child's growing autonomy. So, there must be space between the mother and the child for emotional and symbolic bonding to emerge and the father, as "the third" (see Wright, 1991), facilitates the symbolisation of the connection with the mother, if he can exist with the transitional space between mother and child for periods of time. All this extends developmentally to space between self and other in interpersonal relations later on. First, an attuned other must be present with adequate transitional space between the self and this other, who, in earliest development, is the mother. I speak of transitional space, not interpersonal space, because the focus of the mother is there for the infant's inner self, not for her own self.

Melanie Klein and psychic space

Unlike Winnicott, Klein never conceptualised a theory that explicitly deals with space. Yet, as with all his other theories, roots of Winnicott's theory on transitional and psychic space can be seen in Klein. Klein is constantly dealing in dimensions of psychic space when she speaks of an internal world and of split-off and dissociated parts of that internal world. She is constantly dealing with space when she speaks about psychic integration. Psychic integration streamlines a personality through the ownership of truths that reveal themselves through the fantasies of the psyche. These psychic fantasies relate to parts of the developing self that exist in psychic space.

I would also like to believe that Melanie Klein would be one of the first to agree with my own theorising when I visualise space as potential forms that internal objects can take, just as time can be conceptualised as such: that is, as either persecutory or holding in dynamic internal object form (see Kavaler-Adler, 1996, in the theory of the "creative mystique"). I imagine in my own theoretical reverie that space can appear in at least three psychic fantasy forms as internal objects.

1. The first form of space as an internal object would be as a holding object, related to the symbiotic mother of earliest infancy. Associations to the holding mother in relation to external holding objects (self-objects or subjective objects) would usually operate on an unconscious level unless revealed through free association in psychoanalysis.
2. Space can also be experienced as persecutory by intrusive objects (similar to Winnicott's impinging or too omnipotent other/ mother).
3. Space can appear as a transitional stage "mothering" other, a symbolic mother object that facilitates separation–individuation, and facilitates the internalisation of the developmentally facilitating good enough other in symbolic form. In this way, the self can house adequate self and object relations at its core. Such self and object relations, symbolically held within the internal world, can promote relatedness and all the psychological growth that comes through relatedness.

Klein's way of thinking seems to have been visual. Championing the critical role of psychic fantasy in her theories seems related to Klein's acute visual sense. Klein focused this visual sense most assiduously on the terrain of the internal world, where the core self develops through the evocation of self and other relations. Because Melanie Klein's theory is so visual, it is more conducive to theorising about psychic space and its parallels occurring in Winnicott's area of transitional space than is Freudian theory. Therefore, where Freud spoke of instinctual impulses, Klein speaks about psychic fantasies of self and other relations, with a vast cinema screen that she designates as the internal world.

In examining the Klein–Winnicott dialectic on psychic space, I shall demonstrate through clinical and literary examples how what is implicit in Klein on space interacts with what is explicit in Winnicott on space. I shall also explicate the transitional object role of the analyst, along with the analyst's role in translating free associations drawn from dreams and psychic fantasies into conscious symbolic formulations that we designate to be psychoanalytic and object relations interpretations. In the following clinical examples, both female and male patients in psychoanalytic object relations treatment will speak and interact with the analyst serving in his dual role of transitional object and symbolic interpreter. Illustrations will demonstrate how mourning evolves in a developmental context, becoming the overall process I term "developmental mourning". We shall see how such mourning naturally evolves as a primary therapeutic route to opening up both psychic and transitional space in treatment, and to simultaneously opening the route to free associations and mutual interpretation of these associations by patient and analyst. We will contrast this natural evolution to a state of pathological mourning and psychic arrest that compels perpetual re-enactments. The active role of the analyst in opening psychic space is explored, in terms of the analyst creating a transitional space for vulnerable feelings, such as tenderness.

A look at Louise

In Louise's treatment, we see the key to dream analysis in terms of the theme of space. Louise's dreams spoke of conflicts and losses that could be deciphered by analysing the themes of space in her dreams. When she and I analysed two significant dreams along these lines, Louise had reached a symbolic level of experiencing psychic conflicts and loss through a critical mourning process in her treatment. She had mourned layers of grief related to the loss of her father in childhood, and had reached earlier levels of loss related to emotional abuse and emotional disconnection from her mother. Such loss and abuse extended back to Louise's two-year-old period, during the critical developmental phases of separation–individuation that overlaps with Winnicott's transitional stage.

In order for Louise to tolerate the pain of an emotional withdrawal from her mother during her pre-oedipal toddler years, she needed to relinquish provocations that were directed at me as her analyst, provocations that were like proto-symbolic enactments. These enactments defended Louise against the pain of her two-year-old "abandonment depression" rage and loss (see Masterson on "abandonment depression", 1976, 1981). Louise's provocations towards me as her analyst appeared as an identification with the aggressor in terms of having had a mother who, beginning with the transitional stage of her development, when the mother could no longer enjoy merger with a cuddly baby, was rejecting through cold, contemptuous, and condemning judgements. In Kleinian terminology, Louise's repetition of the persecutory aspects of her mother could be understood as her provoking the analyst in ways that sometimes induce countertransference enactments through projective identification. Louise projected her childhood aggression in the form of hostile and whining demands. As her analyst, I tried to feel and process my reactions to her provocative and sometimes taunting and devaluing aggression. When I failed, I would be swept up in a critical attitude of coldness, contempt, and devaluating distain, even if I did not outwardly exhibit this attitude. This mirrored Louise's attitude towards me in the transference, when she re-enacted her mother's behaviour towards her. When this reactive introjective identification occurred on my part, in Klein's terminology, I was not able to be a transitional object in Winnicott's sense because there was no transitional space between Louise and I that would allow me to comfortably process my feelings and thoughts as I would if I was successfully being a "psychic container", in Bion's (1970) terms. Instead, I lost my psychic space and could not freely reflect upon the clinical experience. I felt impulsive urges towards Louise, and at those times I could not yet identify my own feelings and thoughts behind my internal impulses. In fact, similar to Joseph (1989), I temporarily lost my ability to know I was feeling feelings and thinking thoughts. Instead, I felt a sadomasochistic reactivity as my psychic space was assaulted. I was affected by how Louise could not, at those times, allow transitional space between us. She was too caught up in her compulsive maternal re-enactment. In retrospect, I conclude that this foreclosure of transitional space between us reflected Louise's foreshortened internal psychic space caused by the pressures of her unassimilated transitional stage experience with her mother. I realised later that Louise was compelled to re-enact and relive her past sadomasochistic relationship with her mother, which did not allow her to be aware of feeling feelings and thinking thoughts. This oppressive reactivity foreshortened both psychic and transitional space. The effect on me from this reactivity, and within Louise due to her reactivity, was to induce impulses to retaliate. At this earlier stage of treatment I did not have the psychic and transitional space to think, feel, and then respond to the messages from Louise's internal psychic fantasy world, which hid behind Louise's compulsive provocations, reactive to her split-off impulses.

However, as I was gradually able to desist from retaliatory reactions, and was able to feel the two-year-old helplessness that was behind Louise's provocations, I could feel the anguished impingements within Louise that alternated with abandoning indifference, or abandoning detachment. It was these painful impingements that Louise was warding off within her internal self. Louise's defensive attitude of contempt—one of Klein's manic defences—served to help Louise split off and avoid the childhood pain that lay behind her attacks on me. Behind the re-enactment of the contemptuous mother was the inadequate mother that had been internalised as a devalued self-constellation. All this was dissociated through the combination of splitting off feelings and then projecting her pain outward through a manic defence attitude of contempt.

As Louise's analyst, I was gradually able to decipher the pathological mother–child reactions that lay behind Louise's compulsive behaviour toward me in the present. With time and the holding environment that the treatment sessions provided for both of us, I was able to empathically reach behind Louise's hostile, distancing behaviour. I could then find the injured helpless child self within Louise. Louise constantly feared this vulnerable child within her. She felt helpless in the face of anything that threatened to reveal her vulnerability.

Once I could speak to the two-year-old child in Louise, I was able to unconsciously become a therapeutic transitional object for Louise. I was able to stay attuned to the vulnerable place inside Louise where the pain of her early abandonment trauma resided. As I became more and more attuned to this pain, I could feel Louise. I reached out to her by speaking of the pain I could feel behind her cold, devaluing, and hostile manner, and how it was pressuring her. I also told her of the sadness I could feel within that pain, a sadness that had been buried for a lifetime, but which I believe had begun at the age of two. That was when the loving and holding mother of Louise's infancy had turned cold and withdrew from empathically bonding with her daughter. As I stayed with Louise in this way, by contacting her formerly feared and warded-off feelings, and by speaking to the little girl in her about the profound sadness behind her defensive rage, Louise began to become more and more alive with me. She began to expose her affect states, even though she had to face so much pain and rage that lay behind her defensive coldness and hostility. As I put my sense of her formerly split-off and dissociated two-year-old self into words for her, Louise began to understand the pre-oedipal conflicts between her need for contact, connection, and understanding, and her fear-driven defensive attitudes of coldness, contempt, and distancing.

As I spoke about her conflicts, Louise understood that I could feel the opening of space between us; space for each of us to feel and think, to communicate our thoughts and feelings in words, so that we could have meaningful conversations. We began to experience the growth of a psychic dialectic between us, where formerly there had only been provocative and reactive monologues.

Melanie Klein never actually acknowledged this kind of opening of space for dialogue and contact between analyst and analysand, at least not explicitly. However, Kleinians such as Betty Joseph did understand the internal psychic space of the analyst could be foreclosed by the negative impact of the patient's aggressive proto-symbolic projective identifications, as opposed to symbolic level projections (Joseph, 1989). Joseph, a modern-day Kleinian, understood that such projective identifications were part of the splitting and dissociation of a paranoid–schizoid position, in which a constant enactment was compulsively aimed at the analyst. She understood that compulsive re-enactment was an avoidance of conscious remembering (in both cognitive and body experience terms), since remembering threatened to overwhelm the patient with feelings of pain and loss.

Bion (1963, 1970) spoke of containing the affective impact of such an assault and of translating it into symbolic language. Similarly, Joseph (1989) spoke of having her mental ego functioning assaulted by a patient in paranoid–schizoid fantasy enactment, with sadomasochistic dynamics. She tried to survive this assault in order to understand what the patient was reacting to in the transference, such as a reaction to the unconscious fear of the analyst's vacation that might repeat a parental abandonment from childhood. What neither Klein nor the neo-Kleinians explicitly state is that such paranoid–schizoid enactments and provocations—severely assaulting the psychic space of the analyst—are generally the consequence of actual pre-oedipal trauma. They often hold this out as a possibility, but never see the degree of probability in such a conclusion.

Winnicott's perspective on Louise

For Winnicott and his followers, however, the re-enactment of trauma is most generally seen as relevant to the foreclosing of psychic space, first in the adult patient when a child, the adult patient's behaviour with the analyst, and the analyst's reactive foreclosure of psychic space. Even more distinct from the Kleinians is the topic of transitional impact at the time when psychic space in both analyst and patient is reactively foreclosed. It is the area between the patient and the analyst that Winnicott and his followers might focus on. Seeing things in developmental terms, they might see the development of an analyst to be a transitional object, one attuned to the patient, and yet separate enough from the patient to feel and suffer all he or she needs to endure.

Louise's development: resolution of treatment in Klein's and Winnicott's terms

I was able to stay increasingly present with Louise as she surrendered to the powerful affect states of her abandonment trauma. I could become a transitional object by being separate enough to allow her to suffer her rage, pain, need, shame, and guilt. Ultimately, she experienced profound sadness related to all the losses she had undergone, but had not yet consciously experienced in her lifetime. As Louise yielded to consciousness of this sadness and mourned the developmental stage object loss that she had suffered, she began to assimilate her experience. Then she was less likely to split off her affect states and to experience them through projections of persecutory attitudes. In Kleinian terms, Louise began to own all her impulses and affects. In Winnicottian terms, Louise began to allow transitional space for her own self-reflection and free association. Thus, Louise increasingly entered and sustained a depressive position self-integration process. She became increasingly self-aware. Yet, as Louise now increasingly contained her inner experience more, she also evolved a normal repression process whereby her childhood fears, needs, and longings could haunt her again—but now on a symbolic level—through her dreams and fantasy life. Two dreams in particular occurred as she reached the symbolic level of the depressive position and began to have associations ("free associations") to repressed phenomena that she now could, for the first time, contain within her own psyche. It was in the sixth year of Louise's treatment that two important dreams emerged in which the theme of space played a prominent role. They expressed pre-oedipal abandonment trauma in symbolic terms. In Bion's terms, split-off proto-symbolic beta enactments had been transferred to alpha level symbolic statements. This alpha level symbolism needed interpretation by the analyst to translate the unconscious meaning behind the dream images (Grotstein, 1996).

Interpretation of space dynamics within dream imagery

Dream no. 1

Louise dreamed her office was invaded by a man who possibly occupied it without paying rent. To compound the invasion, this man had a female associate who tried to steal the key to the office so as to eventually displace Louise altogether. Louise remembered screaming with a helpless, hysterical, tantrum-like cry. She felt no psychic space to think anything through in her mind. She felt claustrophobically encapsulated in an infantile state. Her rage at the woman stealing the key for the young man manifested as a helpless, impotent screaming at a mother figure—a mother figure that was irrationally and narcissistically lusting after control of her. She felt abandoned, excluded, robbed, and impotent all at once. When she awoke, a sense of heart-choking terror seemed to penetrate and spread through her, as if she was being assaulted by a persecutory bad object inside her.

When I, as Louise's analyst, interpreted the theme of space that dominated the dream, Louise was able to begin a free association process that led to enormous relief. I interpreted the theft of her space, which made her feel as if she was being exiled to an external void where she had no self-anchoring ownership. I also interpreted her terror of losing control when she felt abruptly displaced and outnumbered by the male and female collusion. To lose control would be to be thrown out of a containing or holding space, and to be thrust into a vacuum. The vacuum reflected insatiable oral infant cravings without an available mother for nurturance.

Louise felt my empathic connection through this interpretation. For the first time in the psychoanalytic session, she felt released from a visceral, panic-inducing frenzy of helplessness. She seemed to wake up to cognitive thinking and linear and symbolic thought. She then named the female and male figures in the dream, whom she began to interpret as representatives of people in her current life. She became aware that these people related back to primal mother and brother figures by whom she had felt dominated, excluded, and betrayed.

Dream no. 2

Working together, Louise and I interpreted another of her dreams, one that yielded particular meaning in terms of themes of space. Understanding these themes opened up psychic space within each of us as well as transitional space between us. This second dream was about Louise receiving a request for money from a male friend who, during the period when he had been actively in Louise's life, had played the psychic role of a father figure for her. In the real world, Louise had lost touch with this man. Then she learnt of a tragic accident in which his daughter was killed. She kept thinking about sending him a card, note, or missive of some kind to express her horror and sadness, and offer her condolences to him.

Suspended in the guilt of not yet acting on her intention, and the loss of him as a fantasy father who would protect and admire her, Louis woke up from a deep sleep one morning with a feeling of panic not unknown to her. The panic was similar to that which she had experienced after the first dream, reported above, when Louise had felt alone, abandoned, and helpless. Louise contrasted this feeling with how she had actually felt in the second dream. She realised that in the second dream she had found a renewed connection with this male father figure. Yet, the moment she woke up she felt as if she had lost the connection. She felt bereft and alone, as if abandoned for being bad, which was an old familiar childhood motif in her dreams. She believed she was being watched by an external other, one who saw her through the eyes of condemning judgement. This sense of persecutory invasion and judgement was accompanied by an aching pain and a feeling of being empty or blank inside. The power of the outside judge grew in intensity, until the pain became an active grief that made her cry. Only when she reached the feeling of grief did she feel that she had an inside again, where internal psychic space existed. Before that, she felt excluded from the inside of herself, as if a black abyss pervaded her insides (see Dickinson, 1960; Kavaler-Adler, 1993a). The persecutory external object, which haunted her, felt like Sabina's lie detector in Anaïs Nin's (1974) *Spy in the House of Love*.

In this second dream, Louise had at first felt a warm, safe feeling, believing she was included in her former male father figure's private world, as if she had a home there. This feeling arose in her dream by having this male friend send her a card with photos on each side, which appeared to her to be like a family album with her being included in the family portraits. In the dream, she saw a photo of herself with her husband in the male friend's photo album. The male friend's greeting card, with the enclosed photo album, was accompanied by a request for a financial gift. In the dream, the request for help related to tragic object loss, the loss of a daughter. Louise realised, as she looked at the picture of herself and her husband in this family-like album of pictures, that she looked quite good in the picture that this man had carefully placed in his little card/album of photos. She noticed that her hair and makeup, and even her lipstick, looked "just right". In the picture, Louise saw her face was warm, self-assured, relaxed, and calm, as if she had felt centred well within herself while still being fully open to relatedness at the time when the picture photo was taken. The presence of her husband in the photo implied that her male friend was in the background taking the photograph. The photo made Louise feel as if she, her male friend, and her husband, were all one happy family. As she described the dream and the photograph, she realised that she had placed this male friend in her current life as if he was in the position of her actual father. She realised this because it was her father, in her childhood, who was always taking pictures of her and of others in the family.

Louise also remembered that in the dream she had decided to send £100 to this man to help him during his time of need. In the dream she felt happy to be included as one of the friends to whom this man, in his state of loss, had sent the photos, along with his request for help. She felt the warmth of inclusion and acceptance. This feeling was sharply broken when she woke up suddenly, and realised that in actuality she had not had any direct communication from this man for a long time. Also, she had not found any way of communicating with him after his daughter's death, although her wish to make contact and to express her sympathy was frequently in her mind. The theme of space entered our psychoanalytic dialogue when I proposed that the dream suggested that Louise had a space in this man's life that she no longer had. I added that this was just like her having had a major space in her father's life that she no longer had, because her father had died. She agreed with me.

Louise and I then explored how the loss of that imagined and projected space in her father's world might cause her to feel as if she was an insubstantial and excluded being who lacked her own internal psychic space. There was no transitional space for her in the movement from her dream to her waking state. Louise felt cast out of the family when her father no longer existed in childhood, just as she felt cast out from the family when she woke up from a dream and realised that the connection with the father figure that she wished to recreate in her dream was actually lost, or broken off. As I interpreted this, I believed that Louise heard me. She associated to being cast out from the family and into hell — the black abyss she associated with her last dream. The connotation of hell went beyond the theme of exclusion from a containing space in which a father–daughter relationship or an overall family relationship could reside. Louise's association to being cast into "hell" suggested a primal sense of "being bad". We had come upon this primal sense of guilt before in discussing her relationship with her mother, the parent who remained for her when her father died.

Louise's mother continually scapegoated her daughter through projective identification projections of "badness" and inadequacy.

When imprinted with her own introjections of her mother's pathological and persecutory projections, Louise felt flattened out, as if all the
good, alive substances in her had been drained out of her, leaving her
as a depleted projection screen for her mother. In this introjected state
of badness, Louise experienced a distinct lack of internal space, of
having been emptied out of all joy and love, and, thus, of existing as
a hollow shell. As Louise's internal space was lost so was her sense of
interpersonal space, what Winnicott called transitional space or
"potential space" between mother and toddler or patient and analyst.
In Winnicott's view, such loss of psychic or "potential" space generally indicated childhood trauma, and specifically transitional stage or
separation stage trauma.

As Louise's analyst, I had often felt this loss of transitional space
with Louise, when she would lose her internal psychic space capacities to reflect on herself, and when she lost her abilities to define her
thoughts, feelings, and images (which Klein would call psychic fantasies) symbolically. Louise would then become either withdrawn or
overwhelmed. When her internal psychic space was lost due to the
unconscious reliving of the loss of her father, she would behave like a
two-year-old in a tantrum. That is why only tears of grief brought
relief, for only in feeling this grief could she reconnect to the lost other,
who represented her deceased father, and only through grief could
she find the feelings of love she had once had and shared with him.
When the themes of loss of psychic and transitional space could be
depicted in dream imagery, Louise was able to sustain the transitional
space in her analytic sessions with me. We could also call this transitional space "analytic space", in Winnicott's terms. With analytic space
opened up, Louise could formulate the symbolic meanings that are
found through free association. She could analyse her dream images
through her associations so that she could become separate enough
from the images to share her thoughts and feelings in the transitional
space dialogue evolving between us.

Klein–Winnicott dialectic in Louise's treatment

Unlike Winnicott, Melanie Klein assumes the level of psychoanalytic
capacity for free association in her patients, without developmental
considerations. However, I believe she would understand when the

transitional and psychic space for symbolic level free association was blocked by psychic conflict or trauma. Klein had worked with children in play therapy and understood how the play of children could be blocked by psychic conflict, such as the conflict over the expression of aggressive impulses and their related psychic fantasies of hostile assault. I believe that Klein would be less likely to acknowledge or focus on the developmental blocks to transitional, analytic, and psychic space rooted in trauma and developmental arrest than would Winnicott, but clearly her theory interacts with such clinical phenomenon.

Louise regressed within her dreams and in her affect states whenever she woke from dreams related to primal developmental trauma. These dreams stemmed from the separation–individuation period of pre-oedipal development. The psychic conflicts of connection and disconnection were similarly grounded in this period, even though later oedipal level themes occurred at times. Even when oedipal level themes did occur there were frequently more overriding themes of abandonment and exclusion related to separation–individuation stage trauma, or, in Winnicott's terms, related to transitional stage trauma. As she became an actively "interpreting subject" (Ogden, 1986, 1994), Louise demonstrated Klein's depressive position form of development. She could reflect on—and symbolise—her experience simultaneously with feeling the grief affects of the depressive position. Her associations also revealed the separation, loss, and grief of Winnicott's transitional stage, and the primal father loss that triggered an earlier two- year-old abandonment panic from trauma during this transitional stage.

Space themes in the case of Richard

After many years in once a week treatment, Richard was starting to experience a conscious sense of me as both his analyst and as a transitional object. He begins to play with certain conflicts related to the transitional space between us in the treatment session. Leading up to this time, Richard experienced a multitude of poignant phases of developmental mourning in which he reconnected with early love for his father, who left his family when Richard was just one year old. He also reconnected with love for his stepfather and teenage girlfriend, both of whom he had lost over the years. Most critically, Richard mourned the early loss of his mother, a woman who seems to have had difficulty maintaining emotional support as a holding and transitional stage mother once she lost her husband through divorce.

In the ninth year of treatment, Richard was on the verge of leaving therapy in a common characterological distancing reaction. In the previous session, I had suggested that he might benefit from attending sessions more often. Richard's reflexive reaction was to think of leaving. Right in the midst of articulating his impulse to leave, however, he began to experience the other side of his transferential conflict taking place between fears of being trapped with an unavailable mother and his fears of loss that unconsciously echoed his primal paternal abandonment. As his analyst, I was able to allow transitional space for him to experience this conflict while with me, as I remained quiet and separate from his own inner turmoil. In the next moment, while still on the couch, he suddenly surrendered. The doors to his primal grief opened and he sobbed and sobbed on the couch, while simultaneously articulating the new conscious awareness of a love that he had lost through his repressive and dissociative defences against the pain of loss. Often living under the cloud of abandonment depression in the past, he was now most fully on the point of freeing himself as he relinquished his primal grief and surrendered to contact with his internal self. He also surrendered to me, his analyst, in the psychic and transitional space that opened once he could yield his warding-off and distancing defences.

In the past, Richard had spoken about an impinging and persecutory father as well as an impinging, clinging, and possessive mother. However, in this moment, when he began to leave me, as if to leave the disappointing aspects of both his parents, he then pivoted into the transformative affect experience of his primal grief that would become his overall developmental mourning process. Through his tears and sobbing, Richard cried out, "My father could be contemptuous and manipulative, but he also had some wonderful qualities!" He started sobbing with tears of grief and loss, feeling sadness he had blocked off for a lifetime. I was with him, but quiet. I could resonate with his sadness while also remaining silent. In this way, I allowed Richard the transitional space he needed to open his core self to developmental mourning. As Richard filled the transitional space allowed by both my silence and my emotional presence, he cried that underneath all the rage he had spoken about, related to his father, he had always loved him. As he now welcomed this feeling of love, surrendering his usual distancing mechanisms with which he fought attachment through detachment, he said, "Maybe now I can love my wife, now that I've discovered this love inside me for my father."

Richard did not speak directly to me at this point, and neither did he speak about me. He was not yet conscious of his feelings towards me. His past transference had revealed that he feared I would be secretly contemptuous and judgemental of him as he had felt his father had been in his childhood. At other times, he had imagined me to be the disappointing and disappointed mother who had felt rejected by him just as all his girlfriends—including his teenage girl-friend—had felt rejected by him.

However, as Richard opened to his core love for the father and for the father–mother union of his infancy (first year of life) he began to remember all his relationships with a new clarity and a new passion. He woke up to how angry he had been all along with his teenage girl-friend, who had left him and then finalised her departure by joining a cult abroad in Europe. He realised in this ninth year of once-a-week treatment that he had gone through the motions of trying to retrieve his lost teenage girlfriend. He had offered her family his services in trying to rescue her from the cult. He realised now, however, that all during that time he had been emotionally and psychically numb. He related how out of touch he must have been to not have felt the anger and rage he felt now as he recalled his girlfriend's departure. He recalled her indifference to his feelings when she had called him in a frenzied state of ecstasy to tell him that she had joined the cult. He had felt guilty that he could not feel happy for his former girlfriend, even though it had been obvious to him that that was what she had wanted him to feel. Now he wanted to cry out everything that he had neg-lected to say to her then. He said he wanted to scream to her, "What about me! I miss you! I want you to come back!" Thus, as Richard woke up to his feeling self, he felt all that had been numbed within him. He felt all that he had kept removing himself from through his distancing defences. He woke up to all this through the grief for his lost father, and for his wish to love and be loved by his father. The early parental abandonment that he had run from all his life came alive. Richard then experienced memories of love and loss in relation to the many women that he had left abruptly. He realised now that he had been unconsciously doing to them what he felt had been done to him by his teenage girlfriend, and earlier by his father.

As Richard's feeling came alive through this psychotherapeutic mourning process he also had psychic fantasies come alive that reflected unconscious memories. Some of these memories were from early preverbal infancy and so could not be conceptualised before his core grief and core love opened psychic space within him, and, as Klein would say, within his internal world.

During his tenth year of treatment, Richard dreamed that he was a small child, perhaps an infant or toddler, being washed in a sink by his mother. The dream turned to a nightmare when the sink he was being bathed in broke and he crashed down to the ground. The sink fractured into pieces, just as he felt he had fractured psychically into pieces when his mother might have dropped her bond with him when he was one year old—perhaps withdrawing into herself after feeling abandoned by her husband, who left the family at that time. Richard suspected there had been a detachment in his mother even earlier because she was carrying unmourned childhood trauma and sexual abuse within herself.

Richard was able to have associations to this dream, and, in doing so, he realised that he had felt emotionally dropped by his mother. As he consciously faced this painful and fragmenting experience of being psychically abandoned as a child, he became increasingly aware of why he had spent years distancing himself from me, from his wife, and from all intimate relationships. He realised he had lost any sense of safety and trust with his mother. He also realised that he had later felt unsafe with his father as well, because he had been emotionally attacked throughout his childhood by his father whenever he came to visit.

As Richard awoke into consciousness of his early maternal trauma he also felt more alive in the world. A sense of greyness lessened and colours opened up. He commented for the first time that he was actually aware of me as a person, and he said that I was someone who liked to dress in a lot of colours. He also developed empathic feelings for others in general. One day, he talked about the burden of grief he was carrying in relation to the suffering of humanity in the face of worldwide problems. He said, "The Israelis are being murdered and we all feel the weight of it!"

Although increasingly waking up to consciousness of his internal self, Richard had not fully surrendered in his thirteenth year of treatment. Then he began to speak to me about his conscious experience of me. He articulated how vividly he now experienced me as a transitional object, as a separate person, and also as a woman who could arouse his sexual desire. He felt the sexual desire when feeling gratitude towards me that also made him feel love for me. Richard's gratitude emerged in the transitional space I encouraged by being present with him as a transitional object without imposing needs of my own. Issues of conflict over psychic and transitional space arose when Richard spoke about desires that could awaken early childhood fears of incest. Yet, Richard remained able to have his free associations at this time, and was able to symbolise and verbalise his desires, fears, and psychic conflicts. There was no evidence of a foreclosure of psychic or transitional space. Through mourning with me over the years, Richard had worked through his early infant trauma, as well as his toddler stage separation trauma. I had been present as a supportive other for him.

In his thirteenth year of object relations treatment once a week, Richard and I had a pivotal discussion. That discussion exemplifies the evolution of intimacy that can follow a critical developmental mourning process in which all the major traumas and losses of one's life have been consciously confronted. In this session, Richard reached out across the transitional space between us and began to share very personal feelings that recognised the analyst as both a transitional object and a love object.

Over time, Richard's mourning process had opened up his internal psychic space through assimilating both the aggressive and loving parts of his personality. In a Kleinian sense, he had been moving progressively towards increasing psychic integration, which enabled transitional space to open between us. Richard had learnt to observe his own feelings and thoughts, and, hence, became aware of the anxiety, shame, and sexual excitement that he felt in our personal communication. With adequate psychic space provided by the analyst as a "good enough" transitional object, Richard had adequate psychic space within himself to sustain free associations. He began to free associate as the space for a conscious awareness of the conflicts that come with intimate communication and feelings.

In simple yet eloquent terms, Richard expressed the importance of my presence, specifically recognising my transitional object role, and how it allowed him to consciously feel sexual arousal for me—as well as an intense longing to receive maternal love from me. He was able to see, and comment on, how all this longing, mixed with sexual desire, might be foreclosed by feelings of haunting guilt about incestuous associations and fears of the humiliating rejection of unrequited love.

Richard: Last week I really felt you. I've been feeling more accepting, and I know it's related to you. I was thinking of you just now. I sensed that you were going through an experience of loss last week, and I could feel you.

Analyst: Thanks for letting me know that.

Richard: I experience you as being very emotionally present with me—very responsive—and accepting, and helpful to me. I think it's been very helpful to me to be here and think with you. It's helped me to feel more safe or more free to be more present—to be more vulnerable and more open with you—and somehow by extension with myself. So that makes me feel gratitude towards you!

Analyst: That has music in it.

Richard: What's the music?

Analyst: The flow back and forth, the interplay. The inner feeling of what you feel when you express gratitude towards me. It has music in it. [Richard had a passionate interest in music.]

Richard: It's kind of an exchange of energy—of feeling—maybe of love. I'm a very sexual person. With you I feel anxiety. If I let myself love you, then a warm melting feeling will come. Then I'll want to have sex with you.

[Richard laughed just then—one of amusement, as much as self-consciousness. He is able to look at himself in the area of transitional space between us. He continues:]

It could be a lot of fun. But saying that makes me feel shame. I feel it's incestuous. Maybe it has to do with shame in general. I'm very sexual but very vulnerable to humiliation unless there's mutual interest. Maybe that's why it's easier with younger women. The older women pull for the shame and mother anxiety . . . So I'm going to come back to talking about you. I'm really wondering what the anxiety is about, about incest? Talking to you about you turns me on a little bit. I feel closer to you. Now I feel excited.

There's something about feeling gratitude towards you. I'm aware of feeling some reluctance or conflict about that—maybe because it makes me feel more vulnerable and more dependent. I don't know. It's sort of based on the sense that you actually care about me. Then I think, "What if you don't care about me and I'm just making it up?" That would make me an idiot or a fool. When young I fell in love with someone and she apparently didn't fall in love with me. I'm thinking of the girlfriend I had in my teens. Now I'm thinking about my mother. Did I feel rejected by my mother?

Analyst: That's an interesting question. You generally think of the other side of it, with you as the guilty agent of rejection in reaction to your mother's clinging. Yet, on the other side of it, you might have felt rejected, just as you did with your teenage girlfriend, and as you are now afraid of feeling with me. [Richard proceeded to relate this association to early mother rejection, to pre-oedipal phenomena, as opposed to oedipal stage exclusion and conflict.]

Richard: I do think you're right about some early rejection. I drank a baby bottle until I was five. I don't think I drank it all the time, but I had a hard time letting go of it. That translates into my having strong sexual desire. It translates into my intense hunger for connection. I imagine that I didn't get what I need from my mother, and so I was left with this longing!! It makes me think of my early experience of not being attuned to, of not being safe— of not being able to trust. But now with you, after so long, I'm aware of something about feeling this greater sense of safety. It feels like wholeness. It leaves me feeling more empathic—maybe like the music you were talking about. What goes around comes around. Since you've given me empathy and acceptance I can now feel empathy and acceptance towards others. So I have some kind of an impulse to want to play with you.

[Richard laughed and cleared his throat. The sexual implication of "playing with me" seemed to have aroused his anxiety again, possibly coupled with the associated incestuous longings that were just then becoming conscious. Also, the intensity of the preverbal oral cravings, that were formerly dissociated and projected, might also play a part in this anxiety.]

Richard: It's a very simple thing, but it feels like an important breakthrough.

Analyst: Yes it is a breakthrough for you to be saying these things
directly to me. Now it's time to go.

The analyst's breathing opening transitional space and breathing in the patient

As psychoanalysts, we sometimes do things intuitively that only later
do we begin see as contributions to therapeutic technique and the
therapeutic action of psychoanalysis. It is just such a context that I
now assess a non-verbal kind of intervention that positively affected
the treatment process of a woman with an intense homoerotic transference. Having completed this treatment many years ago, my own
psychic space opened up over time, enabling the reflections that
follow. Given the topic of psychic and transitional space, it occurs to
me that my work with this former analysand, Shelly, offers a unique
perspective on the analyst's capacities to open up transitional space in
treatment.

In Shelly's case, a patient who had regressed from symbolic to
proto-symbolic transference, verbal communication provided the
opening of transitional space. This happened in the course of a treatment process that touched on core pre-oedipal trauma and its resolution through developmental mourning, combined with interpretation
related to transference work. The intensity of all the formerly rejected
pre-oedipal cravings, combined with the oedipal level longings,
required a developmental progression in which the patient could
articulate in the symbolic language of words that which she had felt
as a pre-oedipal toddler about her mother. Shelly spoke in lusty, adult
sexual language about the oedipal level homoerotic fantasies that
disguised her early pre-oedipal level of intense need, vulnerability,
and formerly warded-off tenderness. As her analyst, I accepted this
level of romantic and sexual desire, as well as the symbolic messages
in Shelly's verbal expression. However, I also listened closely in order
to see behind the manifestation of such verbal level erotic imagery that
Shelly experienced in the conceptual language of psychic fantasy.

My part in opening transitional space for Shelly in an area in
which it had been foreclosed concerns the profound longings of a
woman to disclose her earliest core needs and longings. Although
Shelly was courageous in her expression of sexual fantasies about me

as a desirable woman (and as a transferential idealised mother figure), she was terrified of the more vulnerable area in her psyche that housed the most exquisitely tender feelings of transitional stage toddler love. This earlier toddler love might be the kind of pre-oedipal sensual love that Wrye and Welles (1998) have written about in their book, *The Narration of Desire*.

For three years of object relations psychoanalytic treatment, Shelly seductively articulated aggressive and competitive fantasies of engaging in sex with me. She articulated fantasies of being involved with me in a sexual situation where we were both being penetrated by a man. She expressed fantasies in which I appeared as the child part of her, as well as fantasies in which I appeared as a powerful and sensual woman, who sometimes had a penis. After three years, Shelly began to open to a new stage of vulnerability in her treatment. At this point, she conveyed to me a whole other level of desire. Her progression to this level of trust in me seemed to be related to her ability to have opened up the pain of many childhood memories of suffering rejection by a very creative, but narcissistically self-absorbed and preoccupied mother. Her mother's verbal and physical assaults on Shelly were suffered intermittently with some very tender, nurturing times with her mother. She had shared in her mother's whole range of feelings and thoughts, thus becoming a very special confidant of her mother. Consequently, her mother's narcissistic rages left Shelly—after having been held close in her mother's confidence and having strained to meet her mother's impossible needs—feeling betrayed and abandoned, and with an extreme vulnerability to narcissistic injury. She also had been compelled to relive the kind of depressions that she had first experienced in the company of her mother, who was also frequently depressed. Yet, buried under the repressed pain and unspoken rage of those long-ago times—in which Shelly felt weighted down, even buried, by her mother's depressions—were earlier experiences of her mother's tenderness, nurturance, and care-taking. Shelly had fantasies that seemed to echo repressed memories of her toddler days when she was two and three years old. Once, Shelly had come in wet from the snow and was tenderly caressed by her mother, who then patiently undressed her and embraced her with the warmth of her concern. Another time, Shelly sat quietly in her mother's lap while she spoke lovingly to her and gently brushed her hair. This was a contented mother that Shelly rarely experienced.

In the transference, Shelly relived the long repressed memory of being in her mother's lap. She began to articulate her image of having me hold her in my lap, and of me tenderly touching her hair. As the fantasy mother, she imagined me to brush her hair away from her face with my hands. In her fantasy, I might look at her as would a mother deeply engaged in eye contact with her child. But then Shelly abruptly stopped and sat up from the couch. She wanted to express her love for me, she said, but had suddenly felt faint and then suffocated by the powerful affects that threatened to erupt from her memories of these early time of tenderness—memories that she had defended herself from for so long. In subsequent sessions, Shelly tried again to express her transitional stage love for me, feelings she wished she could have expressed to her mother. But by the time she could do so, her mother had begun attacking Shelly, and so speaking with her mother about this earlier period of tender, nurturing love had become too danger-ous. Only during her third year in psychoanalysis (three times a week), could Shelly begin to attempt that which had been impossible throughout her childhood and early adult years—to express the early passions of love for her mother by attempting to express it to me.

The analyst's breathing and the patient's unconscious

As Shelly tried repeatedly opened herself to her deepest level of feeling, after having once or twice stopped because of the terror she felt of fainting or being suffocated by her feelings, I found myself meeting her on a non-verbal level. Without conscious intent, my breathing deepened and my lungs began to expand; I found myself responding to my subliminal body consciousness, opening the psychic doorway to Shelly's unconscious communications while she laboured through the throes of struggling towards consciousness, so that she might express in words her love for me. Opening that psychic doorway involved the opening up of the transitional space between us. As Shelly gained access to the feelings at her deepest core—a core enveloped in deep grief—she began to cry, sobbing uncontrollably. Slowly, she became able to articulate the cherished and formerly hidden words of love, the words of a sweet and vulnerable two- or three-year-old. I witnessed her painful struggle, the agony and fear of exposing that which had been too dangerous to expose all these years.

I heard the pain and then I heard the love itself. Shelley almost choked on her words at times, but, as I opened my breathing, she continued. She said, "You mean so much to me. I feel like I have to tell you how much I love you." My unconscious body response became conscious. I could now see that I played an active, albeit non-verbal, part in opening the transitional space needed between us, allowing her deepest self to come into the world. Risking all, it was the first time ever she had uttered verbal expression of her preverbal longings.

Transitional space in the internal world: the case of Jennifer

As I look back on my work with another female patient, Jennifer, I am struck by how a woman's psychic being can open up from a dramatically foreclosed state. Early in her psychoanalytic treatment, Jennifer described the foreclosed state she lived in. She said that it was as if her body had a lead pipe extending from her head down to her toes, blocking out all emotional sensation in her body core, including her genital area and torso. How did she come from that foreclosed state to one in which she became alive with rich, visceral, body sensations? How did she evolve from her foreclosed existence to a place in which she could have the most vivid psychic fantasy imagery—imagery that introduced both of us to a lush, resonant, and tranquil internal world? How did the psychic space open up within her? How did the engagement between us occur in the transitional space responsible?

I shall briefly summarise certain trends in Jennifer's treatment that allowed her to progress towards an expansive and rich internal world that was evidence of the evolution of both psychic and transitional space. In doing so, I indicate how a psychic dialectic between Klein's view of psychic integration and Winnicott's view of the transitional object role of the psychoanalyst allowed this woman to grow in terms of the psychic dynamics of space. The dialectic of the Kleinian and Winnicottian clinical processes can also be viewed from the developmental perspective that I propose in terms of an overall "developmental mourning" process.

When Jennifer first came to an analytic treatment that would last over eight years, her disconnection from herself was symptomatically seen in her experience of being cut off from her body. As mentioned, instead of the experience of inner space and of a self or inner voice, she felt as if her head was on top of a lead pipe that extended down to her feet and toes. She had occasional fantasies of attacking herself with a knife, as if to commit a kind of hara-kiri suicide. This fantasy illustrated to what degree she projected on to herself an internal bad self, one that related to the sense of carrying the leaden weight of unconscious childhood guilt that needed to become conscious. She wanted to attack the closed off internal self and kill it, punishing it for the unforgivable crimes she believed that she had committed. The greatest of these crimes fantasised was of having psychologically murdered her own child when she left him with her mother in Europe when she came to America. Like the weight of lead that she fantasised inhabiting her body space, she carried a burden of guilt.

Jennifer spoke of seeing herself as a criminal and so it followed that she projected on to herself and on to her body the view of having bad stuff inside her. Believing that everything inside of her was tainted by badness, she had no internal space for a "good enough" internal object bond, or for relationships within her internal world. Thus, her potential internal world was foreshortened and foreclosed. In the terms of the British theorist Fairbairn (1952), it was split off and sealed off. While projecting all the badness on to herself, and rationalising that her "killer rage" made her bad, indicating that the childhood sources of this rage remained unconscious, Jennifer projected all her "goodness" (what Klein would call her internal good object) on to me, so that for a period of time she saw me through the lens of an idealising transference. She wanted to be an extension of me in the beginning of her treatment, which lasted until she began to value her own differentiated identity. Through her idealising transference fantasies, Jennifer attempted to live either vicariously through me or in a psychic merger in which she felt as if she was becoming a part of me. This probably repeated the way her mother had used her as an extension of herself and had resisted her separating from her, causing Jennifer to have developmental trauma from the two- and three-year-old separation–individuation period, in Winnicott's terms, the critical transitional stage era. In Klein's terms, Jennifer was splitting her internal good and bad objects and projecting the bad ones on to herself (or interjecting it) and was projecting the early infant idealised object (Klein's "breast"-mother, or Winnicott's "holding" mother) out on to the analyst.

In order for Jennifer to connect with her internal self and body self, she had to open the psychic space and transitional space needed to integrate her bad and idealised objects to create a Kleinian "good object", or a Winnicottian "good enough" object. For her to get there, however, she first had to use me as a transitional object for her developmental needs. She would do so, however, by viewing me through the Kleinian lens of an idealised transference object. Whereas Klein might see the idealised transference purely in defensive terms, to ward off fears of the analyst as a persecutory mother and to ward off awareness of her own hostile aggression towards this transferential mother, it is necessary to see the developmental use of the idealising transference that evolved, vividly so in Jennifer's case. Although it interacts with defensive idealisation, this idealisation, when projected on to the analyst as a transference object, is also a means—in the developmental terms of Winnicott—to reparative growth. Winnicott could see the transitional object role of the analyst in receiving the idealising transference views and helping the patient consciously articulate the fantasies related to this transference idealisation. Kohut's (1971) American view of the developmental use of the idealising transference can be cited here as well.

How did this all take place in Jennifer? When Jennifer began treatment she viewed me as having the courage to be out in the world in a way that terrified her. She feared being destroyed by others if she were to put herself "out there". Yet, vicariously, she could enjoy seeing me as being "out there" and as having all the successes that she wanted to be a part of by viewing them in me. Later, this would dramatically change and she would want to be the one out there, but only after she had integrated herself through analysis and the separation–individuation mourning process.

From the beginning, Jennifer was on the couch. However, she would sometimes also see me at public events and lectures. Whenever this happened, she would study me intently, feeling thrilled if she thought I was excited and enthusiastic about my presentation in public and an audience's reception. She would also have vivid psychic fantasies about me, when her psychic fantasy life was still impoverished. She would imagine that she was seeing through my eyes and hearing through my ears and that that I was writing knowledge into her mind as she was reading books that I had written. Through me, she saw herself succeeding in the world without having to take the risks of exposing herself by being "out there" herself. At a period in the treatment of strong symbiosis within the idealising transference, she imagined I was a shaman who could see things inside of her in an almost magical way.

As long as Jennifer stayed in this realm of idealised transference fantasy, and saw herself as the inadequate or bad one, she could not open her inner psychic space. However, as she began to feel that she wanted to have more of an identity of her own, she also began to open up the rage, pain, and object loss of her childhood. She recalled a mother who opposed her developmental needs for separation and a father who attacked her from a position of devaluing narcissistic contempt. As her affects opened up along with memories, I became more of a transitional object with whom she could feel all her feelings and think all her thoughts and memories.

I became less of an idealised extension for Jennifer. Consequently, Jennifer could also begin to see my faults as well as my talents and abilities. She also realised that the guilt she had about her "crimes" and her "killer rage" could be examined. Eventually, Jennifer saw that she did not empathically understand what had compelled her to act as she had—for example, to leave her child behind. As memories came back to Jennifer, she realised that she had been literally trapped with her mother and family. She began to understand her actions in relation to this situation from her past. Gradually, then, she could begin to have compassion for herself.

In this way, she also came to make reparative moves towards her relationship with her son, and eventually was able to have him come to live with her. With my presence and my empathy, Jennifer followed the developmental course of her affects in the course of treatment. She became fully conscious of what all her "killer rage" had been about. Jennifer recalled specific memories of her mother's attacks on her when she would have friends other than her mother. She also recalled her father's belittling comments that attacked her self-confidence and attacked her femininity. When all the critical memories that triggered her current rage were felt, talked about, and defined in the transitional space between us, she was able to surrender to the deep need for love that lay behind the rage.

It was at this point that Jennifer opened the oceans of tears that told the story of the deep sadness within her. This was the deep grief related to her agonising childhood need to be loved even as she separated and became an individual. Jennifer's insight would often bring the backlash reactions from her unconscious of visceral and somatic pain and sickness that recapitulated early infant illness as a retaliatory punishment for her growing awareness, and for her growing individual identity that evolved through consciousness. In the transference, I could be the mother who would be enraged by Jennifer's progress in forming her own identity. Believing this, Jennifer would turn against herself to punish herself with attacks as a way of warding off the feared mother's or father's attacks. Nevertheless, Jennifer could express the frustrated developmental needs of her childhood in the transitional space of the treatment process. With me as a transitional object, she reached the expression of her deepest cry, and, with it, her earliest memories and associations. She would speak of feeling healed by this deep crying and by the mourning of all the losses of her life.

As Jennifer faced the formerly dissociated pain of her primal losses she no longer needed to split off her inner potentials and capacities on to the analyst as an idealised other. I no longer had to represent all that she had thought was only in me, but which was actually there within herself as well. Simultaneously, feeling her rage consciously and understanding it, Jennifer no longer needed to project images of criminals and of "badness" on to herself. She could now own her aggression as energy, vitality, and self-assertiveness, rather than experiencing it as the curse of criminal badness or as self-undermining sabotage that had convinced her that she was inadequate.

In parallel with this growth, she began to own her potentials, which included potentials to love and create, and to more freely accept and express the full range of her feelings and fantasies. She became increasingly whole through the self-integration process based on feeling the grief of pre-oedipal object loss within "developmental mourning".

Klein–Winnicott dialectic in the transitional stage of psychic transformation

One day, Jennifer had a dream that her body had separated itself from my body. I realised that this was a critical turning point in Jennifer's overlapping self-integration process—as viewed from a Kleinian perspective—and her transitional stage separation–individuation process, as viewed from a Winnicottian perspective. Her dream stated the critical point of separation in her developmental journey, following the mournful grief over her losses, longing, and regrets. After telling me about this dream, we had a different experience together in the transitional space between us. Instead of me continuing to feel feelings similar to hers along with her, as I had in the past (such as when I had felt my lungs expand as she felt her lungs expanding), I began to have distinctly different feelings to those she had.

While she was feeling happiness and joy, I felt mild depression. Also, within her own psychic space Jennifer felt quite differently. Like Richard, she began to feel heights of enthusiastic energy as well as exchanges of energy between us. Jennifer spoke of feeling "so-o-o-o connected". She had dreams of her female and spiritual self emerging: women dancing in whole rectangular forms, dressed in orange and yellow colours. She dreamed of a part of herself in a spiritual lapis lazuli blue colour. She also had dreams of sexual and sensual fulfilment.

Klein's internal world

Then Jennifer began to have psychic fantasies about the nature of her internal world itself. She saw her internal world as a deep cave beneath the ocean, with a low-key tranquillity. She felt in my presence as if she could visit this ocean cave within her, where she would feel a sense of peaceful harmony. Along with vivid self-sensation and self-awareness that she had never experienced before, her internal psychic space came alive along with the transitional space between us in treatment. She began to move towards a termination process in which she could trust that she could be "out there" in the world as a motivational speaker, or as a leader of other sorts, all on her own, without me.

The Kleinian self-integration process of the depressive position had taken place. Jennifer navigated through the developmental mourning process that my own theory describes. This allowed her to face her aggression as a subjective and reflective self within the Kleinian depressive position. Consequently, Jennifer no longer spoke of herself as a murderer with "killer rage". Instead, she was able to contain and use her aggression in the service of self-agency. As she controlled impulses to retaliate on the son with whom she had become reunited, she began to associate herself with those—such as Martin Luther King and Gandhi—who contained their aggression for constructive purposes. Then she also found the symbol of a Black Madonna, who represented to her a full range of integrated erotic, feminine, and aggressive parts of herself.

Winnicott's developmental internalisation in interaction with Klein's phenomenology

Jennifer found the love at the core of her that had been there from the earliest infant time. She found the love offered in a maternal connection that resided in her psyche from before the time of her transitional separation–individuation stage traumas.

In Kleinian terms, by owning her aggression, facing her psychic fantasies consciously, and mourning her guilt and loss, Jennifer was able to survive the depressive position struggles. She could then psychologically develop past the regressive phenomena of the paranoid–schizoid position that threatened to pull her back into pre-symbolic enactments.

In Winnicottian terms, she had internalised enough of the "good enough" aspects of the transitional object relationship with the analyst to be able to have a secure internal connection with a good internal object. Thus, she refound the early good object that was there all along, behind the warded-off pain, and behind the splitting process and the defences, as Klein would have predicted. Then she was also able to internalise more sustained good object connection so as to build up her core self, as Winnicott would have predicted.

CHAPTER SEVEN

Dynamics of transitional space: pathological foreclosure *vs.* expansion in clinical treatment

In this chapter, a psychobiographical example is given to illustrate how the Winnicottian dimension of transitional space, which corresponds to the internal world's psychic space, becomes foreclosed in those who are arrested with severe character pathology, without the intervention of object relations psychoanalytic treatment. Then, several clinical vignettes are offered to illustrate the contrast of how two patients who underwent an in-depth "developmental mourning" process in object relations psychoanalytic treatment were able to open up the transitional space in their lives, corresponding with the internal psychic space in their intrapsychic life.

The psychobiographical example pertains to the lives I have studied in my former books. In *The Creative Mystique: From Red Shoes Frenzy to Love and Creativity* (1996), I have an extensive study of the life of Virginia Woolf. In this chapter, which was published earlier in my newly edited *The Compulsion to Create: Women Writers and Their Demon Lovers* (2013), I cite some of the life phenomena that show the tragic foreclosure of transitional space in the life of Virginia Woolf. Following this, I offer clinical case vignettes from patients who pursued extensive object relations psychoanalytic treatment. It will be seen that these psychoanalytic patients (or analysands) were able dramatically to expand the dimensions of their lives, despite early pre-oedipal trauma, as well as later childhood trauma. Their internal worlds can be visited because they offered so much evidence of their growth from reporting dreams and fantasies from their internal worlds, as well as illustrating the expanding dimensions of their lives (their transitional space) in the changes within their external lives.

By studying a well-known writer such as Virginia Woolf, an artist who reached out to the world through brilliant, symbolic expositions of her internal world of darkness, we come to appreciate the need for an object relations treatment for primal pre-oedipal stage psychic trauma, the "basic fault", to use Balint's (1979) succinct term. By examining the biographical evidence to be found across the span of an entire individual human life, we can see a macrocosm of what we might otherwise only glimpse in a microcosmic context from the slivers of life we are privileged to view in our patients (Kavaler-Adler, 2013[1996]).

Virginia Woolf

According to her biographers (Bell, 1972; Bond, 1989; De Salvo, 1989; Gordon, 1989; Panken, 1987; Rose, 1978; Van Buren Kelley, 1971), Virginia Woolf had only one positive memory of being with her mother. It is so early a memory that only someone with pre-oedipal trauma and psychic arrest could recall it, since only in such cases has the normal psychological protection of repression failed.

Virginia Woolf remembered herself as an infant lying in her mother's lap listening to the rhythmic sounds of the ocean waves as they swirled and crashed beyond the window of her family's summer home (De Salvo, 1989). There is a musical and sensual ecstasy in Woolf's memory of being in her mother's presence at this time, one that she will always yearn for, but never re-experience. For a moment, her mother was the good enough "holding mother" of Winnicott. But by the time Virginia was ten weeks old, her mother had chosen to abort contact with her by refusing to continue to breastfeed or hold her (Bond, 1989). This decision was supported by her husband, Leslie Stephen, who did not want his wife to be uncomfortable. In another biographical report of the same memory, Panken (1987) writes of Virginia's terror in the moment of lying in her mother's lap, rather than of any ecstasy. In Woolf's diaries, the memory of the same moment that she had earlier written about as sensual delight is transformed into infantile dread and visceral terror (De Salvo, 1989).

How ironic that this abrupt and certainly traumatising withdrawal from breastfeeding by Virginia's mother, Julia Stephen, should symbolically parallel the abrupt withdrawal of breastfeeding by Winnicott's own mother, who stopped nursing her male infant when she felt sexually stimulated by such an intimate encounter (Rodman, 2004). However, the symbolic parallel might have ended here because, with the withdrawal of the maternal breast, Virginia Woolf encountered the coldest emotional abandonment possible. She was placed in the children's nursery, where the nurse fed her by propping up a bottle. Here was the proverbial wire mesh mother incarnate. There was no mother, no nurse, no terrycloth mummy, and no person in any capacity at all to hold Virginia as an infant. No wonder the child began to scream violently, becoming known in the family for her nursery rages.

There were, of course, perfunctory daily parental visits that punctuated Virginia's time in the nursery. However, Virginia was tortured in the nursery. She was provoked, intimidated, and assaulted with the verbal attacks (and probably physical, as well) of her older brother and sister, Thoby and Vanessa.

By virtue of her young age unable to communicate in the face of such early abuse, Virginia is reported to have resorted to turning all her rage and wrath inward against herself. She submitted to the abuse of her siblings as a way of punishing them with the vision of her masochistic pain to match their sadism, even though doing so would have also assured them of their power advantage over her as well. In one instance, she was in a fight with her brother Thoby, when suddenly Virginia gave up the fight and let Thoby pummel her with his fists (see Kavaler-Adler, 1996).

Where was her mother during this time? Generally absent. Virginia Woolf's mother only entered the nursery for ritualised visits. Equally telling, whenever the family gathered together, Virginia could never be alone with her mother for a moment; one of her siblings would always intrude. Woolf (1927) depicted just such intrusion in *To the Lighthouse*, a work of biographical fiction. The abrupt, murderous shock of intrusion that can disrupt an intimate moment is also delineated in her novel, *The Voyage Out* (Woolf, 1915), where, at the brink of intimacy, Terrance and Rachel are suddenly interrupted by a knock at the door. When Rachel breaks the spell to answer the door, Terrance fantasises that an old hunchback woman with a knife will stab her when she opens it. Spoken through her alter ego character, Terrance, this fantasy demonstrates the intense and murderous aggression that Virginia Woolf turns upon herself, represented in the surrogate character Rachel. It also shows how the "potential space" (Winnicott, 1971a) for intimacy between two people collapses, as a traumatic disruption interrupts. Terrance envisions a woman with a murderous impulse and a knife. This is interesting, because as an infant, Virginia was similarly "stabbed" by a woman when her mother abruptly ceased breastfeeding, and then deprived her of all emotional holding and support. Without adequate maternal holding, living in a "transitional space" (as during Winnicott's transitional stage) becomes impossible. This transitional stage corresponds to the critical separation–individuation phase of Mahler (1967, 1971), during which traumatic disruption results in character disorders. In the fantasies and behaviours of her fictional characters, in the portrayal of the intense disruption of their potential and transitional space, Virginia Woolf provides us with a compelling study of how such disruption afflicts those whose lives are diminished by them, and how they can result in character disorders.

Despite being born into a highly literary family, if it were not for her father, Virginia Woolf might never have written or published a thing. She existed only as a supplicant to an elegant but cold mother. Virginia was granted the privilege of bringing jewels to her mother as she dressed for dinner, but she had no direct affectionate encounter with the woman. In one memory, Virginia turned her attention away from her mother to focus instead on the rich, sensual colours of the room's flowered wallpaper (Woolf, 1978). The wallpaper might have symbolised some sensuality that Virginia desired to touch in her mother, but from which she was banned. She was just an observer. The only place that Virginia found any form of a Winnicottian "holding environment" was in the attention that she received from her father as she began to read and write.

Virginia Woolf and her father

Virginia ("Ginny" to her father) soon became Leslie Stephens's favourite child. Her father was a respected author, and, as a man of

letters, was quick to recognise and encourage his daughter's precocious literary abilities. During her oedipal years, Leslie held Virginia
on his knee and allowed her to display her affection with kisses
(Panken, 1987). Quentin Bell (1972) claims that Leslie Stephen was
pleased when his daughter would say "kiss" and offer him the affection that he probably very much lacked in his relationship with his
wife. As Leslie and Julie Stephen struggled to impose their individual
subtle undercurrents of sadomasochistic power on each other, the
marriage became something of an intermittent cold war. But with his
little girl Virginia, Leslie Stephen could relax and fully enjoy her
company. He frequently took his daughter on walks in the country-
side around their summer estate. Bell's (1972) poetic words capture
the oedipal lyric that both Virginia and her father might have felt
when they walked together at St Ives during her childhood summers:
"This was the time when Virginia could walk out with her father to
the . . . fairyland of great ferns which stood high above a child's head,
or to Halestown Bog where the osmunda grew . . ." (p. 34). This
oedipal stage lyric would continue. While her brothers attended
university, Virginia learnt to read and write, and studied Greek, Latin,
and English literature under the tutelage of her admiring father. When
auditory hallucinations foreclosed Virginia's psychic space in her
early twenties, following her father's death, she heard birds singing to
her in Greek (see *Mrs Dalloway*, Woolf, 1925). In her very first suicide
attempt, she acted out her early compulsion to turn aggression against
herself by jumping out of the window. With no primal internal object
connection to sustain her, it is probably safe to assume that Woolf
strongly felt like jumping out of her skin. Virginia's father had been an
external compensatory self-object or "subjective object" (Winnicott,
1971b), and losing him left Virginia with no psychological compensation for the lack of an internalised "good enough mother" (Winnicott,
1975) from her primal years.

Bond (1989) focuses on how Virginia lost the lap of her mother
permanently at two, losing a chance to return to her mother for refuelling during the practising stage of separation–individuation, as well
as during rapprochement state, when a child usually returns to her
mother with the evidence of her autonomous adventures (Mahler,
Pine, & Bergmann, 1975). Bond (1989) theorises that Virginia Woolf
returned to a maternal lap that was already occupied by her younger
brother Adrian, the future psychoanalyst, who seems to have received

preferential treatment from the mother because he was a boy. This preoccupied mother was also the cold mother Virginia Woolf remembered in the symbolism of her cold hard jewels (Rose, 1978), as well as the stern and cold figure who, as she lay dying, left Virginia with the pedantic instruction: "Hold yourself straight, my little Goat" (Woolf, 1985, p. 84). ("Goat" was a family nickname for Virginia.)

Due to the mother's emotional abandonment of her daughter, Leslie Stephen's paternal affection for Virginia cannot be overemphasised. Even though Virginia Woolf's core body self had been arrested, leaving her with a life-long underlying fragility and vulnerability that could manifest as psychosis and suicide, her father's affection allowed Virginia to develop a sense of self at the symbolic and literary level. Even so, Virginia's verbal and symbolic self would inevitably split off from the sealed and traumatised primary organic self. This split meant that her internal true self-potential could not be directly experienced in interpersonal relations, although it could be experienced in a sublimated form—as in literary creation and discourse. While Virginia Woolf's verbal and literary abilities were innate and spontaneous, they could only serve to create a secondary self, not a primary core Winnicottian "true self". To develop the primal true self (which originates when an infant is lying in its mother's arms, and is body based), Virginia would have needed the contact and support from her mother or from a maternal connection in her earliest years. However, as described, not only was her mother detached, but so were her nurses.

Sexual abuse

Virginia Woolf was sexually abused at a very vulnerable age. Following a life-threatening bout of whooping cough at the age of six, her half-brother Gerald molested her (De Salvo, 1989). Gerald set a dinner tray on a window ledge that faced a mirror. He then sat Virginia on the tray and proceeded to fondle her genitals. This experience erupts in her psyche many years later, at the time she was writing her last novel, Between the Acts (Woolf, 1941), and not long before she committed suicide at the age of fifty-nine. For the rest of her life, Virginia was cursed with a paranoid terror of mirrors (De Salvo, 1989). Because mirrors terrified her, Woolf loathed drawing rooms that had mirrors, believing that the other people in the room were gazing at her and

judging her. Her phobic shame sensibility was great, and when combined with the retriggering of her early childhood object loss, could
result in psychosis. Virginia feared, in a highly paranoid fashion, the
caustic judges of the social arena (Bell, 1972; Kavaler-Adler, 1985). Bell
(1972) writes, "She went through agonies of embarrassment, miserable humiliating evenings when she couldn't find a partner, ghastly
meaningless conversations which got bogged down and left her
blushing and wordless" (p. 77). Virginia Woolf escaped some of her
phobic terrors by becoming part of the well-known literary and intellectual Bloomsbury group during her twenties. Leonard Woolf came
along during this period of her life and, not long after, married her,
thus becoming her guardian. He became the external "subjective
object" (Winnicott, 1971b) or self-object (Kohut, 1977) who provided
compensatory positive mirroring, as her father did. Lucky as she was
(for having had her father during early childhood and Leonard as a
husband), Woolf was at the same time a victim of her dependence on
both men as compensatory self-object mirrors.

Virginia (Stephen) Woolf's story vividly illustrates how the nurturance of a father, especially at the oedipal stage and beyond, fails to
replace the mother. Her story contests Kohut's (1977) proposal (in
Restoration of the Self) that the idealisation of the father can compensate for lack of primal mirroring for the self by the mother. By disprov-
ing Kohut's tenet, Virginia Woolf's story supports the theory of Winnicott that so emphatically values the primal contribution of the
primal or chthonic mother (a Jungian term), as well as the mother's
role, in conjunction with the parenting role of the father, throughout
childhood.

Virginia Woolf: opening and closing
of potential and transitional space

The moments of hope in Virginia Woolf's life are reflected as potential
space in her creative writing and literary works. The aborted and brief
nature of this hope, which translates into the foreclosing of potential
psychic and transitional space, is seen within her literary work as well
as it is seen in her life, as portrayed by Virginia Woolf's biographers.

Virginia Woolf barely survived her childhood. The acute loss of
her mother's breastfeeding at ten weeks, the weak recovery from

whooping cough at six, the sexual molestation by her older step-brother Gerald, and her mother's cold, dying last words to her at the age of thirteen, all took their toll. Unable to mourn and assimilate the profound nature of such early loss, Virginia suffered her first psychotic episode following her mother's death. After Julia Stephen died, Virginia's older sister, Stella, took on the mothering functions, until she married, soon after which she died. These events all occurred by the time Virginia was in her early teens. When her father died, the one who had loved her as much as anyone in her family was capable of love, Virginia was just twenty-two. Virginia's father Leslie had loved her mostly as an idealised part of himself, someone who would eventually ensure his literary immortality by becoming an author. He found his daughter enjoyable and talented, and had given her affection. His death in 1904 provoked Virginia's manic and depressive psychosis, as well as her first suicide attempt. The "outer roar" of the whole world became intrusive. Hearing "birds singing . . . in Greek" and sensing her father's presence in their song, she jumped out of the window. The window was close enough to the ground, and she was not seriously injured. Her suicide attempt thus seemed more a "cry for help" than a serious attempt to end her life. But not long after her father's presence was gone (indifferent as he might have been to the care-taking of his daughters, since the profound loss of his wife left him detached and depressed), even the symbolic archetypal promise of his protection gradually disappeared from her frail young life (see Kavaler-Adler, 1996). Following Virginia's failed suicide attempt, her other half-brother, George, attempted to sexually molest her one night in the bedroom she shared with her sister Vanessa. Virginia Stephen escaped this matrix of horrors and losses by moving to Bloomsbury and entering the world of the Bloomsbury Group and the life of Leonard Woolf.

Bloomsbury and Leonard

Virginia Stephen's escape from her parents' home (and the abusive guardianship of her half-brother George) gave her independence unknown for women in her day. It allowed her to become footloose and fancy-free if she so chose. Potential psychic and transitional space appeared to open when she and her sister Vanessa moved to

Bloomsbury. The hope of having her "love affair with the world" (Greenacre, 1957, p. 57; Mahler, 1971, p. 410) after a depressed and numbed-out childhood might have begun to emerge at this time.

With an upper-class education in the social graces, some inherited financial security, and (at least in Virginia's case) a literary education, the two single women soon had frequent visits from the university men who were friends of their older brother Thoby. Many of these young men would become the leading intellectuals of the day, among them Bertrand Russell, Aldous Huxley, and Lytton Strachey. Strachey actually proposed marriage to Virginia, but the proposal lapsed within twenty-four hours. Strachey's intellectual enthusiasm for Virginia's literary brilliance and companionship were outweighed by the necessity of coming to terms with his true homosexual nature. This disappointment might have led to despair, had not Leonard Woolf entered Virginia's life shortly after Strachey's withdrawal, and proposed marriage. This proposal was made with its own form of reluctance and ambivalence, but Leonard followed through on his promise.

In Woolf's earlier novels, such as Voyage Out (1915) and Night and Day (1919), we get a glimpse of the mental terrain of both Virginia and Leonard during their courtship and early marriage. Aside from the disruption of any moment of intimacy between Ralph (Leonard's alter ego) and Katharine (Virginia's alter ego), the main characters in Night and Day (1919), we also learn how Leonard experiences his love for Virginia in a very mental, non-physical, form. Ralph imagines Katharine in her own sphere of solitude, and feels an affection that draws him towards her. Panken (1987) notes that Ralph and Katharine pass through each other's minds, rather than touching and interacting as two sensual or sexual bodies. This dynamic is exposed in Virginia Woolf's own words (from Night and Day): ". . . They seemed to pass in and out of each other's minds, questioning and answering. The utmost fullness of communion seemed to be theirs . . ." (Woolf, 1919, Chapter XXVIII). They begin to include each other in their separate interior worlds and mental landscapes. Marriage seemed like a logical consequence. But Virginia's hopes for a fully alive sexual (as well as intellectual) marriage go unrealised. There is a brief period of hope, just prior to the honeymoon, when Virginia opens a psychic space in her mind, with the hope of a fully intimate and sexual marriage. She envisions a union that would produce real children, as well as "children of the mind" through literary accomplishments. Virginia writes to

Leonard that her "flanks and rump are now in finest plumage" (Panken, 1987, p. 65). She feels rich with this plumage. Her hope is soon dashed, however, for (like so many others who suffer early disruptive trauma that repeats over and over again through psychic repetition compulsion) she has chosen a partner with similar or complementary developmental problems. The hope, which temporarily expands Virginia's psychic space, falls victim to the reality of the honeymoon. Leonard Woolf is inexperienced sexually, and Virginia fails to have an orgasm, a failure that the Bloomsbury band blames on Virginia.

Virginia's sister Vanessa had experienced sexual climax in an early marriage to Clive Bell and in her liaison with Duncan Grant (despite his homosexual preferences), a painter like herself. Keep in mind, too, that Vanessa, unlike Virginia, was not molested in her childhood. In addition, Vanessa's lovers might have been more equipped for love-making than the schizoid intellectual, Leonard Woolf. Just as in the nursery of her childhood, all the disparagement and aggression was turned against Virginia. Seeking the mothering she had lacked, Virginia often turned to Vanessa, even though Vanessa never responded to Virginia with anything but contempt and indifference, if not outright hostility. Rather than offer the comfort and solace Virginia wanted, Vanessa (through her gossipy criticism among the Bloomsbury literati) turned on Virginia, just as she had with her verbal taunts in the childhood nursery. Given the family history, it would not be difficult to imagine Vanessa leading the chorus of critics who ridiculed Virginia for her lack of sexual fulfilment.

As usual, Virginia reacted by withdrawing socially and turning against herself in her own mind. As her marriage takes its course, she creates Septimus, a suicidal male character in the novel *Mrs Dalloway* (Woolf, 1925). Septimus kills himself over a wife who, perhaps, like Leonard with Virginia, did not want to see her role in her spouse's breakdowns, and because of his conflict over his homosexual obsession (Panken, 1987). In her novels, Virginia Woolf's unconscious mind could speak freely, in contrast to her conscious idealisation of Leonard, while simultaneously shielding him from her wrath. However, at a more conscious level, in her diaries, Virginia Woolf speaks of the contraction of her hopes, perhaps as a way of not feeling conscious rage towards Vanessa and Leonard. These diary entries found their way into *Mrs Dalloway*, where she gives a vivid depiction of the loss of transitional and potential space between her and Leonard. Clarissa, Virginia's alter ego character in *Mrs Dalloway*, describes how her marital bed has become a place of cold isolation. Through the fictional character Clarissa, who says that she had become like a "nun withdrawing . . .", we can glimpse Virginia Woolf's true feelings: "The sheets were clean, tight stretched in a broad white band from side to side. Narrower and narrower would her bed be . . ." (1925, p. 45). Leonard has failed to be a competent lover, let alone a passionate one. When the doctors advise him that Virginia cannot handle the excitement of either lovemaking or motherhood, he actively withdraws from her. Instead of encouraging an active engagement in life, which might have helped Virginia feel more whole, Leonard deferred to the doctors who preached isolation and removal from the excitement of life as a deterrent to renewed episodes of mental illness. This advice frequently extended beyond the bedroom and into the sphere of Virginia's literary solitude. At times, pen and paper were denied her, as a precaution against self-harm, and she had to fight to write. Although writing could not cure her, preventing her from doing so would surely make her more paranoid and terrified in her isolation (Panken, 1987).

In Virginia Woolf's (1931) novel *The Waves*, we encounter many isolated figures. Each fears that the entrance of another into his or her psychic and physical sphere will result in a compulsion to merge with the other, and that the consequence will be the obliteration of a sense of individual identity. In *The Waves*, Virginia Woolf writes,

> How curiously one is changed by the addition, even at a distance, of a friend. How useful an office one's friends perform when they recall us. Yet how painful to be recalled, to be mitigated to have one's self adulterated, mixed up, become part of another. As he approaches I become not myself, but Neville mixed with somebody – with whom? – with Bernard? Yes, it is Bernard, and it is to Bernard that I shall put the question, Who am I? (p. 59)

From such characterisation, we can see that Virginia's loss of connection with her primal mother affected her from the earliest time, perhaps even before the early toddler differentiation stage in Mahler's era of separation–individuation, resulting in manic depressive psychosis, not just borderline, narcissistic, or schizoid character disorder. In conjunction with this defensive individual isolation, and to preserve a fragile sense of identity, were merger fantasies related to a pure terror. In opposition to togetherness of humans (who can connect through the developmental achievement of a true self), in *The Waves* birds compulsively flock together in a state of communal terror. Whereas Virginia Woolf's humans evade one another, observe each other with fear and hostility, or isolate themselves in a state of deadness or depersonalisation (e.g., the alter ego character, Rhoda), her birds flock together in a massive terror-induced hysteria. This flocking together did not bring peace or harmony or a containing sense of communal presence—quite the opposite, in fact. Woolf's birds flock together out of a need to escape terror, much like the terror of humans in her later novel, *Between the Acts* (Woolf, 1941). The fragile fabric of life seems to disintegrate, as the stage, play, and programme of the actors fall apart in *Between the Acts*. In Woolf's novels, humans do not comfort each other and neither do the birds comfort one another. This is not surprising, when we consider that as an infant and child the author had no mothering presence to calm her, and certainly nobody to sustain her. A single memory of lying pleasurably on her mother's lap as an infant might have been all that Virginia Woolf had.

In the image of the birds flocking together, we see how Virginia's sense of potential and transitional space was foreshortened. The birds' flight-from-terror merger captures the raw instinctual terror of the human who has not, in Winnicott's sense, internalised a benign and tranquil presence from the mother in the first three years of life (i.e., during infancy and the transitional stage of separation–individuation). There was no space between the terrified birds, and no space to feel, think, or reflect on feeling or thinking. Without such potential space, which reflects the lack of both internal psychic space and quasi-interpersonal transitional space, there is no internal world of live subjective beings that can create meaning through the evolution of interpersonal conversation and interaction. The internal world is foreclosed by bad objects, malevolent attacking objects, such as the lady with the knife who is imagined to be killing Rachel in *Voyage Out*.

Despite all this, Virginia did gain some potential and psychic space from the marriage that made her "Mrs Woolf". Commenting on their manner of daily life, Woolf said that Leonard and she were "too close and not close enough" (Panken, 1987, p. 246). Leonard intruded on Virginia's body space by keeping records of her menstrual cycles as a means of watching the orbit of her mind. He would then report his findings to the doctors he consulted about her mental health. In so doing, Leonard became the self-object (Kohut, 1977), or "subjective object" (Winnicott, 1971b), who would nurture the entrance of her literary works to the outer world.

Together, Leonard and Virginia established Hogarth Press, a company that published all of Virginia's books. Leonard intimately involved himself with the children of Virginia's mind (if not of her body) by reading and editing her literary work. When he was not depriving her of pen and paper in compliance with doctors' orders for her to rest, Leonard was actively encouraging her work. When he was not hyper-vigilantly protecting her from herself, he was applauding her creative self-expression. He was allowing her to have a literary voice that compensated for her lack of an interpersonal or social voice.

In interpersonal situations, Virginia defended the shame-ridden child within herself by making sarcastic quips and cynical comments that often pushed others away, including Leonard. She especially pushed away the literary rivals, such as Katherine Mansfield, who died quite young, leaving Virginia Woolf to produce so much more. According to one biographer of Katherine Mansfield, Mansfield had experimented with literary forms that influenced Virginia (Kavaler-Adler, 1991b). It was in the sustained, even if overly protective and controlling presence of Leonard, that Virginia Woolf blossomed as a literary author, just as she had blossomed in the presence of her literary father when she had learned to read, write, and analyse literature with him. When Leonard was with her, serving as an external self-object, Virginia Woolf had hope, which allowed her a sense of "vision" in her work. Leonard's external supporting presence substituted for an actual symbolisation of a good enough mother. In her novel *The Waves*, Virginia Woolf (1931) has several part-object characters, each seeming to reflect different aspects of her life. Creating alter ego characters provided her with a meaningful experience of self, even if it was not one integrated or cohesive self on the internal primary psychic level, which she could use in interpersonal relations.

In *The Waves*, the character Bernard seems to express the artist in Woolf that (up until the writing of this novel) has survived psychic disruption and primitive splitting. Bernard learns that he can deal with his frequent disappointments as an artist, desperate to find meaning in life by accepting the inevitable fact that his visions need to be created repeatedly. He realises that each time one vision is destroyed, it needs to be rebuilt, and in accepting this existential fact, he (Virginia) finds hope.

In the same novel, *The Waves*, Virginia Woolf confronts the encroaching despair she suffered after the death of her brother Thoby, with whom she spent her childhood in the nursery. Through her characters, Virginia expresses her vision that rectangles and triangles speak of some underlying pattern in our nature, a pattern that the artist realises by focusing inward on unconscious phenomena. To see geometric patterns in nature seems to provide Virginia Woolf with a sense of something that joins us all together beyond individual human experience, beyond our failing differentiation. [Her infancy impaired her basic sense of differentiation, as seen in Bernard.] In joining us together on a psychic level, this pattern allows us to see beyond our own individual mortality into the wider functioning of the universe that extends forever further than any individual death or loss. However, such a sense of vision could easily fail for Bernard (Virginia). The connection with this deeper reality was dependent on the continuing support of an external self-object (or subjective object) in her life, such as Leonard. Consequently, Bernard has to face his disillusionment, as his vision fails. He is able, though, to rediscover his vision in another form, so that he ultimately has the hope that his vision can be recreated, and, thus, his creative work, with the meaning it provides through the artistic vision, can be renewed, even if it may be temporarily vanquished by psychological blocks and by (unsymbolised) bad-object intrusions. As Virginia Woolf expresses this through Bernard, she provides evidence of the opening of the psychic space for creative artistic vision, a vision that can only come in parallel with the opening of transitional space between oneself and other human beings in the interpersonal world. Although Bernard (Virginia) fears losing his fragile sense of differentiated identity when he greets a friend coming down the street (because he unconsciously wishes to merge with him), he manages to salvage his sense of identity by articulating an artistic vision. (Perhaps this merger wish is a wish to re-create the early maternal symbiosis that was so tragically interrupted.) Artistic vision allows Bernard to bring uniquely defined meaning into the world through his artistry, which, for his creator, Virginia Woolf, was her literary craft.

In contrast to Bernard, the character Rhoda is so insecurely located in her body that she slams her feet against the bedpost at night in order to reassure herself that she exists. Unlike Bernard, Rhoda represents the dissociated and suicidal part of Virginia Woolf, which cannot sustain a mind–body connection without an external self-object (Winnicott's "subjective object") to make up for the lack of an internal mothering presence from infancy. Rhoda, unlike Bernard, succumbs to despair and commits suicide, just as, ultimately, Virginia Woolf will do when her psychic and transitional space closes later in her life. Ultimately, Virginia Woolf's artistic sense of recreating vision and the world's response to that vision is vanquished. The terror of the birds flocking and flying together seems to express the internal state of Rhoda/Virginia, who is swept up in terror due to a dislocation from her core body self and a consequent dislocation from any interpersonal context and structure in her life. There is no differentiated identity or interpersonal connection in the birds, only a symbolic joining together in terror and manic, despair-driven motion. The title of the book, *The Waves* (Woolf, 1931) seems to speak of life in terms of a metaphor for existential helplessness in the face of the overpowering waves of life that inundate one with anguish and paralysing terror and shame. Perhaps these are the waves of fortune that are never tamed by the feeble wishes and will of any one individual.

The character Lily in *To the Lighthouse* (Woolf, 1927) is obviously another alter ego self-portrait of Virginia. Lily is described as a painter who can only paint when she risks the emotional terror of jumping off a psychological cliff. The hope and faith that allow her to leap off a psychological precipice is only possible if she can imagine that her mother is standing behind her. She risks articulating herself through painting, with fragile hope that the world would respond to her work and recognise her through this.

Virginia Woolf lost her mother at the age of thirteen. To gain faith in her own ability to initiate the expression of a true self from within, Virginia would try to conjure up her dead mother's psychological presence. What else could she do but imagine a mothering presence? Yet, her mother's presence had been so fleeting. Perhaps that one memory of lying in her mother's lap at the house by the sea gave her enough to temporarily conjure up an image of a mothering presence, even when her mother's presence was never trusted to remain with her for long. It was heroic for Lily/Virginia Woolf to take such a risk with just the fragile fragment of a mother she could evoke from within. Her heroism punctuated her creative process, helping her live in the moments within it. As an artist she had no choice but to be alone in the creative moment, which meant surrendering any dependence on her external self-object, subjective object, Leonard.

The subject of transitional space seems to be addressed directly by Woolf (1929) in *A Room of One's Own*. Known as a feminist text, this extended essay is a proclamation of freedom for the artist, and particularly for the female artist. Although the twentieth century had begun by the time Virginia Woolf was an adult, she none the less lived in a post-Victorian world where women were prohibited by law from having anything of their own. No matter how rich their family of origin or the family of their marriages, women were economically subject to male domination and to an overarching patriarchal system. (The women who formed political protests for female suffrage were intensely persecuted in both England and America, and their later victory was long in coming.) No matter how grand the home of a married woman, and no matter how many servants were at her disposal, she was subject to the domination or indulgence of her man.

Virginia's marriage with Leonard Woolf was unique in many ways. The fact that she came from an upper middle-class family of some literary reputation must have had a great deal to do with her ability to have a room of her own where she could pursue her literary craft in solitude. Virginia Woolf spoke at a local women's college, in a day when most of the world consisted of male-only universities, such as Cambridge and Oxford. In such a rarefied atmosphere, Virginia Woolf lectured on what was required for a woman to be able to pursue a literary career. A room of one's own was necessary, combined with so many pounds sterling a year. Virginia's college audience must have been waiting to be inspired by a married woman actively publishing fiction with the full support of her husband.

I propose that Virginia Woolf's declaration that a room of one's own was required spoke to the most profound psychological need that Winnicott had proposed and championed for psychic and transitional space. Virginia Woolf's revolutionary lecture was psychological as well as political. She declared that external space allowed for the mind's psychological space to engender its own true self-expression through an evolving creative process. How ironic, then, that Virginia Woolf would be defeated by her own psychological demons, despite her unique—and courageous—arrangement to have her own writing room during the post-Victorian world.

How much did her courage to speak out for women's rights interact with her newfound lesbian love affair with Vita Sackville-West? For the first time, with Vita (who had an even more unusual marital arrangement with her husband), Virginia became a sexual being. She discovered that she had both feminine and masculine sexual desires. And, again for the first time, Virginia Woolf actually had sex. She came alive in her body, and if only for a very finite period of time, she understood what sexuality felt like. She had become temporarily liberated by her connection with a woman. The homosexual nature of the sex allowed her to find her object of desire to reflect the female body that she had been forced to live in, with all its traumatic molestations and intrusions. Unlike Leonard, who loved her mind but shunned her body, Vita Sackville-West loved Virginia's body and allowed Virginia to adore her (Vita's) body as well. Virginia wrote to Vita, "I like your energy, I love your legs, I long to see you" (as quoted by Panken, 1987, p. 169). Adoring Vita and relishing a physical aliveness through vicarious as well as interactive pleasure, Virginia's mind became alive with a pregnant feeling that had been aborted with Leonard when they first married.

Virginia began to experience her literary creations as babies in her womb, as if a ripe pear was about to drop from the branch of a tree with all its grand fecundity. She wrote that her next literary work was "impending in me, grown heavy in my mind like a ripe pear; pendant, gravid, asking to be cut or it will fall" (Woolf, 1953, p. 136). Like the birth of an individual body, Virginia's creative process gives birth, "giving the moment whole" (Panken, 1987, p. 187). Here Woolf describes her true self's spontaneity, that is, the spontaneity of being in the moment within her creative process. This occurs during the time that Virginia Woolf allows herself to experience her sexuality with Vita Sackville-West. For a period of time, Vita becomes the intimate other to whom Virginia can open her mind and body. Following this awareness of the birth of the creative moment, Virginia Woolf writes, "so I have something instead of children" (as quoted by Panken, 1987, p. 187). She compares her work to Vanessa's pregnancies, and to Vanessa's nurturing of her children (Panken, 1987). This view of creativity provided a feminine mode of experience that she had hitherto lacked in her life (Kavaler-Adler, 1996). From the brief moment of sexual connection with Vita, the transitional space opens between them; this in turn opens the psychic (or "potential") space within Woolf's mind. She experiences a mental sexual orgasm through her creative process. On the phallic side of her sexuality, she experiences "spurts of thoughts coming as I walk, as I sit; things churning up in my mind and so making a perpetual pageant, which is to be my happiness" (Woolf, 1953, p. 66). Then, after the arousal and erection, there is the metaphorical moment of orgasm. In *To The Lighthouse*, Virginia writes, "then her thought, which had spun quicker and quicker, exploded of its own intensity; she felt 'released'" (Woolf, 1927, p. 24).

Of course, the fact that Virginia experienced pregnancy as external, like the genitals of a man that were more related to the branches of a tree than to a female womb, says something about the confusion and diversity within Virginia's internal world of sexual fantasies. In her novel *Orlando* (1928), Virginia Woolf depicted a psychic journey that had her alter ego heroine transforming into male figures and back to female—demonstrating the gender fluidity of her own sexuality. The body became less important than the psychological experience of creation. She wrote that she "no longer wants children since 'ideas possess' her" (Panken, 1987, p. 172). Virginia was brought to life during the brief honeymoon period of a love affair that would quickly become tempestuous and ultimately disappointing. It was not long before she was crying out to Vita through the pain of rejection that "There is something that doesn't vibrate in you!" (Panken, 1987, p. 139). From such a statement, one can imagine that Virginia was once more experiencing the wall of distraction and indifference in Vita that she had once experienced in her mother. Instead of the rich exchange of energy that had brought her such joy in the beginning of her love affair with Vita, she now felt the deadness of someone psychologically walled off from her. In saying that something in Vita did not vibrate, she was saying that there was no response to her from this female other. What a repetition this must have been of her early infant experience, particularly from the time of the suspension of her mother's breastfeeding, and then probably through the times of differentiation and separation–individuation that were so arrested by her mother's lack of attunement to her developmental needs.

The ultimate foreclosing of both potential transitional and psychic space in the life and work of Virginia Woolf

The Years (Woolf, 1937) was supposed to have been a disappointing novel for Virginia Woolf. According to Quentin Bell (1972), Leonard

Woolf felt compelled to support the book in order to preserve Virginia's sanity, because he anticipated a suicidal reaction if she thought the book was a failure. Even though Leonard also saw the work as a failure, Bell (1972) reports that he felt it was not as much a failure as Virginia thought. When Leonard finished reading the book he was able to deliver enthusiastic verbal applause, exclaiming, "It's extraordinarily good!" It is interesting to compare Virginia at the time of writing *The Years*, a book she openly believed was a failure, with Virginia who wrote her last work, *Between the Acts*. The comparison is particularly poignant because *Between the Acts* precedes her ultimate suicide attempt, the last and final attempt that results in her death (see Kavaler-Adler, 1996, 2007). There is still a sexual vitality and self-cohesion in *The Years*, which is missing in Virginia's last novel, *Between the Acts*. The symbolic evidence for this can be seen in the transition from housing her self-identity in the image of a racehorse in *The Years* to housing her self-image in the fragmented and regressive image of maggots in *Between the Acts*. A racehorse suggests a vital sexual energy, perhaps more masculine than feminine in nature, but cohesive in its overall capacity to express energy and individual personality together. Maggots suggest deterioration into a fragmented image of self, where the individual personality is lost, and where the pure survival hunger replaces any sense of individual pride or accomplishment. Maggots feed on human decay, whereas racehorses are cared for by humans. The image of maggots, therefore, suggests the absence of any relationship that could be compared to a human relationship, as well as implying the absence of self-pride and individual identity.

Looking at the life events that seem to have been responsible for Virginia Woolf's psychological regression and deterioration from the time she wrote *The Years* to the time when she wrote *Between the Acts* is revealing. By the time of the latter book, Virginia's relationship with Vita had disintegrated, along with her short-lived joy of living comfortably and energetically in her own body. Virginia's body reverted to being a warehouse of dissociated traumatic pain, pain that could not be contained through psychological processing. She then descended to mania and paranoid psychosis because of her lack of psycho-physical articulation and neutralisation of the rage associated with pain she experienced.

In *Between the Acts* (Woolf, 1941), Virginia has several alter ego characters. One of them is the artist self, the author who has prepared a script for a minor play to be performed by amateur actors in a literary pageant for the populace. She sees her piece of art reduced to ruin and audience ridicule. Because the actors and audience both fail her, and because of the recent fight she has had with her homosexual lover, she becomes distraught. Here we see Woolf in relation to her deteriorating love affair with Vita. Without the external support of her female lover who, like Leonard, had become a subjective object or self-object for her, this character obviously mirrors Virginia herself as she sinks into a severe state of self-doubt. The playwright becomes overwhelmed with restlessness and confused agitation; she is filled with anxiety and with the loss of any sense of self-coherence and self-boundaries. As the play she has written falls apart (this is the "fragmenting self" reaction frequently described in relation to the narcissistic character) and the actors jump ship before the play is done, the woman is left with no boundary between her and her audience. In writing this book, Virginia Woolf feels she has been ridiculed, just as she was in the nursery of her childhood where she dissolved into purple rages. In *Between the Acts*, Virginia's alter ego playwright is not applauded. The audience applauds the actors and others, but *never* the author. Turning the rage against herself, as she did as a child, the female homosexual character helplessly erupts with bitter and disillusioned comments about her theatrical world, which she sees as a reflection of the disintegrating world at large. Indeed, the world around the author of the play *in* the book, as well as around the author *of* the book (Virginia Woolf), was exploding and disintegrating as the Second World War began to erupt around her.

Hogarth Press, the publishing house that Leonard Woolf created for her, had to suspend its operations during the Second Word War. As a result, Virginia Woolf lost her relationship with her audience. She writes then that she lost her writer's "I". She speaks of losing the "echo" of herself that was provided by her readers, her self-object audience as an external mirror to make up for the lack of early internalised maternal mirroring. Along with losing the "echo", Virginia loses her sense of identity as a subjective "I" that she had formerly found through writing. She lost the compensatory mirroring of the writing process that her father had provided when he responded with applause and support for her literary efforts.

Losing her subjectivity, Virginia Woolf feels invaded by an outside world that has ceased to support her. Her fragile connection to her internal self leaves her with little to defend against the outer world's invasion. Her boundaries disintegrate, along with her individual identity as a subjective self. This loss of subjectivity exposes Virginia's alter ego character in *Between the Acts* to experiencing the external world as a rapacious assailant rather than a penetrating phallic experience that stimulates her. In her diary, she writes of an "outer roar" invading her. As when her father died and Virginia Woolf heard birds speaking to her in Greek, all becomes an outward assault, mimicking the early sexual assaults of her childhood and early adulthood. But probably all this went further back to the loss Woolf experienced when her mother ceased breastfeeding her daughter at ten weeks, as well as the subsequent experience of the cold bottle propped up in her crib by a nurse. In Winnicott's terms, with no "primary maternal preoccupation" and no maternal holding environment, the world impinges upon Woolf's sense of self. Unlike the compensatory transitional object of one of my former patients who, as an infant in her crib, clung to a bottle of hot tea contained in a sock to protect her from too much heat, Virginia Woolf did not have even this kind of simulated maternal warmth.

At the end of her life, Virginia felt that nothing but "just" little books would remain after her passing. We can feel here an encroaching despair. In losing her writer's "I", Virginia had lost any sense of the subjectivity of herself within her books. She lost the sustainable sense of meaning that had been provided by the subjective experience she found before in the writing. Everything is foreshortened in her mind, as the transitional object of her literary audience is lost, and the transitional and psychic space necessary for the formation of a subjective or "true self" is abbreviated. Consequently, self-reflection fails. Instead of feeling a psychological link with the essence and meaning of the words in her books, Virginia views them from the outside as just dead static objects. This is related to viewing herself as an object as she loses the psychological links to her external self-objects. It is also related to her being outside of her body again as she fails to find containment for bodily sexual desires, and their pre-oedipal erotic origins, in the transitional space of a love relationship with Vita. She loses Vita, and her sister Vanessa continually fails to be there for her as the maternal, related, and caring figure that Virginia wishes her to be. Abandoned as an adult just as she was as an infant, Virginia turns her rage inward, just as she did as a child when she physically turned to attack herself in the nursery to protect Vanessa and her brother

Thoby from her rage. Virginia continues to idealise Vanessa and Leonard, even though both fail her at the same time that her relationship with Vita Sackville-West disintegrates.

It is all there in her last book, *Between the Acts*. Aside from the homosexual playwright, there is the character of Isa, who represents Virginia Woolf's heterosexual self and her heterosexual dilemmas. Isa's depressed and suicidal despair is reflected in her obsessions. One set of obsessions is about a newspaper story on rape (see Kavaler-Adler, 1996). Isa cannot get her mind off it. It is easy to see how Isa's preoccupation reflects an alter ego aspect of Virginia Woolf, who was never able to express the traumatic experiences of being molested when she was six by her half-brother Gerald, or the later molestations by her half-brother George when she was in her late teens or early twenties. As Isa peers into a pool of water, she sees the soiled and perverted sexual imagery of her own mind and the duckweed that cannot be drained away. "Duckweed" is a symbolic reference to Woolf's half-brothers, whose last name was not Stephen (as was Virginia's maiden surname), but Duckworth. So, Duckworth is converted to "duckweed" through Woolf's alter ego character Isa as she stares at the sullied water. The eruption of Woolf's dissociated and partially repressed trauma from the inner containment of her memories of sexual abuse colours the waters that Isa gazes into with the blackness of a suicidal despair. The primary process overwhelms the secondary process of the author. Her writer's "I" that could formerly symbolise metaphors to contain the overflow of her internal psychic trauma is drowned as she imagines herself to be in the polluted pond in *Between the Acts*. After she completed this book, Virginia Woolf acted out the suicidal fantasies of her alter ego character (Isa) by drowning herself.

As we get to know Isa in *Between the Acts*, there are frequent references to suicide. Unlike the suicides of the more minor characters Septimus in *Mrs Dalloway* (Woolf, 1925) and Rhoda in *The Waves* (Woolf, 1931), the character of Isa faces us directly with her foreboding thoughts of suicide. Isa lacks the positive counterpart of Bernard that Rhoda has in *The Waves*. Isa murmurs, ". . . what wish should I drop into the well? That the waters should cover me" (quoted by Panken, 1987, p. 247). The biographical derivations of this fictional development can be found in considering the fact that Isa's despair is in response to her alienation from her husband as well as the echoing memories of past betrayals by men in her childhood.

Isa's perseverating suspicions of her husband's infidelity leads her to thoughts of stabbing herself with a knife. She turns her rage and aggression upon herself, as does her creator, Virginia Woolf. Describing Isa, Woolf writes, "Picking up a knife from a plank, she recites: 'from her bosom's snowy antre drew the gleaming blade. Plunge blade! She said. And struck. Faithless, she cried, knife, too! It broke. So too my heart!'" (as quoted in Panken, 1987, p. 248).

Isa, like Woolf, seemingly wishes to murder her conscious awareness of her husband's deeds rather than experience the natural psychic impulse to murder her offending husband. Virginia Woolf is seen so clearly here; she is now in her fifties, suffering from the knowledge of her husband's affairs and the failure of Leonard Woolf's love for her. Leonard moves from sexual dalliances with women (that he euphemistically calls "lunches") to an actual love affair, falling in love with a woman other than Virginia. In *Between the Acts*, Isa has the thought that the only way to save her marriage is to fight "like a vixen" with her husband (Kavaler-Adler, 1996). However, because Isa is masochistically constructed, she does not fight back. She turns her rage and aggression on herself. Rather than engaging in marital disharmony, Isa chooses to imagine a flight into suicide by stabbing herself with a knife.

The parallels with Isa's creator are inescapable. Virginia Woolf, similarly masochistically constructed, protected everyone from her rage throughout her life, beginning with her nursery experiences, with Vanessa and Vita as a child, and with Leonard in adult life. At a loss as to how to communicate when she is compelled to continue her relationships with those who have served as idealised objects in her mind, such as Vanessa and Leonard, Virginia chooses flight.

During the war years, Virginia Woolf loses her publisher, her audience, and her husband, as Leonard not only surrenders the publishing press, but also psychologically abandons her for another woman. In doing so, he has ceased to play the part of the husband nurturing the literary book babies of his wife (Panken, 1987).

According to Virginia Woolf's psycho-biographer Shirley Panken (1987), Leonard Woolf had been blocked and frozen in his own writing efforts during the time he supported his wife in developing literary artistry so that she might reach an audience that could provide the "echo" and response she had never received in infancy. Once he freed himself from subordination to his wife's ambitions (and his role as

Virginia's external self-object or subjective object) through a love affair, Leonard became more introspective and began to write himself. This left Virginia feeling bereft. Through the character Isa, we see that Virginia and Leonard were not going to fight "like a vixen". Virginia must have had no choice but to turn her unneutralised childhood rage against herself, as she had done in the past. This renewed "purple rage" seems to be an expression of what Masterson (1979, 1981) has called an "abandonment depression", that is, a pre-oedipal separation–individuation stage trauma, the rage of a dissociated childhood self that had suffered the intrusion of sexual molestation and had never mourned the consequent loss of self, and the rage and shame of being abandoned by a husband who had served as a narcissistic self-extension.

Virginia Woolf herself reported that her husband had been over-protective of her throughout their marriage (Nicolson & Trautmann, 1975). Leonard Woolf kept careful watch on his wife's mental and physical vicissitudes, the better to ward off the paralysing depressions that could lead to manic psychosis and suicidal despair. He purposely lied to her about the worth of *The Years* to protect her, declaring it a great success even though he thought it a failure, "but not as much of a failure as Virginia thought" (Bell, 1972). Before the advent of Leonard's love affair, he was fully engaged in supporting Virginia's literary efforts as well as her mental health. But how could such a husband then later not notice when his wife came home drenched with the water of the lake clinging to her clothes? How could Leonard have believed Virginia's lame excuse that she had been caught in the rain?

That was the day Virginia Woolf attempted suicide again, this time by drowning. Despite her efforts to stay down, she could not keep from floating to the surface. She vowed then that the next time she tried, she would succeed. On her final, successful suicide attempt, Virginia Woolf made sure she would stay submerged by wearing a jacket with two pockets, each filled with weighty stones. Before she left home, she left a note for Leonard to discover. "If anyone could have saved me it would have been you" (Woolf, 1979, p. 481) she wrote, protecting him to the end, and especially in this final instance, from any guilt he might feel over her death, despite his recent indifference to signals of her despair and suicidal thinking, which would not have escaped him in the past.

In her suicide note, Virginia Woolf also wrote of her need to end her life because the haunting voices were coming back (Nicolson &

Trautmann, 1975). What could these haunting voices be if not the internal split-off parts of her that could not be openly vocalised? Voices of anger that she had never dared to express in speech, despite her hostile and sarcastic verbal quips. Voices that led her to sacrifice her own life rather than endure them, even though her alter ego Isa (in *Between the Acts*) had dared to think that she could be saved if she and her husband fought "like a vixen".

Psychic bulimia: the case of Linda

In the first case of psychic bulimia, the female analysand had once been physically bulimic prior to her physical separation from her mother and family. She had to leave her country of origin in order to separate. Once in this country, the analysand, whom I will call Linda, was no longer physically bulimic. Yet, she still evidenced other behavioural symptoms (such as compulsive shopping) of her psychological failure to separate from her family and from the primal mother that her whole family unconsciously represented to her. When Linda entered psychoanalysis (two and three times a week in the first two years, and then five times a week in the following three years), she evidenced feelings of nausea and impulses to vomit in sessions. Such visceral dramas played out a psychic form of bulimia that was expressing her conflict over wishing to swallow and incorporate the transference object, whom she consciously experienced as an idealised symbiotic mother, and her simultaneous impulse to swallow and regurgitate the transference object, who was experienced unconsciously as the traumatising mother who resisted her developmental moves towards separation. The bad object aspect of the transference mother was experienced in many displaced forms with other people in Linda's life, while Linda defended the analyst from this projection, except at times of significant disappointment with the analyst.

Linda would feel like vomiting when she spoke of the demands and needs of others, and in the beginning of treatment she would refer to these "needy" others (in part her own neediness projected) as "vampires". These vampires would rearticulate for Linda her own mother's needs and demands, now operating upon her in her internal world from the time of her childhood. Linda's mother had provoked and induced states of guilt whenever Linda attempted to separate, whether to see a neighbour or to play with another child. The mother would also become punitive if she could not keep her daughter in a state of regressive symbiosis. When Linda succumbed to her mother's control and to her emotional blackmail, she would have to live with a feeling of deadness and numbness in her body. Becoming bulimic was an attempt to come alive from this numbed-out state. In swallowing the idealised mother in the form of food, and then spitting her up as she turned into the "bad" possessive other within her digestive tract, Linda would never be alone without her mother; her body would be overwhelmed by powerful forces rather than just remaining dead. With the loss of her physical bulimia, the numbness returned until Linda entered treatment and opened the door to experiencing the powerful and intense affect states of the abandonment depression related to acts of separation and wishes for separation. As Linda began to come out of her state of numbness in treatment, she did so through her capacity for deep grief crying; she could gradually individuate and separate from her internal possessive mother. In addition to this grief crying, Linda felt a powerful rage emerging from within her, a rage that had always been projected out in the past. The rage was a response to the internal mother's possession of her, and to the mother's guilt-provoking tactics.

However, before Linda could directly feel and express this rage, she experienced it in a somatic form in the body impulse to vomit. All the while she was idealising the analyst and attempting to merge into her through introjections and identification, Linda was seeking to find her own capacities through the analyst, as Linda herself would later interpret it. Linda's idealisation of the analyst could take the form of twinship transference: "I see what you see. I want to feel what you feel." It could also take the form of a merger fantasy: "when I read something you've written I feel like you're writing in my mind." Linda used the idealised transference mother as a container for her violent somatic and emotional reactions to the internal demon mother. She wanted to slap and be slapped by this internal demon mother. She wished to swallow her and escape from her at once, perpetually feeling an impulse to vomit her up as she appeared in displaced forms in many figures in her life. Sometimes, Linda would come into more direct contact with her ambivalent feelings for the analyst, and she would experience the impulse to slap her or to vomit up the rageful anger she felt towards the analyst. Her impulses to slap and vomit had an erotic aspect, which could eventually be interpreted. When the father transference emerged, it appeared to overlap with the split mother transference, forming a vivid view of a demon-lover figure. Linda expressed her responses to the masculinised and eroticised demon-lover mother, now dressed in the personality of her internal father and father transference as follows: "He aroused me and seduced me and then rejected me with an attack that felt like a powerful killing slap and a killing rage!" Linda's capacity to tolerate this ambivalence directly within the transference increased with repeated cycles of deep grief sobbing. Linda's form of total body sobbing helped her to contact her deep infant self as well as her toddler self, which lived with a perpetual psychic need to separate and individuate.

Complicating Linda's body–mind experience of merger and separation was the body repetition compulsion of an infant illness. When Linda was about eighteen months old, her mother took her to the hospital with high fever and vomiting. The doctors told her mother that Linda was too ill to be helped. They asked her mother to take her home so that she could die there. Linda's mother was distraught and in deep despair when she left the hospital with her baby daughter. On the train home, she held the infant on her lap, while the baby vomited on her all the way home. As the mother held the baby continually, the infant Linda began to cry until she cried herself to sleep. From there on, Linda got better.

Linda would repeatedly relive the symptoms of her infant illness in treatment, having psychically fused the experience of the illness with her reactions to separation anxiety and with reactions to the rage about her internal mother's resistance to her separation. She would not only relive the ongoing impulse to continually vomit, but she would also revisit the emotional sense of feeling that she was literally dying. Separation experiences in the analysis, such as the analyst's vacations and even weekend separations would bring up this set of psychophysical reactions. Later in treatment (during the sixth year), Linda would relive the sense of dying as a defensive punishment for her very real moves towards increasing separation in relationship to her transference objects, as seen played out with the analyst.

The entire enactment of physical impulses to vomit, along with the psycho-physical sense of nausea, becomes a demon-lover complex in this analysand. Linda's demon-lover complex can be seen not only in the light of her responses to a split primal mother image, but also as elaborated in treatment by overlapping father transference. This father transference first appeared as an eroticisation of the aggressive mother, who had responded to Linda's moves towards separation with physical slaps and raging screams. Linda's impulses to slap and vomit had an erotic aspect that could eventually be interpreted. As Linda's capacity to grieve and mourn through the separation process in treatment advanced, with the containing of her primitive aggressive affects in the holding environment, she increasingly experienced conscious and differentiated feelings and images related to her sexuality. Then the father transference could emerge, presenting a distinct view of the father as a demon lover. Linda's words articulate this: "He aroused me and seduced me and then attacked me with a powerful verbal slap and killing rage." Verbalising this demon-lover father transference allowed Linda to separate from a sadomasochistic attachment to her father, an attachment which had the pathological consequences of propelling her sexual desire into sadomasochistic enactments with her boyfriends and with the husband she had married during treatment.

In addition to the pre-oedipal mother transference and the oedipal and adolescent father transferences, Linda experienced an intense homoerotic transference in treatment. She dreamed of clashing and interpenetrating vaginas that she associated with herself and the analyst. Consciously, she became intensely curious about women's bodies. She had conscious wishes to be intensely close to her female analyst, wishing to extend an emotional intimacy into a physical and sexual intimacy. Linda exclaimed to me at this time, "Wouldn't it be wonderful if we were both gay women so that we could be as close as any two people can get, inside each other's bodies as well as inside each other's minds." Later, Linda's sexuality became more of a response to men in her life, and she began to enjoy sex with her husband, forgoing the raging fights she had before each sexual encounter in the past. Linda's powerful oedipal erotic desires emerged increasingly. Her sadomasochistic enactments around sexuality lessened and disappeared, except in symbolised fantasy. Her impulses to vomit became refined psychic signals through momentary nausea, such signals alerting Linda to her anger or to the anger of others. As Linda became increasingly separate and differentiated in her new identity, she began to experience men as positive male figures and men in authority as positive male father figures. Women became less aggressive and more vulnerable in her new perceptions. They no longer appeared to her like psychic vampires, as they had when she had first begun her treatment six years earlier.

Psychic vampirism in an oral level demon-lover transference

Ms Z was a female psychoanalytic psychotherapy patient whom I treated for nine years. From the beginning of treatment she exhibited an aggressive oral and devouring hunger towards the analyst through sarcastic and demeaning verbal attacks. This behaviour was accompanied by dreams that highlighted the "bloody" violence in her oral hunger, which reflected Ms Z's wish to incorporate the analyst and to be her, hidden behind the self-protective aggressive distancing behaviour manoeuvres that we spoke of as "backlash reactions" in the early process of her treatment. Ms Z would rage with hunger, demonstrated by her "stealing" flyers from the analyst on workshops she was offering, and by her angry scribbling on these flyers, reminiscent of Melanie Klein's descriptions of the infant wanting to rip open the mother's body in order to get back inside it, or Klein's psychic fantasy of ripping and tearing up the breast. Intense envy combined with intense hunger in Ms Z's attacks; however, she would only later become conscious of this when words began to have meaning. In the beginning, Ms Z warded off the symbolic content of words, putting up a wall against the analyst, who would often react by repeating what she had just said to Ms Z. Ms Z would then experience the analyst as a "battering ram", which became a metallic part object breast-mother in one of her dreams, a metallic breast that was ripping and tearing a hungry infant's body apart, shoving the metallic breast in the mouth of the infant. Interestingly, the conscious transference perception of the female analyst as the metallic breast, or "battering ram", was reversed in Ms Z's unconscious view of things as seen in her dreams. In her dream of the metallic breast-mother with the infant, Ms Z was actually the one in the position of the mother with the metallic breast. She was the one pounding into the infant, through the infant's mouth, to the point of murderous annihilation. This reflected her actual aggressive behaviour with me in which she would constantly taunt, insult, accuse, and generally abuse me with verbal assaults. Ms Z perceived herself as the victimised infant. In the early months of treatment, she was in a constant cold, hostile, and bitter rage that she could not control. Her hunger was too great. Only much later could she acknowledge her hunger in conscious wishes to have my body, to be me, to have my talents, my legs, my way of dressing, and my ability to be sexual in a sustained relationship with a man. When Ms Z became more capable of owning her sense of agency, increasingly entering a depressive position state of mind and becoming strong enough to relinquish a paranoid stance for longer periods of time, I was able to interpret her fear of guilt and grief. I told her that she wanted to "ruthlessly attack me without incurring a sense of guilt". At first, Ms Z was very upset by this statement, but she began to embrace the meaning of it and to use it. She began to see that she did want to rip me apart (which I countertransferentially experienced as her having long, fang-like teeth) when she was hungry to become me and to have my body, a body that she experienced as sexually arousing her in sessions. She began to see that her attacks were compulsive and that her lack of choice in the attacks was self-sabotaging. She learnt that she pushed me away when she was most hungry for me, and that she prevented the real emotional contact with me that could be psychologically nurturing to her—when and if she allowed it.

In the eighth year of treatment, when Ms Z was operating more and more on a symbolic level and could reflect on her own behaviour, she had a powerful and authentic moment of regret accompanied by the grief characteristic of regret. She was able to tell me that she was aware that at that time I was not doing anything to her or even appearing to her in any way that she had contempt for (the contempt being a continuous manic defence against her envy and shame, both of which were dealt with increasingly over time), yet she still felt the impulses to attack me. Unlike in the beginning of treatment, she was able to contain her attack impulses and began to reflect on her fears of emotional contact, her fears of wanting me. She became capable of consciously reflecting on who I was to her in the transference. She began to realise that I was not only the metallic breast-mother to her, but I was the metallic pole withholding mother, an anal stage image, and I was also the mother with a metallic penis, and the father who was seductive but secretly dangerous and rapacious. The metallic mother–father was Ms Z's own unique form of a demon-lover figure, highlighting her pre-oedipal oral stage trauma, and which turned the desired father that she was tantalised by—and which she sought compensation from—into another layer of a threatening primal maternal figure. Her dreams highlighted this as she fantasised kissing me in the transference, being seduced by me as a male analyst, and then being raped by me in many masculine forms, where I appeared as a group of little boys or as a seductive father figure. Ms Z externalised her own sexual impulses, which she had great difficulty in containing, and she viewed me as a woman possessing the sexuality that she believed she did not possess, as she characterised herself as the daughter of the metallic mother, schizoid and devoid of feeling (read more about this in Kavaler-Adler, 2004).

Ms Z had pleasurable memories of play that had incestuous overtones with her father. Nevertheless, when she was in the grip of her demon-lover father transference, which interacted with and coloured her demon-lover mother transference, she would have memories of her father losing his boundaries, as when he washed himself in front of her in the bathtub while she sat on the toilet in the bathroom. Ms Z then chose to visit a former male psychiatrist that she had seen for five years, just to reprimand him for not having helped her see her father's "sexual abuse". She wanted to blame her father rather than to see that her inability to remember whether or not her father actually washed his penis in front of her might have had something to do with her own wishes and impulses while sitting in the bathroom with him. Consequently, her expectations in the father transference with me were distorted. When Ms Z wished to kiss me and embrace me, she had fantasies of me being a male analyst seducing her. When she felt the intense sexual longings towards me as a separate object right in the moment she merged her motivation together with mine and declared, "We're going to act out!" Then she cut off her feelings, and retreated into a position of being vaginally and anally aroused by my body as soon as she walked into the room with me. She would often defend against these feelings, but they would always come back. When she could verbalise the body arousal, rather than just "stealing it" (as she stole my flyers) to take home and masturbate with, she could define vaginal and anal sensations that allowed her to temporarily own her own sexuality. At these times, she would be less inclined to attack me, as she could be in her own body and have her own body. At these times, her oral compulsions to devour or bite me with impulses and words would recede. They would then manifest as a displaced form of anal and vaginal longing when they did appear, rather than being the primary oral vampire lust that they had appeared to reflect in the beginning of her treatment. Nevertheless, Ms Z would retreat into the defensive stance of being the mother's daughter, claiming she could have no sexuality because her mother had none. She would then again feel intensely envious of me, and would think of attacking me, although she never did. We could speak about her conflict at this point, because I was becoming more of a whole object to her and less of a caricatured demon-lover figure. She was aware that I was vulnerable and not metallic. Ms Z hated having to suffer the psychic conflict created by this knowledge. Yet, she was becoming more and more human and less and less like a vampire. Her mourning process proceeded from there. (For further explication of this case, see "Vaginal core or vampire mouth, the visceral level of envy in women", Kavaler-Adler, 1998).

Ms Z's fears of receptivity to emotional contact could eventually be interpreted in terms of states of fusion between oral hunger and oedipal desire, which provoked fears in Ms Z (paranoid–schizoid position fears) that she would be overwhelmed or destroyed by her projected impulses. Ms Z's negative assaults on both the analyst and on herself brought despair. However, later they could be felt with a sense of regret reflective of a depressive position capacity for concern, following the repeated grieving of early loss. These verbal and mental assaults became understood in treatment as defensive barriers that she attempted to erect against the powerful and primitive fears that were embedded in the demon-lover complex and in the body's manner of reacting to it.

CHAPTER EIGHT

Winnicott's contribution to the understanding of mirroring as a developmental process: the Klein–Winnicott dialectic within

I n 1967, Winnicott wrote his paper, "Mirror-role of the mother and family in child development". In doing so, he brought a primary aspect of developmental functioning to the awareness of psychoanalysts. Freudian and Kleinian analysts (who thought solely in terms of interpreting unconscious impulses or fantasies to make them conscious through interpretation) would greatly resist the developmental perspective that Winnicott was introducing into the British Psychoanalytic Society. Analysed by a Kleinian analyst, Joan Riviere, Winnicott would constantly find his ideas and their developmental focus on the environmental other, the mother and, later, the analyst, rejected and misunderstood. In America, Freudian analysts who congregated as medical elite in the conclave of the New York Psychoanalytic Institute, were even more rejecting (Rodman, 2004).

Anna Freud was more sympathetic, as shown through Winnicott's correspondence with her, cited by Rodman (2004) in his biography of Winnicott. She validated Winnicott's contribution of the idea of the "transitional object" to the world of analysts at large.

It appears that Winnicott tried to create his own transitional space between Melanie Klein, his supervisor and teacher, and her rival, Anna Freud. He wrote to each of them, testing their reactions to his new ideas. After the rejection of his ideas on environmental influence by the Kleinians, Winnicott had no choice but to break away from the Kleinian group. Nevertheless, Winnicott tried to preserve his appreciation of Melanie Klein's profound contributions, as noted by Rodman (2004).

Winnicott's background as a paediatrician dictated his very different perspective, one in which the actual mothering of the infant and the actual behaviour of the psychoanalyst with her/his patient counted a great deal. Following Klein, Winnicott seems to have assumed that the psychological infant was still alive in the unconscious of the individual adult. Although Winnicott acknowledged innate drives—with great gratitude to Freud for his contributions in this area—as well as innate psychic fantasy as taught in the theoretical and clinical contributions of Klein, his own perspective was one in which the actual behaviour of the mother dominated over any innate contribution to psychic fantasy. It was through Winnicott that we first learnt of the internal world that had psychological images, functions, and avenues of motivation that reflected the primal impact of the real mother of infancy and childhood and, in extension, the real family of childhood origin. The impact of the real mother, parents, and family did not occur in a vacuum; it took place within the matrix drive impulses and drive-based passions and fantasies.

Winnicott saw the impact of the mother, in particular, as having a course dictated by nature. This was not, however, the "nature" of drive instincts cited by Freud. Neither was it Klein's concept of nature, in which portrayals of good and bad mother images in psychic fantasy emerge as reactions to drives. Winnicott's idea of nature was a developmental journey that had a psychological evolution beyond biology that could be compared to Lorenz's (1974) imprinting, but which went far beyond such imprinting in its psychological sophistication. Winnicott believed that the mother was the facilitator of nature's developmental journey, and he wrote many essays on how the mother either succeeded or failed at this task. Given Winnicott's perspective, it is no wonder that he was quite upset, even livid, when he first heard Melanie Klein's (1957) paper, "Envy and gratitude". Although Klein's "Envy and gratitude" was a brilliant clinical paper, and psychoanalytic insight into envy and gratitude was profoundly needed, Winnicott did not accept Klein's idea that children (as well as the child part of adult psychoanalytic patients) were innately programmed for hostile, aggressive, and unconsciously envious attacks on the mother and her later representatives, as these were justified by Klein due to the innate power of the death instinct. Winnicott, like many of us today, might have valued the clinical phenomena cited by Klein, but at the same time felt the toxic imposition of her metapsychological belief in a hostile and attacking psychic energy of the death instinct. This was Klein's own form of a death instinct, quite different from that of Freud. Actually Klein's "death instinct" metapsychology was not explicitly expressed in "Envy and gratitude", which sustained a clinical focus. Ironically, "Envy and gratitude" was also the paper in which Melanie Klein first acknowledged the impact of the real psychoanalyst (and, thus, of the real mother) in her writing. In "Envy and gratitude", Klein (1957) writes about an analyst (herself) transforming a patient's (analysand's) experience of infant and child deprivation, coloured by the patient's own hostile and envious impulses and projections, into a more benign experience of mothering through the analyst's accurate interpretations. The psychoanalyst understands the patient's dream of having a woman in front of her in a line for food who takes the two precious cakes that she wanted—like a maternal breast drinking its own milk. She related this to the analyst being seen as taking two psychoanalytic therapy sessions for herself when the patient was too sick to attend. Klein writes that the female patient, an older woman, was for the first time able to experience the session when such interpretations were offered as creating a nurturing experience, which in turn influenced the patient to revise her view of her childhood. With her new sense of being understood in her analysis the patient decided that her childhood had not been as depriving as she had thought. Here, Klein is admitting that the psychic fantasy related to one's childhood is affected by the environment, and, in this case, by the environment of the analyst in relation to the patient. Although Klein does restrict her view of the analyst in the therapeutic environment to that of the interpreter of unconscious experience so that the unconscious may become conscious, she fully recognises that the impact of the analyst, as part of the patient's analytical environment, comes not just in providing the patient with insight, but in providing the patient with the experience of being nurtured by the offering in itself of correct interpretations. In this way, Klein was actually moving towards Winnicott's more extensive view of the analyst as provider of a critical holding environment for the patient, thereby hypothetically providing for the developmental needs of the patient, just as the "good enough" mother of infancy and childhood provides for the psychological needs of her child.

Nevertheless, Winnicott's view of Klein's (1957) paper "Envy and gratitude" did not include this subtle entrance into the therapeutic environment that Klein expressed at the end of the paper. In fact, when Klein first presented the paper in the 1930s (with Winnicott in the audience), the end of the paper might not yet have been written, as it was in her later publication of the paper in 1957. Whether or not the end was written as it was in its published version, it is clear from the reports by Grosskurth (1986) of Winnicott's reactions to Klein's first reading of the "Envy and gratitude" paper that Winnicott was profoundly disturbed by Klein's clinical assertion of her death instinct metapsychology in which the child or the patient could be blamed for having all kinds of hostile impulses and projections that were not necessarily provoked by the actual behaviour of the mother, other, analyst, or general relational environment. At the juncture of Klein's "Envy and gratitude" reading, Winnicott might have believed Klein saw her patients as having solipsistic unconscious drive systems, in the form of psychic fantasies, which could be brought to consciousness and, thus, controlled, but which could never be traced back to difficulties in a developmental journey that related to the mother, care-taker, or psychoanalyst. Although Klein would certainly have proclaimed that her intention was to inform the patient through interpretation of unconscious fantasies that would control the patient unless they could be made conscious (and, therefore, that she was interested in helping the patient become more of a free and aware agent in his or her own life), it is quite probable that Winnicott only heard her interpretations of envious hostile wishes towards the analyst from the patient as a way of blaming the patient. He probably viewed Klein as failing to understand the original situation that provoked the hungry and envious instinct in relation to the mother, and that was now being experienced in relation to the transferential mother analyst. He would also have proposed that the analyst's sole role of interpreter and bearer of psychoanalytic knowledge would be a provocation for the patient's aggression in itself, in as much as he later wrote about the "too omnipotent" mother or analyst. This paper was probably largely inspired by Klein and the Kleinian group. Winnicott's view *vs.* Klein's view of the clinical material in "Envy and gratitude" can, therefore, be seen as a pivotal focus for an overall dialectic between Winnicott and Klein, and part of what I refer to as the "Klein–Winnicott dialectic".

Winnicott's paper on "Mirror-role of mother and family in child development" and the Klein–Winnicott dialectic

In his 1967 paper, "Mirror-role of mother and family in child development", Winnicott draws on his developmental view of mothering to grapple with a fascinating phenomenon. He is curious about how the self is facilitated in its natural evolution through the mother's reflection back to her child of his/her own internal state and need state. He speaks of the mother's face reflecting the child's state back to him when he is still an infant, even prior to verbal connection. Winnicott refers to Lacan's view that it is only by looking in a mirror that a child can begin to see his whole self come together, but quickly goes beyond Lacan's view by stating how Lacan neglected to understand the role of the mother in being the first mirror for the child, implying that the mother provides a mirroring function that a glass mirror can never provide. In fact, Winnicott understands that making use of a glass mirror is only as effective as that which has been internalised already in the psyche through the mirroring face and demeanour of the primal mother.

Essentially, what Winnicott is claiming in this paper is that we come to know ourselves through the empathic reflection of ourselves that we can receive from our mothers. From Winnicott's perspective, the mother feels and perceives us in our reality, in our true, authentic, and evolving nature. However, in contrast to the function of mirroring that the mother provides, there is the danger of having a mother who does not see us. He speaks of the mother who is so depressed or preoccupied that she sees only her own state of mind when she looks at the child. Consequently, the child is forced to see the mother, rather than his/her own self, prior to having formed a self based on the mother's mirroring reflection. This results in a void in the experience of self. The child is compelled to substitute the image of the mother, and her state of mind, for his own, rendering the child reactive and false, rather than spontaneous and true in his self-development. The child reacts with a depressed mother, according to Winnicott, by feeling compelled to repair the mother, rather than, in his words, being concerned with himself and with repairing himself. In other words, when the mother who is preoccupied with herself and, hence, has not been responsive to the child's internal state (by reflecting that state through her facial expression and behaviour back to the child), the child becomes preoccupied with the mother as a defensive way of warding off the empty void within.

The child of the depressed or preoccupied mother who cannot mirror the child is forced to defensively ward off an internal self that cannot be tolerated when experienced as an empty void or a chaotic terrain that has not been organised by the mother's mirroring response. The child is also forced to reactively organise himself around the mother's needs to try to maintain the psychological bond with her that is essential for him to feel he exists at all. In line with Winnicott's (1960b) paper, "Ego distortion in terms of true and false self", the child who does not encounter a mother who can provide a mirroring function is forced to be a false self—that is, a self that becomes reactive to the mother and her needs rather than to his internal self and his needs. To illustrate the experience of the void behind the reactive and, thus, contrived compensatory behaviour, Winnicott (1967) quotes a patient who said, "*Wouldn't it be* awful *if* the child *looked* into the *mirror* and saw *nothing!*" (p. 136).

Winnicott makes clear his belief that to see oneself in a mirror one must have originally been responded to by an empathically mirroring mother. Then the image of the mother's face mirroring back your own face and feeling state will be with you when you look in the mirror: you can see yourself because your mother could originally see you. It is interesting that Winnicott chose the example of the depressed mother as the mother who fails to mirror the child. He could have chosen any other state of mind in the mother; the state of mind of the narcissistic mother, for example (like Klein's mother), but he chose the mother with a schizoid form of depression, having a void or empty core within (as opposed to a guilt depressive with unconscious rage). Reading Rodman's (2004) biography of Winnicott, it is easy to see that Winnicott's mother was depressed, and that he saw himself as the child who was forced to mirror back the mother's reflection, rather than appreciating his own reflection through the mother's face. He must have also felt like the child who was forced to be reactively attuned to the mother, rather than having the mother attuned to him. Winnicott was most probably the child who is forced to seek repair for his mother in reaction to a profound compulsion stemming from mother–infant bonding. Informing us of this is Winnicott, as an adult, writing poetry that illustrates his resentment towards the childhood mother who placed him in such a developmentally inhibiting predicament. This was a resentment that he might have become aware of only after his own psychoanalysis.

Winnicott wrote a poem titled "The Tree", in which he speaks of the mother who stole his vitality (Rodman, 2004, pp. 13–14, 289–291). He speaks of the depressed mother, who tried to enliven herself through his childhood energy and enthusiasm.

> Mother below is weeping
>   weeping
>   weeping
> Thus I knew her
>
> Once, stretched out on her lap
>   As now on a dead tree
> I learned to make her smile
>   to stem her tears
>   to undo her guilt
>   to cure her inward death
>
> To enliven her was my living . . .
>
> Now mother is weeping
> She must weep
> The sins of the whole world weigh less than this
>   Woman's heaviness
>
> O Glastonbury
>
> Must I bring even these thorns to flower?
>   even this dead tree to leaf?
> How, in agony
> Held by dead wood that has no need of me
>   By the cruelty of the nail's hatred
> Of gravity's inexorable and heartless
> Pull
> I thirst . . .
>
> It is I who die
>   I who die
>   I die
>   I
>   (as quoted by Rodman, 2004, pp. 290–291)

In this poem, Winnicott implies that his mother robbed him of his vitality by her parasitic use of him to energise herself. The internally dead mother (perhaps in a schizoid form of empty depression, as opposed to guilt depression) could not resonate his aliveness, and instead, she is robbing him of his energy. In "Mirror-role of mother and family in child development", Winnicott (1967) speaks distinctly of the developmental need of the child to have a mother who can "give back" to the child his/her self. He then makes the leap to the psychoanalytic clinical situation that is so characteristic of his overall body of clinical theory, assuming a parallel between the mother–child dyad and the psychoanalyst and patient (analysand) dyad. This parallel comparison is based on Winnicott's belief that the environment provided for developmental growth in both childhood and in the treatment situation. This developmental growth is based on the experience of being with the mother, in childhood, and with the analyst in adulthood. Although interpretation by the analyst might make the unconscious conscious, it is the analyst's presence, his or her way of being with a patient, which allows the patient to experience developmental growth, as opposed to just attaining insight about unconscious phenomenon: content and process. So, the mirroring capacity of the analyst, as with the mother, is then judged by Winnicott to be dependent on how well the analyst can "give back" the experience of the patient to the patient. "Giving back" involves feeling and understanding the patient's internal state. By conveying the patient's internal state back to the patient so that it can be cohesively defined, an overall self-image and self-concept can develop.

The psycho-biographical studies of Kahr (1996) and Rodman (2004) allow us to surmise that Winnicott believed his own experience was not given back to him by his mother. Rather, Winnicott's biography, as well as his theorising, presents us with a situation in which his mother sought to feed off his energy rather than to convey it back to him. In addition to draining his energy, Winnicott indicates in an article on the feminine and masculine selves (see Rodman, 2004) that his own innate masculine mode of energy had apparently been ignored and denied by his mother. For example, Rodman (2004) speaks of an incident when Winnicott as a child was encouraged by his mother to play with a doll. Apparently, his father saw this and made a snide comment, greatly injuring Donald Winnicott as the child. In reaction, Donald threw the doll away, with an obvious sense of shame and rage.

His father had somehow made him quite aware of his view that play-ing with dolls was for girls, not boys. Winnicott later blamed his mother for trying to induce him into a female role, trying to make him an image and likeness of her, rather than allowing him to be a distinctly masculine being. He later expressed resentment that his mother tried to channel him in the direction of female development rather than a masculine one. He speculated that she did this in order to force him to become her care-taker.

In conjunction with this denial of his masculinity by his mother, and seemingly as a re-creation of his mother's motivation to turn him into a care-taker for her, Winnicott later married a woman who demanded that he be in the role of care-taker rather than in the masculine role of lover or husband. This was his first wife, Alice Taylor. Alice also, like his mother, could not understand or appreciate Donald Winnicott's true and individuating nature. According to Rodman (2004), Alice totally disparaged his activities as a psycho-analyst, complained that he was too tired when he got home, and would have liked to mould him into being a "normal GP" (general physician) like her father and brother. When Alice looked at Donald Winnicott, she did not see him and his own form of motivation and inspired creative energy; she saw a man who disappointed her by not being like the other men she knew. She obviously could not mirror back Winnicott's true self to him. This would suggest that Winnicott married a woman who served as another schizoid and depressed mother figure, and one who depleted him rather than energised him. She wanted him to play the role of her caricatured view of a doctor rather than to evolve and develop as his own true self. In other words, Winnicott married the most pathological aspects of his mother in Alice. Guilt prevented him from leaving a situation that was repeat-ing the detrimental effects of his childhood. He again became a reac-tive care-taker, and actually bonded to Alice through this care-taking role. As Alice increasingly became an invalid, Winnicott was forced to become even more of a care-taker, always to his detriment. Alice's limitations were so extreme that Donald Winnicott could never penetrate her sexually, let alone psychologically. He suffered the effects of an unconsummated marriage.

It was not until Winnicott met Claire Britton, the woman who would eventually become his second wife, that he ever experienced his masculine role as a sexual being. At the time when he finally met Claire and had consummated sexual activity, he wrote of the importance of having an opportunity for "ruthlessness" in one's life, and acknowledged the importance of the sexual drive and the freedom to express it in lovemaking. In Claire Britton, he chose an entirely different kind of woman than Alice or his mother. Claire had a full range of vitality of her own, and showed it in intellectual, sexual, and physical ways. Donald and Claire enjoyed spontaneous play and dancing together as well as sex and spirited intellectual discussion and debate. Furthermore, Claire could mirror Winnicott in a way he had not experienced before. Claire shared Donald's interests and joined him in the psychoanalytic world through entering her own analysis and psychoanalytic training. She was also engaged in social work projects to which she could bring a psychodynamic understanding. In addition, Claire could respond enthusiastically to Donald Winnicott's ideas and motivations. She could not only reflect the meaning of his words and ideas back to him, as well as his masculinity, but she could expand on his own ideas with her own knowledge and experience. She could mirror, but also expand mirroring through interpersonal interaction, debate, and dialogue.

Winnicott nearly died in his marital servitude to Alice Walker before he could make the break from her to commit himself to Claire. He spent many years having an affair with Claire, half living with her, but always dutifully (out of guilt, and concern as well) returning home to Alice. This was a dramatic moment in Donald Winnicott's life, when he suffered a few heart attacks and physical illness, and, as his former patient and colleague Marion Milner stated, Winnicott would surely die if he would not leave Alice (see Rodman, 2004). Finally, seeing how dire his situation is, he says goodbye to Alice, moves in with Claire permanently, and marries her. This does not prevent Winnicott from continuing to financially support Alice, probably out of genuine concern for the woman he lived with for so many years, having, in his words, a marital "corporation" with her, besides his neurotic guilt (Rodman, 2004).

The omnipotent mother and another form of deprivation in developmental mirroring

Another form of mothering that interferes with developmental growth, and specifically with the capacity to offer the developmental mirroring function proposed by Winnicott, is the narcissistic mother. When Winnicott encountered Melanie Klein as his teacher and supervisor, he started writing about the mother who was too omnipotent (see Winnicott, 1974). He obviously experienced Klein in her transferential role as a maternal authority as the prototype for the "too omnipotent" mother and the "too omnipotent" analyst that he began referring to in his writing. Not only did Winnicott start to explore the idea of the analyst who forestalled true self-development in her patients by knowing too much and not letting the patient discover him or herself through personal experience in the therapeutic session, but Winnicott also began to write about the too omnipotent mother who substituted her "gesture" for the spontaneous and self-initiated gesture of the child. Once again seeing the psychoanalyst and the actual mother in a parallel scheme in his mind related to his sensitivity to developmental thinking, Winnicott focused on that which disrupted a natural developmental progression occurring in therapy and in life. Melanie Klein seems to have served as a negative model for Winnicott's metaphor of the "too omnipotent" mother or analyst. Winnicott cited Glover's comments that in her writings, Klein portrayed her own psychic fantasies ("phantasies") as those of her analysands (see Rodman, 2004). To cite Glover in any way was certainly an assault on Klein, because Glover had been Klein's greatest opponent in the British Psychoanalytic Society. Glover had frequently attacked Klein, along with her daughter, Melitta Schmideberg, when he was supposedly analysing Melitta (see Grosskurth, 1986). All this demonstrates that Winnicott intended separating from Klein to pursue his own theories. However, when Winnicott uses Glover's (1945) comments about Klein offering her own fantasies to substantiate her theories (rather than using fantasies of her patients), he is also pointing to a contemporary, living example of his more abstract statement that the analyst needs to avoid substituting his or her own interpretation for the gesture of the patient, just as the mother needs to avoid substituting her own need or gesture for that of her child. Winnicott also stated in his writings that the analyst must formulate his or her interpretations in a fresh way, based on the moment of living or being, as Winnicott believed in a "fresh" experience-based approach with a patient (see Rodman, 2004).

Views on technique

Winnicott's view countered a traditional classical approach that, in his opinion, could offer stale interpretations that were rehashed and iterated from past thinking, interpretations that were preformulated rather than spontaneous outgrowths of the analyst's clinical experience with the patient. Consequently, Winnicott opposed interpretations drawn from theory that was conceptualised outside of the treat-ment situation with the patient, and outside of a shared experience with the patient that could be felt in a mutual way, in favour of those that could be formulated *in vivo* in the atmosphere of treatment shared by analyst and patient. By criticising psychoanalytic technique without directly implicating Klein, Winnicott begins to support *clinical* technique. In the psychoanalytic world, in which technique had been little formulated since Freud (other than by Ferenczi, who had been all but banned from psychoanalytic training and reading), Winnicott brought new observational insight to psychoanalytic technique. To further his observations of the psychoanalyst being too dominant and imposing knowledge in a session rather than allowing it to evolve, Winnicott comments (as cited by Rodman, 2004) that patients seem to be indoctrinated by their analysts, not only on a conscious level, but also on an unconscious level. He observes that Freudian patients have Freudian dreams, Jungian patients have Jungian dreams, Adlerian patients have Adlerian dreams, etc.

I suppose that Winnicott believed that an analyst who was "too omnipotently" indoctrinating his patients could not possibly be successfully mirroring them. The analyst who is encased in an omnipotent position, assuming to know all about the unconscious and any one patient's unconscious ahead of time, cannot be present for the fresh clinical moment to take place. (This is overlapping with Bion's (1970) understanding of a fresh clinical moment, in which the analyst is present "without memory or desire".) Then, the analyst is also not present to take in and to "give back" the patient's self-expression being experienced in the moment. Such preoccupation and omnipotent anticipation in the analyst can be likened, in Winnicott's terms, to a "doing" rather than to an organic "being".

Klein's contrasting technique and its biographical derivatives

The analyst cannot give back to the patient what he has not allowed himself to experience. This is another form of failure in providing a developmental mirroring process that Klein herself might have experienced with her mother, and then replicated. Klein did not have the failure of a depressed mother like Winnicott. She had a too omnipotent mother, who was encased in narcissistic character defences, as Grosskurth's (1986) biographical research on Klein illustrates. Grosskurth drew on her own first-hand research related to letters of Libussa, Melanie Klein's mother. These letters show that Libussa was extremely envious of her children. In fact, it seems that in her wish to live vicariously through her daughter, Melanie, Libussa burrowed herself into her adult daughter's married life. Seeing her daughter as being what she herself wanted to be, Libussa could not possibly have adequately mirrored Melanie. She could not have emphatically "given back" a genuine response and a genuine understanding of what her daughter was experiencing. Neither could she have given back a resonant sense of who her daughter was, and that she had a separate image. Instead, Melanie Klein's mother seems to have tried to mould her daughter to an extreme degree of her own images and projections, a goal illustrative of a narcissistic mode of operation.

This narcissistic rather than developmental mirroring can be seen in relation to Libussa's son, Emanuel, as well, who tried to live up to Libussa's fabricated image of him being an artist. Emanuel was supposed to be the grandiose heir of his mother's literary ambitions. Consequently, when Emanuel died young, Libussa denied that he had failed at his literary work, as documented by Grosskurth (1986). Libussa programmed her daughter differently. Melanie, who became Mrs Klein through marriage, was to become her mother's extension. As her brother had been, Melanie also was disposed of by her mother when she interfered with Libussa's plans to replace Melanie as the central person in her own life. Libussa had sent Emanuel on long-distance journeys, even when he was severely ill and reported to feel miserable there, to fulfil some kind of Byronian literary vision. According to Grosskurth (1986), Libussa got Emanuel out of the way so that she could concentrate on marrying off her daughters to those that the mother found suitable, in terms of her own ambitions. Then she proceeded to get Melanie out of her way as well, once she was married, pregnant, or engaged in being a mother. Libussa did not only command Melanie to go to health spas, but, when Melanie was pregnant with Melitta, Libussa actually dictated a regime of behaviour that threatened to extinguish all of Melanie's self-motivation and self-expression. For example, Libussa even cautioned Melanie not to play the piano when pregnant, as described by Grosskurth (1986). Certainly, Libussa's attempt omnipotently to control her daughter's life could be understood as characterological behaviour, with which her daughter was then psychologically compelled to identify. This identification could serve a dual role: first, as an unconscious way of internalising her mother and, second, as an unconscious reaction to envy provoked by her mother's powerful role of domination. Consequently, if Melanie had (in Winnicott's terms) a "too omnipotent" mother, she would, in turn, become the prototype of such a mother. She would certainly fit the bill of being Winnicott's "too omnipotent" analyst/mother then. Hence, it could only follow that Melanie Klein might have been inhibited in her abilities to mirror back to the patients their own self-evolving developmental experience, even though she could understand her patients' unconscious associations and could enquire into their motivations. Perhaps, despite the fact that she was quite a talent at intuitive insight into the unconscious processes and translating of the unconscious into conscious knowledge of her patients, she would not be tuned into their developmental evolution in the treatment process, as was the talent of Winnicott.

What can we learn from Winnicott about healthy vs. pathological mirroring in clinical cases?

Many examples come to mind of patients' descriptions of their parents, and particularly mothers' failures in mirroring. Sometimes, these failures were evidence of a lack of parental attunement that could be related to a preoccupying depression. At other times these failures were evidence of the "too omnipotent" narcissistic intrusions of parents, or were evidence of the parents' own overall character structure being based on their living in a hall of mirrors.

One young female analysand spoke poignantly of moments in her childhood when she would be lost in a spontaneous experience. She would be enjoying herself while playing and fantasising. She would be feeling the essence of being herself in the moment. Then, suddenly, her mother's attraction to her mode of being would become a frustrating disruption of her natural state. Her mother would come towards her with a camera to capture her daughter in the act of being herself in a way that pleased the mother. The camera would face her daughter with the self-conscious awareness of herself, demanding a performance, where formerly there had only been the kind of vitality of true self-spontaneous spirit that Winnicott wrote about. This young female patient's anger at the mother who so disrupted her state of being with an explicit demand for performance, as conveyed by her coming towards her with a camera, was latent and never formulated by this woman until she had the "holding environment" to express her recalled frustration in her analysis. Like a voodoo incantation or hex, my young female patient felt a little bit of her soul being co-opted by her mother at these times. The camera represented to her an instrument that would steal her fire and put her experience in a box, so that she could no longer be lost in herself and perhaps in her "love affair with the world" (Greenacre, 1957, p. 57; Mahler, 1971, p. 410). Here is an example of the too omnipotent mother who substituted an image of the child (a picture) for her child's vivid spontaneous experience of being in the moment. The daughter of this mother substituted narcissistic mirroring for the developmental mirroring that Winnicott believed "mother nature" within the average mother could provide.

Another young woman spoke of the mother that was too often unable to see her because the mother was in a mental state of preoccupation related to her depressed state. Although the mother was perceived as a hyper-vigilant care-taker in some regards, for example, monitoring her daughter's functional habits constantly, such as what she should eat or how much sleep she should get, the mother was all but absent when it came to seeing or "giving back" her daughter's impulses to initiate a desire or to express herself in any way. Consequently, my patient grew to adulthood with a sense that "something is missing in me". She would observe others, such as her boyfriend, having passions to initiate creative projects and to engage in self-motivated activities, without the need for another to be present, and she could only envy them. These people seemed to have a whole state of enthusiasm and excitement that she lacked in her life, missing perhaps what Tessman (1982) has named "endeavor excitement".

In addition to the lack of her mother's reflection when she had the impulse to initiate an activity or to express a feeling state from within, her mother would actually actively stifle her daughter's self-expression. My patient described to me a childhood in which her mother would try to encourage her father to sleep as much as possible, since the father was often inebriated when not asleep. Her mother continuously directed her to be quiet, and to keep still and silent. So, her father was absent most of the time, while her mother was in an avoidant state in relation to the father and in a repressive state in relation to her (if not altogether preoccupied with the depressive worries in her own mind). In the transference, this young woman would be super-sensitive to any slight lack of attunement to her during a psychoanalytic psychotherapy session. She would be particularly outraged if she thought I was sleepy in a session or was not fully awake in relation to her self-evolution in each moment of the session. Although she and I at first related this to her mother's absence in the form of preoccupation, her later associations to her rage, in addition to her fantasies of what she thought in my actual life might distract me or make me tired, revealed that my sleepiness also signified the father's absent state, as he was always in bed asleep. Nevertheless, her mother was experienced as a profound absent and stifling presence. The mother had never given her daughter her due in the developmental terms of a child's need for a mother who could perceive her, not only as tired and hungry, or as needing to do her homework, but as a spirited being with energy and excitement that could be channelled towards constructive enthusiasm and, thus, into creative projects of her own. Without this, my female patient felt that she lacked an essential part of herself. She felt that unless she could be part of a project with the number one other in her life (like her boyfriend), she was boring, dull, dried up, and sometimes filled with the annihilating anxiety (Winnicott's (1965) "unthinkable anxieties") of being in an emotional vacuum within herself.

The narcissistic mother's mirroring of self through projective identification

Another young female patient (whom I will call Carol) grew up in a family where narcissistic character styles interfered with any healthy developmental mirroring. Her father was generally outside, cultivating societal images of himself to promote himself professionally and politically. Her mother slaved away at home, with five children, and was generally preoccupied and unavailable. Carol often felt invisible. Her feelings could not be exposed. She was supposed to be a good little angel child for her mother, who lived in the split-off fantasy world of her idealised image system. Her father sometimes ridiculed her. More often, he was indifferent, except when, as a teenager, she brought a boyfriend home, and then her father started competing with the boyfriend for attention.

If, as a child, she felt pain and needed to cry, she was quickly told to remove herself from her father's sight. To comply, she would disappear upstairs into an attic room where time seemed endless and where she felt too restless to do anything with herself.

As a small child she had been banished by her mother into an outside playpen where she was left for hours. Later, when taking a ride together, her father would stop the car, lock his daughter inside, and then walk off and leave her for a period of time that seemed endless. In psychoanalysis with me three times a week, Carol had to experience states of profound pain related to an internal vacuum state. Being internally in a vacuum, she was also terrified when she attempted to lie on the couch. Without being able to see me, Carol could not believe that I was there unless I actually spoke, and even then, she found it difficult to put together my voice with the person she had seen before she lay down on the couch. Only when she finally trusted my voice enough to yield to the pain and rage within her could Carol begin to feel that she existed in any way other than through images in her mind.

She could not feel herself from within. Carol's first images of herself pertained to her father's demeaning and humiliating dismissal of her. Other images then opened up from memories, such as that of herself sitting on the floor and having a tantrum—for the first time— as a teenager. She had wanted to go to a dance, and her mother told her that she was tired and needed to go to bed. She began to connect with a memory of herself not being able to define anything that she felt because her mother was denying her desire, and Carol was mirroring back to her the mother's own view of what she wished Carol to be feeling. Obviously, her mother was not able to perceive Carol having true feelings, as she wished to control her daughter and not to deal with her daughter's developing sexuality.

Yet, in the midst of all this, there was one trail of mirroring that imprinted aliveness in Carol. This pertained to her mother being mirrored by plugging into her daughter's social achievements through projective identification. As the mother strategically found her way to being mirrored through her daughter by vicariously gratifying her own wishes for social stature, Carol received a selective form of mirroring that followed the line of her mother's quite complex internal narcissistic image system. Essentially, Carol's mother had lived a pretty miserable life, having severe losses in her early years and having suffered continuous neglect and betrayals in her marriage. Yet, there was one golden and gilded area of images that resided in this mother's consciousness, related to a brief period in her young adulthood when she had dined and danced with royalty and people with aristocratic pedigrees. It was this era of narcissistically gratifying social fraternisation that remained embedded in Carol's mother's mind as her true identity, even though her experience during this era had very little to do with the rest of her life. Given the mother's narcissistic ownership of the images of this time, and her total dissociation from all the other experience in her life that might have given an authentic shape to her, the mother was voracious in feeding the narcissistically pleasing view of herself, even if it was distorted and contrived. In order to do so, she readily consumed any image of her daughter that could vicariously flatter her view of herself as being the hidden princess in the tower, or the Cinderella that secretly deserved the attentions of a prince.

To see herself as superior, rather than feeling the horrible waif-like sense of abandonment that actually lived psychically within her, Carol's mother steered her daughter towards sororities, country clubs, and self-important women's societies and groups that could mirror back to her the gilded image that she hungered to see herself through, and that would lend that image a golden glow. Consequently, although feeling dismissed, invisible, or demeaned at so many other times, Carol felt an excited responsiveness from her mother whenever she made the "right" social contact, or joined the "right" social group. What was given back to her at these times was not herself, but her mother's contrived narcissistic image of her mother's self, and her mother's entire narcissistic agenda for Carol's life. Nevertheless, Carol could feel alive at these times, tickled by her mother's excitement. She unconsciously followed the course of her

mother's agenda, never really knowing why, and never knowing why she was so busy with social engagements that she had no
time for creative projects that she fantasised doing, projects that in
fantasy promised to express her own unique and individual self. Only
when she entered psychoanalysis did Carol realise that all these
social engagements that she habitually continued with really bored
her. She realised that she was living her mother's fantasised life
and not her own. Still, she held on to her mother by following her
agenda.

She continued to mirror her mother after her mother's death,
rather than being mirrored by those in her current life for things
that she could actually find to reflect her own interests and her
own potential personality. It was only when Carol decided that she
had completed the trajectory of her mother's secret path of social glory
that she could even begin to allow herself to contemplate
how she might begin to actualise her own creative projects, or to
complete the bits and pieces of them that she had begun in the
past.

In treatment, my mirroring of Carol's desires, giving back her own
thoughts, fantasies, and dreams was very important. However, it
was equally important that I could receive and give back to her the
feelings, images, and memories of her pain, rage, and despair that
she had carried within her. To have just reflected back her unex-
pressed desires and dreams would have threatened to truncate
Carol's personality in the same way that her mother's personality
had been truncated. Carol needed to have all parts of herself affirmed
by responsive mirroring and recognition by the analyst. Unlike the
original mother's response through narcissistic mirroring, it was so
important that the analyst not just see and reflect back to her the
idealised parts of her as the mother had, because it was that narcissistic mirroring on the mother's part which had forced Carol to
narrowly identify only with a grandiose self-image, and to dissociate
from so many other parts of her experiencing self. Carol needed to
have all parts of herself confirmed by the analyst's responsive mirroring. In this way she could feel recognised, not just for the idealised
parts of herself that would cause her to narrowly identify with a
grandiose self-image, but for the vulnerable and needy parts of herself
as well.

*"Giving it back" in the moment of acute clinical
regression that effects personality transformation*

Angelina had been silent and sullen throughout her first year in treat-ment.

She began to show signs of anger and pain during the second year of treatment, but she mostly expressed this off-target, outside of the room, and outside of the transference.

Occasionally, however, she would get angry with me in the session if she thought I was not totally awake and intently focused on her, regardless of how silent and withdrawn she was from any conversa-tion or affect contact. After such anger, she could sometimes open up and reveal some shameful secret tale of her past life, often about her sexual life and past. At times, she confided in me about periods when she had felt deeply humiliated by men.

Angelina also confided how totally worthless she had felt after having called her mother hoping her mother would listen to her, only to be sorely disappointed by her mother's preoccupation with herself (similar to her experience of me when I seemed sleepy). Then one day she came into my office and sat rigidly, totally silent. This went on for at least twenty minutes. During this time, I felt my own struggle not to be lulled into sleepiness by the warded-off affect within Angelina that I could feel behind the emotional barrier that she had construc-ted between us, and between her conscious self and her dissociated inner feeling self. Unable to speak, and seemingly so filled with shame that she could not even say a word about her paralysis to me, Angel-ina suddenly got up and ran out of my office and into the hallway. I got up and followed her. I ran towards her, calling her name, "Angel-ina, Angelina", as she headed towards the stairway. She was about to flee down the stairs when she stopped and looked intently at me, staring, yearning, dying to speak rather than run, but conflicted about whether to run away, just as she always had been conflicted at home whenever she was told to go to bed if she had any painful feelings and needed to cry.

Angelina made a split-second decision and—rather than run away from me and from herself—did a primal affect pivot and unleashed a wailing cry of pain. Having up until then cautiously kept silent as I stood and looked at her to be with her, I could then say, "Come back inside Angelina." Angelina yielded and followed me back into the office. Once inside, she opened the floodgates of full surrender, and gave me her soul as never before. Angelina sat and sobbed and wailed. I sat by her, but across from her, so as not to intimidate her. As she continued to cry and sob out all of the tears that she had been forbidden by parental shaming to express in her childhood, I began to "give back" her own underlying need, to "give back" her own voice, through my own voice as we symbiotically connected in those moments. I merely felt the intuitive message and spoke it. I said for her, "Mummy hold me, hold me mummy!" "Please hold me mummy! Hold me! Hold me!" Angelina seemed soothed by my words that offered my comprehension of her, and allowed her to comprehend herself.

She continued to cry, but not as violently. She surrendered more fully and the crying and wailing continued but softened, until finally she could get up and leave quietly and calmly when it was time to go.

Angelina and I had communed at a level as never before, and this would be a critical turning point for her psychotherapy and in Angelina's life. She would begin to own her own voice, and to find that she had a creative talent, a deeply rich capacity to write. She would discover that she was a creative writer, and that the tragic tenor of her childhood and early adulthood would become the meaning to be formulated and formed in her stories and books. But she would also make the interpersonal connections she could never sustain before. She would even connect with the mother whom she had so hated for not being able to listen or understand her, and, thus, who had failed to mirror her.

She would become the mother's mirror now, "giving back" to the mother herself, as I had "given back" to her. Angelina would also (for the first time) find a boyfriend who was kind and not exploitative or abusive, like the others. But, she was able to do it only after the critical scene with her mother that followed the critical scene with me.

Angelina is "giving it back" to her mother

Angelina's mother was coming to New York for a visit. It was to be a dramatic experience for Angelina, as well as for her siblings, because their mother was coming from abroad. Because Angelina felt more responsibility for her mother than her siblings did, she felt greater anxiety than they did, even though she felt abandoned by her so many times in both childhood and adulthood. In recent years, she even felt abandoned by her mother when she phoned her long distance and her mother could not listen.

Angelina, unlike her siblings, had come to experience brief moments of compassion for the abandoned child inside her mother that Angelina could now imagine, having consciously faced the abandoned child inside herself, more and more with each session in her psychotherapy. So, rather than just feel resentful of her mother when she entered her life once more, as Angelina might have felt in the past, she began to anticipate her mother's visit as a chance for some kind of reparation, although she did not know what she could realistically expect. She was, of course, afraid that her hopes might lead to disappointment, that she would feel frozen out of her mother's life, which was her lifelong experience with her mother. It had only been recently that Angelina could feel a few moments of compassion within herself and possibly capable of reaching out to the child within her mother. Nevertheless, she proceeded to make plans and to take the initiative to plan a week with her siblings in New York for her mother. She wanted her mother to be able to get away from the dark emptiness of her life, where only trips to church broke the endless hours of restless disappointment and—except for her one-sided confessional talks with her priest—extreme isolation.

Angelina's mother lived in a huge manor house on a farm, where her husband had once been an active farmer. Her children had played and grown up on that farm. Her husband was now off with young women having affairs. Whenever he returned home, he expressed his resentment that his wife had the financial status that he had to give up, owning the deed to the farm.

Many years before, at a time when her daughters were teenagers, Angelina's mother had run away from her husband, from the beatings he gave her, his affairs and abandonments of her, her own verbal assaults on him, and from incessant tension that came with the state of war that persisted in the marriage. Angelina's mother went to the city and, for a few brief months that were like an oasis in the midst of the desert that was her life, she studied literature at a university. She tasted the cultural atmosphere of a university and a cosmopolitan city.

But Angelina's mother was drowned by the helpless anguish of trying to provide financially for herself and her daughters. From

Angelina's perspective, her mother had felt herself sinking into a deeper depression than usual when financially (as well as emotionally) feeling alone. Her mother did not think she could make it, despite the inspiration that she felt when attending the classes. On the verge of giving up, Angelina's mother fell back into the old and decayed mould of her marriage. Her husband came pleading with her to return home, to cook and clean for him. He certainly did not line his pleas with any sugary compliments or any heart-felt gratitude. It was very simple. He wanted her to be a housekeeper for him, even though he quite openly declared that he had never loved her. But, in the midst of these insults, he offered her the only thing he could offer, since he could not offer love, concern, or fidelity.

He offered the deed to the farm to her. She would have the status of a landowner, and able to do anything she wished with the property. He, in turn, would live in the house whenever he felt like it, and leave it whenever he pleased, and for as long as he felt like being away. Too beaten down by her own fears and feelings of inadequacy, Angelina's mother capitulated. She sold her soul for the deed to the farm, accepting her husband's blunt offer. She left the books, the studies, and her hopes and dreams, returned home where her children would be free to eventually leave her (at least physically, if not psychologically). In returning home, Angelina's mother willingly entered a life in which each day was a tomb of security. She owned the farm, which provided the security of not having to worry about a place to raise her children, but her husband drank and would disappear for days on end. She cried in church. She was even too distracted to pay much attention to her daughter Angelina when she would call from America.

Still, there were moments on the phone when Angelina's insistence on getting through to her jolted her mother into a state of awareness. Her mother could feel, despite her deadness, that her daughter was changing. She could feel that what her daughter called her "therapy" was making her kinder, more openly vulnerable, with a renewed craving for her mother's attention. She carried this little bit of contact with her daughter to New York, eager to see her children.

The week of her mother's visit went by quickly, with tours of New York and parties with Angelina's siblings and friends. There came a moment, however, that would prove timeless, a moment when mother and daughter finally shared a sense of recognition that would imprint itself upon both of them for life, even if they were never again to speak to each other directly, or with understanding. It came one evening when Angelina managed to be alone on the street with her. Angelina looked into her mother's eyes and saw the pain behind them that she had always subliminally perceived. There was darkness in that pain — but there was also a plea.

As Angelina's mother spoke of all the days alone in her big house at home in the country, tears glistened in her eyes, as if behind a glass barrier of shame. Angelina felt that it was up to her at that moment to reach out, to become like her analyst reaching out to her on the day when she stood frozen by the staircase in the hallway of her analyst's office, ready to flee. Angelina hesitated, but then realising that if she did not respond to the wall of tears streaming from her mother's eyes, her mother could be embalmed forever behind the wall of shame. At last, she said, "It's OK to cry, mum!" As she said it, Angelina felt a spontaneous leap of heartfelt yearning for her mother to feel her own pain and release it. The second she said, "It's OK to cry, mum!" her mother erupted in tears.

Angelina was shocked, but gratified. Her mother sobbed and wailed and released everything at once, crying uncontrollably, much as Angelina had on the day of release in her analyst's office. Her mother felt safe enough to let down her guard and sob. When she was finally free to breathe easily, able to merge into the flow of her own liquid internal life, Angelina's mother looked directly at her and said, "I hope your life will be better than mine!" In those few seconds (that might have extended into minutes), Angelina felt a genuine love for her mother. Here was her mother compassionately wishing that Angelina had a happier life that she had herself, the one separate from that of her mother. Her mother had escaped her life-long wounded narcissism for a moment, and was feeling for another (her daughter), and grateful for her daughter's concern about her need to cry, to mourn, and to feel all the losses of a life spent in disappointment, misery, and as a victim of countless betrayals.

Significantly, then, Angelina's mother wanted to "give back" to Angelina, although that capacity had been all but frozen in her for decades. Within the mother's response was a combination of regret, remorse, and hope for another being's future. She was essentially saying to Angelina that she could face her own regret, about her life if Angelina could have a better life, if Angelina could grasp what she could not. She was also open then to remorse for her own betrayal of Angelina through her betrayal of herself. She could not give Angelina what she could not give herself, but she could offer Angelina the freedom she had never had by giving her a blessing and wishing her well. If only for a moment, she could imagine Angelina's life had some incongruous or magical element in it called "therapy" that could make her life better than it might otherwise have been. Angelina's mother imagined that something called "therapy" could possibly make Angelina's life transcend the limitations of Angelina's mother's life, of both of Angelina's parents, even of Angelina's culture and country.

Angelina and her mother might go back behind their emotional walls later, but nothing would change the communion that took place on a New York street in the darkness of an early spring evening. When Angelina's mother returned to her country, their communion would be sustained long enough for Angelina to say that she understood now that going to church was as important to her mother as was going to psychotherapy sessions for Angelina. In this way, again, Angelina "gave it back" to her mother.

What would Melanie Klein have to say about all this?

Melanie Klein's focus was never a developmental one. She was not interested in how mothers or psychoanalysts would provide developmental functions or provide developmental roles. Klein saw the psychoanalyst's role almost exclusively in terms of interpreting unconscious psychic fantasy ("phantasy"), to allow the impulses and wishes within these fantasies to become conscious, particularly consciously disowned aggressive impulses subject to interpretation. Although Melanie Klein discovered the profound importance of mourning, she related to the mourning process in terms of discovering disowned aggressive fantasies that blocked grief and the release to cry out one's loss. She had less interest in the developmental evolution of grief throughout the psychoanalytic process, which I have studied in all my cases on "developmental mourning" (Kavaler-Adler, 1985–2013). Again, this emphasis seems to have related to Klein's dismissal of a developmental framework that would create analogies between psychoanalysts and actual mothers. In this way, she was totally in conflict with Winnicott.

Envisioning the psychoanalyst solely as an interpreter of unconscious fantasy (or "phantasy", the British term for fantasy from *a priori* unconscious sources), someone who might be internalised as a good object when making interpretations that were perceived as helpful, but who was not otherwise seen as an environmental influence, Klein resisted thinking in terms of the impact of the real analyst and the real mother. Followers of Klein have sometimes given more credence to the influence of the real mother, but have still seen the analyst primarily as the interpreter of psychic fantasies that have *a priori* elements in the unconscious. The real impact of the analyst and conscious counter-transferential issues are all seen in relation to what the patient provokes in the analyst, related to the enactment of their internal world experience, stemming from childhood.

From this perspective, Winnicott's interest in the analyst's mothering functions, and specifically in mirroring function, is not acknowledged as part of the treatment by Kleinians. In fact, they would see active mirroring as often undermining the need of the patient to project his or her internal bad object world fully on to the analyst. Instead of a focus on reflecting back, or "giving back", the patient's true self-experience, the Kleinian analyst would possibly withhold any mirroring from the patient that might gratify addictive cravings for an idealised external other to compensate for an attacking or depriving internal bad object mother. However, authentically felt mirroring might be different than any contrived mirroring based on a Kohutian form of "empathic stance".

This distinctly relates to whether a true vulnerable self is being mirrored or just a grandiose, narcissistic, or contrived self. Many Kleinians did not consider Winnicott to be an analyst, although they often saw him as a brilliant man. The question remains as to how much mirroring is a developmental function in treatment, although—thanks to Winnicott—few today would dispute that it is an important developmental function of mothers. Are psychoanalysts really "giving back" a true part of the self to the patient that will allow a stunted developmental process to proceed, or are they encouraging the development of a grandiose self in attending selectively to the performing part of the patient, and significantly overlooking the more hostile and aggressive part of the patient that the Kleinians are attuned to, as they are attuned to the aggressive objects in the patient's internal world, an aggressive part of the self that could be incorporated into the narcissistic defence of constructing a contrived self-performance?

Related questions arise. Are analysts "giving back" the loving aspects of true self to the patient, or are they "giving back" the narcissistic strivings and achievements of the patient that can be used as manic defences by the patient in the face of hidden and unconscious aggressive components of the personality? Furthermore, do we "give back" the aggressive aspects of the patient in an empathic way that is another part of validating the true self of the patient? And is this different from "interpreting" the aggressive impulses and fantasies?

CHAPTER NINE

Narcissistic mirroring as perversion of developmental mourning

Impingement vs. recognition

N arcissistic parents can pervert developmentally facilitating mirroring into an impinging mode of mirroring, "impinging" being a Winnicottian term. This impinging narcissistic mirroring demands the contrived and "reactive" false-self performance from the child (Winnicott, 1971b). Where the mirroring face of the mother allows for the child's recognition of his inner emotional and self-state, the mirroring of a narcissistic parent reflects back recognition only for the performing behaviour that pleases the parent's narcissistic view. This is not Winnicott's depressed mother who mirrors back her own lousy mood, but the more omnipotent type of mother Winnicott referred to in his writings. And, although Winnicott did not deal with the father, the father has a primal (even if only secondary) effect on development (Kavaler-Adler, 1985, 1986). It is often the father who provides a form of narcissistic mirroring that encourages the child's defensive compensation for earlier psychological lacks, wounds, or deprivations with the mother.

The poet Sylvia Plath and the novelist Anaïs Nin offer biographical literature that illustrates the tremendous power of mirroring in its narcissistic and compensatory kind, which has profound pathological effects on self-evolution. Although Winnicott focused on the false self in the schizoid personality, the omnipotent narcissistic parent offers a pathological form of mirroring. This mirroring shapes a false-self in the child that is grandiose in nature and promotes a contrived perfor- mance, unlike the false schizoid-self of Winnicott that is compulsive in its care-taking, as opposed to in a dramatic performance. Winnicott's ideas on mirroring as a developmental function (1960a,b, 1967, 1971a,b, 1975) find their perverse form in the narcissistic parent's grandiose mirroring, which creates an addiction to the narcissistic image of the parent within the child's psyche. The narcissistic parent might be an envious one if not "fed" the child's flattering perfor- mance. Only when the parent's grandiose self (idealised self) is flat- tered in this exploitive way does the child have a chance of warding off the narcissistic parent's envy and his or her destructive attacks, often expressed as contempt, on the child.

Klein's focus on envy is unnecessary as long as the child remains merged with the narcissistic parent through an addiction to the parent's contrived mirroring view of her- or himself, reflecting back to the child only what is flattering to the parent's grandiose self-image (the case examples presented are of females). Only when the narcissis- tic merger demanded by the parent becomes untenable for the child, breaking the pathological mirroring bond that keeps the child in a state of imprisonment as a self-extension of the mirroring parent do envy, abandonment, and attacks on narcissistic vulnerability become an issue. Only then is the envy of the parent revealed, as well as the envy in the child—the latter written about by Klein. Within the heated-up pathological bond and the bind of narcissistic mirroring, Winnicott's interest in recognition version impingement plays a macabre dance. Nobody displays this dance better than Sylvia Plath.

Sylvia Plath: submission and rebellion
in relation to the narcissistic father

Sylvia Plath's developmental arrest might have begun with her mother's failings in separation–individuation, perhaps due to the sealed-off affect and self-state of her mother. Nevertheless, in her writ- ing, mostly poetry, this is played out with her father, who is more in her conscious memory than is her two- to three-year-old separation period with her mother. Her memory evokes the father for whom she continuously performed to attain a compensatory form of recognition that she craved. Her father becomes both the god and the demon of her primal psychic fantasies within her internal world. The splitting that probably derived from failings in adequate separation–individuation from the mother is prominent. Longings for primal self-recognition (which might have been exaggerated by the mother's lack of responsive developmental mirroring towards her true spontaneous self) are powerfully merged with the oedipal level lust and romantic longings that a little girl has for her daddy. These are further exacerbated by the devastating loss of her father that Sylvia suffered when her father died from a progressive gangrene complication eight days after her ninth birthday.

This early childhood loss seems to have thrown Sylvia back into a regression that combined pre-oedipal starvation for an emotionally unavailable object with oedipal level lust for the object of incestuous sexual and romantic desire. This well-known suicidal poet, who studied with similarly suicidal poets such as Robert Lowell and Anne Sexton, clings to the lost father through the image of the father's mirroring presence. Naming him "Lord of the Mirrors", Sylvia Plath displays herself before her father in her poetry. This is derived from the nature of her relationship with her father in her early life. This relationship is poignantly described by one of Plath's biographers, Butscher (1976). He writes,

> To ensure Otto's attention, Sylvia had to be on stage for him, demonstrating her own worth, earning affection which should have been hers by birthright. It was an unhealthy ambiance of growth, encouraging false values. Learning how to recite those polysyllabic Latin labels, and being regarded by her father's public approval, did have a positive side, an exposure to the reality of competitive relationship, but it also tended to precipitate a vision of knowledge as solely a means to an end, to recognition. Worse, it suggested to the quick witted child that her major worth as a human being depended upon what she did rather than on who she was. Here was the beginning of the model child . . . (pp. 9–10)

These themes of performance and perfection are woven together in the tapestry of her mask, Sylvia's false-self persona. Perhaps, however, the mask might not have been so suffocating if the blow of Otto's death had not struck her when she was so young. Sylvia Plath's incapacity to mourn at that age made her extremely vulnerable to the hazards of narcissistic defence, which she needed to mobilise in order to stave off fragmentation. Due to her father's untimely death, Sylvia could not mourn the disappointments of an idealised father; neither could she mourn the loss of connection with the male who reflected her grandiose self-exhibition. Her image of her father remained distorted, as did her own self-image.

Sylvia Plath's idealisation of her father hid the negative feelings towards him that had to be more deeply buried. After losing her father, Sylvia sought public recognition and approval, apparently in an attempt to retain her father's admiration. Meanwhile, following the loss that Sylvia so demonstratively experienced as abandonment and betrayal, her negative feelings—more deeply buried than ever—became heightened, but it was only later that evidence of this began to appear in her poetry. She withdrew further into the isolating shell of provided by her grandiosity, which she came to perceive as her "bell jar". Even her memories were buried in a tomb of glass insulation. The sharp division that took place in Sylvia Plath at the time of her father's death was between the part of her sealed off from the outside world and the part of her that was in contact with the outside world. In a memoir of her early childhood, *Ocean 1212-W*, Sylvia describes this dissociation in retrospect:

> . . . And this is how it stiffens my vision of that seaside childhood. My father died, we moved inland. Whereon those nine first years of my life sealed themselves off like a ship in a bottle—beautiful, inaccessible, obsolete, a fine, white flying myth . . . (quoted in Butscher, 1976, p. 19)

Instead of grief and loss, there is the wound and the rage. It becomes compulsive. Sylvia continues to perform before her father in her poetry, just as she performed for him each night when he lay in his bed, ill and dying, infected with progressive gangrene. Sylvia's performance before the "ghost" of her father continues after his death. Plath calls the mammoth ghost father "Lord of the Mirrors" in "Lady Lazarus", in her last and most powerful book of poetry, *Ariel* (1965). She highlights the father's role as a grandiose narcissistic mirror, a perverse self-object as opposed to a natural mirroring presence that encourages her true self-expression. Instead of recognition for the total self, she seeks mirroring admiration for her contrived expression of grandiose perfectionism.

In *Ariel*, which was published just before her suicide at thirty, Plath calls her poems the "blood jets", composed at five in the morning, when her children were sleeping, some time after she and her husband, the British poet Ted Hughes, had separated. Plath's pathological jealousies drove the creation of these poems—feelings that eventually found an actual cause. In her poems and in her death, Sylvia performs before the memory of her father: "Dying / Is an art ... / I do it exceptionally well" ("Lady Lazarus", Plath, 1981, p. 245).

The theatre of performance is set and she addresses her mirroring muse and mirroring audience, eroticised with oedipal lust and the narcissistic energy of symbiosis, Otto Plath, her god-size demon lover, her "Lord of the Mirrors". When the atmosphere is one of contrived performance, there can be no true recognition of the mirroring mother's face as described by Winnicott. The performance is arranged to seduce and entrance the mirroring father, who has always been unavailable, but who is now dead. Sylvia continues in "Lady Lazarus": ". . . I am your opus . . . The pure gold baby . . . that melts to a shriek . . ." (Plath, 1981, p. 246).

Here is rage and retaliation as an attempt at resolving the abandonment. It is the poet's attempt to fill the emptiness that is the symptomatic void inside where the primal childhood loss has not been mourned. Sylvia is trying to be reborn here through her retaliation. The retaliation is then turned back on herself. She turns rage into suicidal self-assault. She curls inward, even reclaiming her children as embryos inside her, so that she can enfold everything that she defines as self inward. This is how she prepares for death. This is the schizoid mockery of the failed redemption in the narcissistic solution, which leads to her main "accomplishment", death.

This woman could not take or endure any narcissistic injury—one cannot live on mirroring alone. After Sylvia Plath's writing was rejected for a summer writing class at Harvard, she makes her first suicide attempt. Plath did not have positive recognition for her own natural and spontaneous being, apart from this performance to please the mirroring parent. She did not have relatedness from parents who could be truly affectively responsive. Instead she had a narcissistic reflection of her continued false-self performance—as in reciting poly-syllabic Latin symbols for her father, the professor, the scientist study-ing bees. Such mirroring from the father who mirrored himself could not create or sustain the inner self of his daughter. A distant father, who mirrored Sylvia as a detached and grandiose judge of approval of performance could not help her build the internalised psychologi-cal tools she needed for Winnicott's true self-development. In Winni-cott's terms, Sylvia Plath's "spontaneous gestures" were stifled. The parent's omnipotent gesture was substituted for the child's true self-gesture. Sylvia's father offered an omnipotent and narcissistically selective mirroring, as opposed to reflecting Sylvia's natural exposure of herself. Consequently, he rendered Sylvia visible only in terms of "the perfect" contrived performance. What Sylvia Plath perfected was not true self-expression in the spontaneous instant. Instead of the revelation of true affect, she was conditioned to substitute the contrived exhibitionistic gesture. Spontaneity had to be moulded and, thus, sacrificed in the moment of lust for exhibitionistic appeal to the father god.

Here, Sylvia Plath indulges in anti-libidinal ego attacks. Her inter-nal saboteur is heard in deafening assault. Although falsely dressed in the language of guilt, Plath only articulates paranoid rage and self-attack. In her vulnerability, she rages against narcissistic injury and against the unsealing of the schizoid state, rendering her helpless in the face of exposure. She speaks of a spurious guilt related to paranoid rage, using images of traps and prisons, crossbreeding between Ger-man concentration camps and vaginismus. As her retaliatory resolu-tion turns against her, Plath is paralysed by rage and terror. This is well illustrated in the poem "Paralytic" (Plath, 1981), where she speaks metaphorically about the father-god who loves her, and at the same time is being a cold "iron lung" that sustains her existence.

It is, however, in her most well-known poem, "Daddy", where her paralysis is related to the entrapment in a symbiotic connection to her father. This symbiotic mode of primitive connection—the precursor to connection of two separate beings—can only enrage her and render her helpless, in as much as she still depends on the image of the father-god for the narcissistic mirroring she seeks to sustain her in the face of narcissistic injury. In "Daddy", Plath writes of her life confine-ment in a black shoe, "poor and white", and in a barbed wire snare, "barely daring to breathe . . ." (Plath, 1981, p. 222).

The god daddy and jailor daddy are closely aligned, for her ideal-isation of her father keeps her locked in performing to fulfil his image of her. She has become a prisoner of the mirror, as well as of the exclusive bond that ties her in the fusion of idealisation. It is the idealisation that blocks her rage, and keeps her mask intact. In "The Colossus", daddy is the god of the Roman ruins, "pithy and historical" (Plath, 1981, p. 130).

Trying to sustain herself on narcissistic mirroring from the mythic father-god, Sylvia Plath becomes trapped by the idealising process itself. This process stifles her true experiencing self, and leaves her with the shame of being nothing in comparison to the giant target of her idealisation, the mammoth father-god, who will keep her safe and "out of the wind . . ." (Plath, 1981, p. 130). In the face of his power, the poet projects her envious and hungry child-self on to her father. Then she becomes inarticulate and paralysed, as evidenced in the metaphor of the "iron lung".

Related to Winnicott's idea of the mother who does not mirror her child, but who mirrors back to the child her own mood or her own needs, is the god-daddy of Plath, who demands idealisation if he is to recognise his child. His daughter, Sylvia, now the poet, defers to the god-daddy, as if a supplicant or servant of his own narcissistic stature. Sylvia is trapped by mirroring the "Lord of the Mirrors". Yet, she demands mirroring from her god-daddy to validate her existence. Unfortunately, the god-daddy's mirroring is narcissistic and reflects his own image as he constructs her in his mind, not her true image. He reflects back to her an image of narcissistic perfection that becomes the icon in her mind for her grandiose self and its compulsive, suicidal perfectionism: even death "wears the smile of accomplishment . . ." (Plath, 1965, p. 81).

Like her statement about her husband, Ted Hughes, in relation to being the transferential father substitute, in "Death and Co", she calls him a "bastard masturbating a glitter" (Plath, 1981). When she writes the "Daddy poem", she is also speaking of the father who, like the husband, mirrors himself through her view of him. The poet concludes that her husband, the devastating substitute for her father, is engaged in a form of narcissistic masturbation. He employs "the glitter", the fragmented mirror's glass, to mirror her fragmented sense of self, as she feels abandoned by her mirroring father's death. The idealised father has an enormous power, as he determines who Sylvia is through mirroring, and mirroring is over-dependent on her per-fected performance. To ward off the power of idealisation, Plath negates god and turns her father into the devil (see Plath, 1981, "Daddy"). She speaks of him as a Nazi Devil, since he is German. By turning her adoration for her father into hatred, the poet hopes to free herself of the trap of guilt over her rage, and from the stifling power of image emulation. Yet, without mourning the actual loss of him through death, she is doomed. In her rage and retaliation, Sylvia Plath compulsively reinflates his power. In fact she eroticises his power through her oedipal desire that is compounded by the early infant hunger expressed earlier. In the end, she yearns for an eroticised masochistic submission to her demon god, her cherished paternal sadist, as she constructs him: ". . . Every woman adores a Fascist" ("Daddy", Plath, 1981, p. 223). Yet, she is held tight in the idealisation, which is both protective and suffocating. Then she cannot breathe, and the true self, under the mask, threatens to drain her of life, as the needy child self inside threatens. It becomes greedy with starvation. In "Tulips", she writes of the inner self draining her: ". . . The vivid tulips eat my oxygen" (Plath, 1965, p. 12). In "I Want, I Want", the hidden "open mouthed" child self is again alluded to: "Sand abraded the milkless lip . . ." (Plath, 1981, p. 106).

Turning from mother to father, she is again in the power of the idealised other, who mirrors her. She attempts to revolt against her role of victim, but, unlike the retaliation of "Lady Lazarus", who "eats men like air", her later attempts are clearly unsuccessful.

In Plath's "bee poems" ("The Bee Meeting"; "The Beekeeper's Daughter"; "The Swarm"; "Stings"; "The Arrival of the Bee Box"), the victim becomes the victor, as the queen bee image is used. Sylvia's father was an entomologist, and the poems on bees are all part of her world in relation to daddy. The poet (as her character subject) copu-lates with drones and murders them in the act. The queen bee is also a double for the bitch goddess self, the unliberated feminine strength. Yet, death is tied in with the victory, as Plath describes the murderess that is uplifted "into a heaven that loves her" ("The Bee Meeting", Plath, 1981, p. 212).

In "Daddy", Plath describes how the victim attempts to break the connection with her father, as she writes: "I'm finally through . . ." (Plath, 1981, p. 224). She then kills him off, along with her husband, her daddy's imitation. So, when she kills daddy, she kills them both: "If I've killed one man, I've killed two" (Plath, 1981, p. 224).

Yet, the sadistic revenge is never complete. The villagers stamp on daddy, and now he has a stake in his "fat black heart" (Plath, 1981, p. 224). Yet, still he is not finished. He rumbles with power beneath the tantrum rage assassination. There is no revenge without self-annihilation. The bitch goddess is forever wailing against a wall of blocked grief. The inner self fragments, and the images of fragmentation are many. Often they are mixed with the bloody red wound, which appears to be an early wound of narcissistic injury, concretised as a physical wound, despite its obvious psychological origins: ". . . red lead sinkers round my neck" ("Tulips", Plath, 1965); "squeezing the breath from the blood bells. . . ." ("Medusa", Plath, 1981), and "red blossoms" ("Tulips", Plath, 1965). Other images of fragmentation are also seen. The bees are "honey-drudgers", "little bits of sweetness and death" ("Stings", Plath, 1965). In "Swarm", they are part of the theme of soul-division and self-cohesion breakdown: "The bees argue, in their black ball . . ." (Plath, 1965, p. 65).

Many poems of Sylvia Plath reflect the inner disintegration. In "All the Dead Dears", Plath writes of "Stars grinding, crumb by crumb". In "Lady Lazarus", she turns against herself; the blasts of self-division are tied up with self-hate, and with an inner sense of ugliness: ". . . What a trash . . . What a million filaments . . ." (Plath, 1981, p. 245).

Sylvia Plath's ritual suicide attempts every ten years remind us, morbidly, of the sculptress Camille Claudel, who began to smash her sculpture every year after she left her romantic and creative alliance with August Rodin (Kavaler-Adler, 1996). After her father's death, such behaviour led to Camille's incarceration in an insane asylum, where she languished until her death. Her brother was the agent of her incarceration (at the mother's behest), and her mother emotionally abandoned Camille since her earliest childhood. Like Plath, she was only rescued by her father's mirroring, but it could not help have a narcissistic cast to it, following the emotional abandonment of a paranoid and narcissistic mother. The father's compensatory mirroring must result in compulsion within this light, and Camille succumbed, as many other artists did, including Sylvia Plath, to the "compulsion to create" (see Kavaler-Adler, 1993a).

For Sylvia Plath, injury from the father as an idealised self-object becomes intricately joined with self-destruction. The mirror of adoration, reflective of her daddy's admiring applause, can, thus, turn against her, and become dissecting and critical—the route to annihilation. The mirror rules and retains its power.

The theme of the mirror and theme of the daddy are explicitly united in an oedipal fantasy. First, Sylvia is wedded to the father-"bridegroom" under the sugar roses in "The Beekeeper's Daughter". In "Purdah", he is joined with his role of mirroring self-object. The word "purdah" means "veil", which presents the function of the false coated mirror of a narcissistic image reflection. The veil symbolises the false self. It is the trap of fusion with her god-daddy. To marry daddy, she must appear as the image daddy projects through his narcissism. He mirrors his own projected image. This becomes the trap of the false self that she is entombed in, her death-in-life. If she hates daddy and tries to get free, the guilt over her hatred traps her. Yet, her hatred is an attempt to exorcise the weighty idealisation, and the profound attachment that goes with it. Fused with her father's narcissism, her own self-absorption keeps all other men out. In "The Other", she writes of her lover that there is no place for him "between" herself and *herself* (Plath, 1965).

Plath merges her husband with her father, bringing the intruder into her internal world of image reflection. In "Daddy", her father and husband were merged in her desire to kill. In "Death and Co.", they are merged with the double image of death. She makes death into a twinship, similar to her own false and true selves. One lord of death is the classic Greek Aristotelian, who kills with intellect, and the other is sated with narcissism, and kills with self-absorption. One is her father; the other is her husband: ". . . of course there are two . . ." (Plath, 1981, p. 254).

Several themes of Plath's poetry are brought together here, and they are cast with a foreboding aspect of prediction. In the line "bastard masturbating a glitter" (Plath, 1981, p. 254), the images of daddy, mirror, and narcissistic false selfhood are all integrated. The "glitter" appears to be a mirror element that reflects fragmentation, as well as image making. The sense of narcissistic self-absorption is conveyed with the use of "masturbating", and its masculine aspect is expressed by the term "bastard". We sense Plath's abandonment here, abandonment by the daddy-god-devil male. He abandons her for his own self-preoccupation. Yet, it is her own "glitter" image to which he lends his masturbatory concentration. The image fuses her with him, and lends the falseness of self to both. She dies while waiting by the side of both the cold "icebox" chill of intellect and the secluded sensuality of the male other.

The death-trap of narcissism is fully sprung. The paralysis of guilt and fusion is complete. The last stanza of "Death & Co." predicts the petrification of death, which is also so vividly touched on in "Medusa", "Paralytic", and, last, in "Edge" (Plath, 1965). The feminine self is annihilated through the frost of the masculine false-self ideal. Plath uses the terms "flow" and "bell" to introduce the aspect of femininity. "Bell" is the southern colloquialism for "girl", and the flower-bell is clearly a victim of the "frost", which depicts the isolation resulting from the exclusion of masculine abandonment, and from the trap of false selfhood. In the end, the two seem merged in anonymity, when she moves from the "dead bell" to the use of the word "somebody" in "Somebody's done for" ("Death & Co.", Plath, 1981). Subject and object become one, just as victim and oppressor are fused. Death ceases to differentiate all identities. In a continuing progression, Sylvia Plath's poems all move from similes and comparisons to the annihilation of identity and to merger. The sadistic male daddy is victimised by the queen bee feminine self, who, in turn, is threatened with death by young virgins, and her salvation leads to the death of the author. All are ultimately equalised by extinction. Perfection and death merge in "the smile of accomplishment . . ." ("Edge", Plath, 1965, p. 81).

Birth and death are also joined. First with the babies in their iceboxes in "Death and Co.", and then in "Medusa", with the womb images that petrify: ". . . a placenta / Paralysing the kicking lovers . . ." (Plath, 1965, p. 39). Afterwards, in "Edge", Plath imagines that all dead children are coiled as Cleopatra's asp, and they are returned ("folded") to the mother's body "as petals" (Plath, 1965).

As the self turns against itself, so does the mirror turn against life. In "Last Words", Plath writes, "My mirror is clouding over . . ." (Plath, 1981, p. 172). And later, just before her death, she writes in "Contusion", ". . . The heart shuts, / . . . The mirrors are sheeted" (Plath, 1981, p. 271). With the death of the mirror, her idealised father's mode of admiration, there is nothing left but the last suicide note . . . Sylvia's words become "dry and riderless" ("Words", Plath, 1981, p. 270).

The end has come following the dry bone image of "Edge". Now, the author's words are dry. The struggle of the life fluid "to re-establish its mirror" (Plath, 1965, p. 85) is over. The final performance is played out all too perfectly. In *The Savage God*, Alvarez (1971) suggests that Sylvia Plath's last suicide attempt, at age thirty, was not intended to succeed. Ironically, it was set up with signs of ambivalence not seen in earlier attempts. Sylvia left a note with the telephone number of her doctor next to the gas oven that she used to kill herself.

Sylvia's poetry was perhaps more final than her last thoughts. Her attempts to purge her of death by catharsis through her poetry were never successful. The rage to retaliate was increasingly weakened, until the failure to mourn brought fixation on the wound, ultimately draining into the aridity of death.

Summary on Sylvia Plath

Sylvia Plath's attempt to live though the mirroring of her father left her with a false self that was pathologically grandiose in its dimension. As an extension of her father, she turned to suicide. I propose that she did so both to join her dead father, whom she wished to marry in her oedipal incest fantasies, and to stave off the fragmentation of herself that she experienced after her father, her "Lord of the Mirrors", abandoned her through death. Sylvia Plath survived her first suicide attempt, even though her mother had to have a search party find her in the cellar corner she had hidden in after taking sleeping pills. Plath tells this story in her memoir-novel, *The Bell Jar*. Plath mythologised herself as an Olympian goddess who could overcome death every ten years.

Yet, in Sylvia Plath's last suicide attempt at thirty, then the mother of two young children, who in poetic fantasy folded back into her womb, she met her untimely demise. Sheathed in the fragile veneer of her grandiose self, Plath could not comprehend her own vulnerable mortality and her plan to be rescued, as she had been before, failed when an *au pair* girl arrived late and did not call the doctor, whose number Sylvia had written down for her before suffocating herself in the gas fumes of her own oven. Sylvia died after a suicide attempt that was in part aimed at retaliation against her husband, Ted Hughes. Hughes was the second man to have left Sylvia. In her poetry, Sylvia Plath merges her husband with her father, as seen in "Death & Co.", (Plath, 1965). She highlights the twinship of their abandonment of her and of the loss of the narcissistic mirroring she had received from both of them.

Addicted to a mirroring other, whom she eroticised as she once eroticised her oedipal father, Plath seems to have fallen into the universal narcissistic illusion that attention is love. She was seduced not only by her father's narcissistically flattering mode of mirroring, but by her own illusion as well. From the accounts of all Plath's biographies, it seems that Ted Hughes had truly loved her and, as per Stevenson (1989), he seems to have worked very hard to empathise with her and her narcissistic vulnerabilities. But it appears that Sylvia pushed Hughes away, thus playing a part in provoking an extramarital affair, in which he impregnated his lover. Sylvia Plath does not address any of this in her poetry. Instead, she seems to defensively reduce her husband to a part-object, a narcissistic mirror, another "Lord of the Mirrors", essentially projecting her internal object-father on to her husband. In reducing her husband to her mirror, she loses him psychologically, perhaps even before his love affair prompted him to leave her.

Of course, Sylvia had mirrored Ted as well, always responding to and publicly promoting his poetry. Ted Hughes seems to have left Sylvia for another woman who, like Sylvia, gave him children, worshipped his poetic genius, and who ultimately killed herself. Like Sylvia, she may have ended up living more in his shadow than in his mirror as time went by.

Behind all the shadows of the demon-lover father and father figures hides the internal world mother that Sylvia Plath harboured. In Plath's poetry we meet her in the stark symbolic form that the internal mother takes as a dark moon, an empty core mother whose subjective self is hidden from all, and from her daughter in particular. The mother hid behind the role of a part-object, self-object for Sylvia, mirroring Sylvia as she once had mirrored her husband, Otto Plath, who had once been her professor, and whom she may have revered as an older male authority figure. (See also Silverman & Will, 1986 on failure of emotional self-repair through poetry.)

In Butscher's (1976) biography, we discover that Sylvia believed that her mother had never mourned her father's death. Her poetry reveals that she viewed her mother as a Pollyanna who employed sugary-sweet falseness to cloak her true feelings. Sylvia Plath's poems often depict just such falseness. In relation to her mother's reaction to

Otto Plath's death, Sylvia writes in *The Bell Jar* (as quoted by Butscher, 1976, p. 180):

> Then I remembered that I had never cried for my father's death.
>
> My mother hadn't cried either. She had just smiled and said what a merciful thing it was for him he had died, because if he had lived he would have been crippled and an invalid for life, and he couldn't have stood that, he would rather have died than had that happen . . .

Expressing these thoughts in her poetry, Plath uses the vivid imagery of a dark moon as the absence of an overt and conscious life feeling in her mother. By saying, "The moon has nothing to be sad about" ("Edge", Plath, 1965, p. 81), Sylvia possibly refers to her mother's denial of her loss and of opening herself to sadness of the mourning process. The poet is painting her mother as the witch-mother, with "her blacks crackle and drag" ("Edge", Plath, 1965, p. 81), the shadow side of her mother that might have lingered in Sylvia's psyche as her actual mother failed to open to her inner self and grieve. The split-off aggression hidden behind her sugary false-self is dark, with witch-like rage and bitterness. Likewise, as reported by Butscher (1976), her daughter Sylvia becomes the "bitch goddess" in her own self-portrayal. The bitch goddess is filled with a split-off rage that gives Plath a witch-like quality in her shadow-self when her grandiose false self is performing for daddy's mirroring (Butcher, 1976; Newman, 1971).

CHAPTER TEN

Loneliness in dialectic with solitude

I n 1963, Melanie Klein was writing her paper, "On the sense of loneliness", at relatively the same time that Winnicott (1958) was writing his paper, "The capacity to be alone", which outlined the prerequisites for solitude. In Rodman's (2004) *Biography of D. W. Winnicott*, he points out this intriguing synchronicity. In doing so, he inspired me to look at the biographical and clinical contrasts pertaining to loneliness and solitude, with the accompanying dialectics that paint a theoretical and clinical chiaroscuro.

As we look at the interplay between Klein's thinking on "loneliness" and Winnicott's thinking on solitude as the "capacity to be alone", we look at a dialectic that represents the larger domain of psychoanalytic thinking. It is the domain of the whole school of intersubjective thinking of self psychology and relational psychoanalysis, and it is related to Winnicott's "transitional" phenomena, in contrast and in interaction with the whole classical domain of psychoanalysis, the domain which has seen its "depth" in terms of journeys into the intrapsychic interiors of human beings. This perspective began with Freud, and it continues in the theoretical contributions of Klein.

My own contribution to this thinking can also be seen in this chapter. I illustrate through clinical examples how Klein's focus on the conscious analysis of formerly unconscious paranoid and depressive fantasies (related to her paranoid–schizoid and depressive positions) is part of a developmental mourning process that promotes psychic integration through the re-owning of intrapsychic projections. I also illustrate how Winnicott's focus on the internalisation of the other in the area of transitional space is a part of an overall "developmental mourning" process (see Kavaler-Adler, 1985). In my view of "developmental mourning", one mourns core life object losses. The primal and internal child self is rediscovered as well, and it makes psychic connections. To make such a psychic connections, the child self must be experienced on an affective level of awareness through the grief affect of sadness.

Melanie Klein's paper on loneliness

Melanie Klein's view of loneliness seems to be that loneliness is an inevitable existential reality in human life. However, according to Klein's (1963) view, loneliness can be ameliorated by a psychoanalytic analysis of paranoid and depressive fantasies that interfere with the creation of a "good object" within the intrapsychic internal world. We can only guess how such theoretical thinking was influenced by Klein's own biographical history, which includes a divorce from an early marriage, while a young mother. Klein remained single, living alone during her extensive professional life in London, following her departure from Hungary and then Berlin.

Klein made quite clear in her paper on loneliness that she knew that one can be lonely in the midst of friends. External others around us cannot modify loneliness, according to Klein, unless we integrate ourselves through integration of our internal world. According to Klein, we can integrate by facing our intrapsychic aggressive attacks on others, which can be revealed in the psychoanalytic transferences. We self-integrate by facing the aggressive threats, often related to disappointments that reside in our psychic fantasies of ourselves and of others within our internal world, as revealed in the transference.

We are always lonely unless we integrate our good object into our psyches, according to Klein. Such integration needs to begin with the good aspects of the mother. Klein essentially sees human beings as lessening their loneliness by re-owning their projections. Through this re-owning of projections, external others become less toxic. Consequently, new internalisations of improved external object relations can develop. However, re-owning the projections is not enough. We also need to face the pain of seeing our re-owned aggressive parts as well as our own weaknesses. In this way, we can make reparation to important others in our daily lives. Through this conscious owning of split-off parts of ourselves or of repressed impulses apprehended through the psychic fantasy of the internal world, we come to forgive ourselves for our aggressive impulses, at least enough to retain consciousness of them in psychic fantasy. Consequently, we lessen the degree to which we act them out. In this way, we can come to accept ourselves.

The clinical context of the paper on loneliness

Melanie Klein's (1963) paper on loneliness offers a theory that is spelled out in the clinical context. Through a case example, Melanie Klein, as both analyst and theorist, hypothesises that an unconscious attack on the maternal object, which exists both within the internal world as an internal object, and externally in a projected transferential form in the analytic treatment, will result in loneliness as the patient "bites the hand that feeds it". Through the transferential attack on the analyst, seen in dream symbolisation, Klein's patient becomes alienated from the primal and universal object connection that influence all relationship connection with others in the external world (external to the psyche). In the paper on loneliness, Klein's patient reports dreams in which he is seen as attacking the analyst, as well as attacking his own feminine side as he imagines the analyst to be a hostile lioness who kills kittens. Klein, the analyst, links this dream imagery, with all its supposed hostile intent, to the patient's past. That which is interpreted by Klein as a hostile attack on the transferential mother is seen as childhood rage toward a mother who is experienced as disappointing due to her inability to resiliently survive the aggressive attacks of her son as a child.

Although an initial loving bond was there with mother as a love object in infancy and early childhood, as the male patient progressed in age, his mother was frequently sick or depressed. Angry at this "weakness" in the mother, the son turned towards "mother nature" to find a compensatory "good object" when the mother failed to survive as a "good mother" within his mind. His turn to nature seems to have been interpreted as defensive by Klein.

Klein's patient maintained that nature had a better mother image, since nature sustained his aggressive assaults (knocking down fences and bird nests) while remaining solid, strong, and generally resilient, having flowers and trees and birds able to grow within its metaphorical womb. Klein the psychoanalyst seems to see the substitution of nature for the actual mother as a defensive idealisation that prevents the patient from tolerating consciousness of his aggression towards the mother, which is then rationalised as a justified angry disappointment. (Klein does not account for the original primal disappointment in childhood as related to reality.)

Klein's patient says to her that he did not see nature as ideal. In fact, he declares that nature was a good object, not an "ideal" object, because nature had nasty things within it, like hurricanes and earthquakes. Nevertheless, Klein sees the substitution of mother nature for the actual mother, where a surviving good object was needed, as a defensive manoeuvre. In keeping with this, Klein interprets the patient's dreams in terms of transferential attacks on her. Such transference resistance operates in terms of the patient resisting, owning, and valuing his own female parts. According to Klein, instead of the male patient (analysand) owning his female parts, he envies them in his analyst, and consequently devalues his female analyst through unconscious aggressive attacks.

Klein tells the patient that he has aggressive attacks on the mother (whom he experienced as disappointing) through his transferential attacks on the analyst in dreams. However, Klein's main point becomes that these compulsive aggressive attacks create a situation of psychic loneliness for the patient, because he is "biting the hand which feeds" him (Klein, 1963, p. 182). Therefore, as an analyst who interprets the unconscious aggression in the dream, Klein is helping her patient to tolerate (bit by bit, with tolerable depressive affect, in the face of such interpretations) consciousness of his aggression so that he might re-own his aggressive impulses and face both his paranoid and depressive fantasies. In this way, Klein hopes to help her patient reconnect with the maternal figure as a good object. In doing so, her male patient can feel affiliated, rather than disaffiliated, with the internal mother within his internal world, and also with the external world mother figure experienced in the female analyst, who can also be internalised.

When Klein analyses the paranoid and depressive fantasies of the patient who relives his inner state of alienation and loneliness, she looks at the fear of the mother's retaliation (as the lioness in the dream) on the one hand, and at the depressive grief and guilt related to his aggressive attacks on the mother on the other hand. Both forms of fantasy need to be analysed to help a psychoanalytic patient modify alienating aggression. Through this process, the primal self can tolerate the renewal of love. Also, the analysed patient can integrate tolerable conscious aggression within the context of love, so that the internal object is sustained internally as "good", in Klein's terms.

Klein and Winnicott on "object survival"

It is so interesting that Klein's view of her male patient's need to internalise a good object which could sustain its aliveness and health in the face of patient's attacks seems to directly relate to Winnicott's (1968) development of his theories on "object survival". Winnicott always speaks of the external mother, or the analyst, as needing to survive the aggression of the child, or of the child in the adult patient. This psychic survival of the mother is described by Winnicott as the mother's capacity to take the aggressive affects of her child without abandonment or retaliation. The same is applied to the relationship of the analyst and the patient. Although the degree of such survival is always relative for both Klein and Winnicott, it is the critical aspect of mothering (or parenting) that allows for the continuing psychic growth and development. It is this mothering that allows for the child's continuing "going on being", in Winnicott's words, without the child succumbing to developmental arrest.

In the paper on loneliness, Klein not only presents us with a clinical case, but she also summarises her observations in her paragraphs of general theory. She explicitly states that children need mothers and parents who can remain full and alive. As such, they would not succumb too severely to paranoia and depression (or sickness as manifestation of such) in the face of their children's aggressive impulses and enacted fantasies. In harmony with Winnicott's (1968) formulation on "object survival", she writes,

> The parents by accepting the existence of the child's destructive impulses and showing that they can protect themselves against his

aggressiveness, can diminish his anxiety about the effects of his hostile wishes. As a result the internal object is felt to be less vulnerable and the self less destructive. (Klein, 1963, pp. 312–313)

Did Klein inspire Winnicott towards his theory of "object survival"? Did Winnicott influence Klein? Perhaps the above quote from Klein captures how much there was actually an interpenetrating dialectical theory emerging between them. It is Winnicott, however, who acknowledges Klein's influence, and this makes sense, since he was Klein's student, and not the other way around.

Continuing with Klein's case, we see that the patient's mother is initially internalised as a good object. However, the mother fails to sustain the psychological capacity of a good object by becoming weakened by sickness, as well as by making her son feel trapped in her debilitated presence. Consequently, nature becomes the compensatory good object. However, nature is idealised, and defensive idealisation interferes with the male patient internalising a good object. By definition (in Kenyan terms), a "good object" is not idealised. As long as nature had remained an idealised object in the patient's psyche, the patient had a split-off grandiose self linked with this split-off idealisation. Klein's thinking seems to be that the grandiose self was used defensively to ward off awareness of the aggression for the patient, and to ward off awareness of the real shortcomings or failings of the mother. This becomes even more interesting if we allow for the possibility that Klein was, to some degree, in this same psychic position in relation to her own mother, as proposed in Chapter One.

Transference

When the maternal transference emerged in treatment with Klein, the patient was made aware of his aggressive impulses towards his mother. These hostile aggressive impulses had not been resolved by having psychic fantasies of nature as a good object that could sustain and survive all aggressive assaults. In fact, Klein's male patient had to experience his unconscious hostile fantasy life while with Klein, as it emerged in dreams in which he tried to kill off his own feminine parts. This patient had projected such female parts into his female analyst (Klein). She was seen in his dreams as a lioness. Then, he had associations to a kitten that the lioness assaults and murders. According to Klein's (1963) interpretations, these assaults on the transferential female parts were unconscious derivatives of her male patient's unconscious rage at his mother.

Although Klein's male patient had to face his aggression towards his father as well, Klein focuses particularly on the mother transference, so as to address the issue of loneliness as an outcome of unconscious aggressive attacks on the primal internal object, the mother, which can emerge through dreams and other forms of psychic fantasy in psychoanalytic treatment. When the patient becomes conscious of his aggressive assaults on the female analyst in psychic fantasy, he feels some depression. He is told about the paranoia in his attacks when he is envious of the analyst's femininity (and her feminine capacity to give birth and nurse infants). Consequently, Klein's male patient suffers consciousness of pain (of owning his aggression) through the depressive position.

Klein's male patient has to experience loneliness when he is harbouring unconscious aggression towards his female analyst, who is a transferential mother figure. Klein is implying that when the aggression towards the analyst/mother is present, but unconscious, the patient must feel as if he is "biting the hand which feeds" (Klein, 1963, p. 182) him. Consequently, he is lonely because he cannot feel close to the internal mother. In Klein's thinking, the internal mother represents all external others needed for his relationships; and while this patient is alienating himself from the mother with secret aggressive and murderous attacks upon her (in his psychic fantasy), he cannot be close to anyone.

Given this clinical example, Klein is making the point that no matter how warm and loving external others are, when one is attacking the internal object, which is based at a primary level on the original (fantasy/real) mother, one is going to be lonely rather than feeling connected and related. Loneliness lessens, however, as we face our aggression consciously and surrender our defensive idealisation. The other becomes less powerful by becoming less threatening as we own formerly projected aggression. As we open to the goodness of the other, rather than project our unconscious aggression, we become less lonely.

Klein speaks of us opening to the love and goodness of the other in terms of us taking in enjoyment and pleasure. Many lack this capacity to take in pleasure. This is true particularly in the case of character disorders. In Klein's view, the more we are able to enjoy, and, thus, to truly experience and internalise the enjoyment, the less lonely we become. Nevertheless, according to Klein, we always return to an internal world where some undigested aggression exists, and, thus, some loneliness exists. Idealisation is no cure. It prevents authentic relationships with others, as well as preventing the relative lessening of loneliness. Self-integration, on the other hand, allows for relatedness that lessens loneliness and that allows for better internalisations in adulthood.

Transition to Winnicott and his "The capacity to be alone"

Although Klein never speaks of a psychic space as Winnicott does, it seems that her view of the integration of the self through the integration of one's internal world (in psychoanalytic process) does imply opening up the interpersonal dimension of transitional space. Furthermore, solitude becomes possible with such psychic space expansion. Relatedness is enhanced as this process of psychic expansion proceeds. This leads us directly to Winnicott's 1958 paper, "The capacity to be alone", written in the same year as Klein's paper on loneliness.

How does Winnicott's "The capacity to be alone" paper speak to us about a dimension of psychic health that we experience in states of solitude? How does this same Winnicottian view of solitude as a capacity to be alone begin a dialogue with Klein's views on the human and existential dimension of loneliness? How does this statement form a part of an overall Klein–Winnicott dialectic?

In "The capacity to be alone", Winnicott's emphasis is on a developmental perspective that contrasts with Klein's perspective, going back to Freud's topographic theory of making the unconscious conscious. Although Klein's focus on self-integration is actually a developmental one, Klein is not explicitly focused on psychic and childhood development as Winnicott is. The patient's associations can be thought to evolve in the early holding environment that is recreated in treatment. Klein, however, in contrast to Winnicott, does not experience the environment between analyst and patient being recreated on any external object relations basis. When the patient experiences Mrs Klein as an analyst/mother, it is assumed by Klein to be a transferential projection, and nothing more. Such perceptions on the part of the patient are generally not seen as related to the actual attitude of the analyst and his/her way of being.

By contrast, Winnicott (1971a,b, 1975, 1986) emphasises the external world environment in which the real, external mother—not the fantasy mother—exists. In fact, Winnicott made vivid to us how the real mother has the most profound primal impact on the child. He then extends this thinking to how the maternal attitude of the analyst impacts the psychoanalytic patient. Winnicott always implies an analogous relationship between analyst and patient to that of mother and child. For Winnicott, the maternal holding environment is recreated not only in fantasy, but also in the reality of the psychotherapeutic treatment rooms.

Winnicott operates within a Kleinian universe, but in theoretical contrast to Klein. He lives in his own mental and psychic space, where Klein's theories provide for him both a stimulating and also aversive maternal environment—a maternal environment that challenges, inspires, and, to some extent, infuriates him. Winnicott is compelled to speak about the contrasting external world influences, the influences of the real other, the real external object, and the real original mother that Klein sees merely as a background compensatory influence. For Klein, the internal world contains the fantasy mother that never ceases to predominate.

As a paediatrician, Winnicott observed daily the external mother–child couple. He is, therefore, both equipped to bring in his external world view into psychoanalysis and, seemingly, he is compelled to do so. This is vividly highlighted when he is forced to leave the Kleinian camp in London, when his written contributions are being rejected by the Kleinians. The crescendo of such rejection is marked by the publishing of a volume of articles particularly meant to celebrate Klein's theories. Winnicott is excluded from this volume. His own analyst, Joan Riviere, an ardent Kleinian, was among those who opposed his putting pen to paper with his unique perspective on the external reality-based maternal environment (Rodman, 2004).

In his collected papers, published in a volume titled *Maturational Processes and the Facilitating Environment*, Winnicott (1965) fully announces his personal declaration of independence. In papers such as "The capacity to be alone" (Winnicott, 1958), and "The development of the capacity for concern" (Winnicott, 1963) he openly celebrates the role of the analyst as an external facilitator of a naturally evolving developmental process. This developmental process is continually drawn in parallel to the role of the actual mother of the patient in infancy and toddlerhood, who is the original facilitator of a naturally evolving developmental process.

Winnicott became famous for his statement that "There is no such thing as a baby" (Winnicott, 1975, p. 99), because there is only a "nursing couple", or a baby and a mother. His view was seen as profoundly polarised in relation to Klein. Klein assumed that the internal world was a self-sufficient sphere, which the external mother influenced with time, but which was originally dominated by an internal mother image and fantasy. However, this view does not deal with the developmental timetable related to the growth of symbolic images, which occurs during the period of separation–individuation (Mahler, 1967, 1971), a view I agree with.

Although Klein believed that the child was always interactive with an "other" from birth, she believed that, particularly in the beginning, this other was an internal other. This was true despite her allowance for the external mother to be playing an important role in counteracting the negative effects of this internal mother, who was built largely from split-off aggressive parts of the child's self. For Klein, in the beginning of life, the external mother was also an enhancing influence on the good internal mother, constructed from split-off loving parts of the infant self. With time, this good external mother became more important in Klein's theories, so that by the time she wrote "Envy and gratitude" (Klein, 1957) and her paper on loneliness (Klein, 1963), she was giving more recognition to the external mother. For example, in "Envy and gratitude", Klein (1957) gave increasing recognition to the external psychoanalyst—beyond projection. Nevertheless, Klein still saw the analyst's role only in terms of making the unconscious conscious, through interpretations. It cannot be overlooked, however, that, despite Klein's failure to give Winnicott more than a footnote of recognition in her writing, she seems to have been gradually influenced by Winnicott's emphasis on the external mother and the holding environment, as evidenced in her later writings. However, Klein's emphasis always remained (as it did in the paper on loneliness) on the overpowering impact of the internal world's psychic fantasies. This made the conscious awareness of such fantasies, as well as their underlying impulses, imperative for self-integration and psychic health.

As Winnicott covertly influenced Klein, Klein also perpetually influenced Winnicott, and this transformed a potentially paralysing polarisation between Winnicott and Klein into a dynamically evolving dialectic. From such a dialectical point, we can take a look at Winnicott's (1958) paper "The capacity to be alone". This paper declared Winnicott's external view of psychological internalisation. Meanwhile, Klein continued to focus on self-integration through the re-owning of aggressive impulses symbolised in internal world's psychic fantasies (or "phantasies"), regardless of whether the aggressive impulses were repressed within unconscious psychic fantasies or were split-off (i.e., dissociated) enactments of fantasy. Viewing internalisation as critical to psychological development in general, and, in particular, to clinical treatment that wished to enhance and re-mobilise this development, Winnicott was indeed declaring a psychological manifesto.

"Going-on-being", presence, and Winnicott's manifesto

Winnicott's manifesto increasingly influenced modern psychoanalysis and, in time, it will totally transform psychoanalytic thinking. Those interested in "right brain" psychology would rally to Winnicott. The gestalt approach would challenge the merely linear in psychoanalysis as well as in other therapies. Postmodernists would look to Winnicott for their own purposes.

"The capacity to be alone" (Winnicott, 1958) became a core kernel of this Winnicottian manifesto. Like Zen Buddhism, yoga, or Tai Chi, it emphasises presence. What is it like for the analyst to truly be in the moment, and what is the consequence of the analyst not being present in the moment? Such questions can now be asked, after Winnicott spoke of the absolute need of the child (as well as of the child within the adult psychoanalytic patient) to be nurtured by the "being" (not the "doing") of the primal mother and all those who play the role of a "subjective object," those serving maternal functions (e.g., the therapists). For Winnicott, continuity and cohesion in the self of the child, which he spoke about as a sense of "going-on-being" (Winnicott, 1960a, p. 587), could only come about when a mother was present with her own alive "being" presence.

As the child of a depressed mother, who had disrupted her bonding with him as an infant during the breastfeeding, and who might have suffered postpartum depression, as well as later depression during his childhood (Rodman, 2004), Winnicott became extremely sensitive to this issue of the presence of an alive, as opposed to a deadened or emotionally detached, mother. With such sensitivity, Winnicott developed an attunement to the degree of "alive" presence in the mothers of his paediatric patients and, later, in his psychotherapy patients.

Presence became a profound factor in treatment of psychological disorders, and what the analyst was actively feeling and thinking when in the room with the patient became as important, and sometimes more important, than the interpretations being made. This is especially true in the case of those with developmental arrests, such as the character disorders. In fact, the art and science of interpretation was transformed by Winnicott's focus on "being," because it was no longer enough to offer intellectual interpretations, which Winnicott clearly viewed as "stale" (see Rodman, 2004). It was no longer enough to speak Freudian or Kleinian language and "make interpretations" based on theories. Following Winnicott, the analysts now actually process a "live" experience in the room with the patient, and that leads to the interpretation.

Winnicott's effect upon the theory of countertransference

Elaborating upon this contribution of Winnicott to American theory, we developed the art of using our "objective", as opposed to "subjective," countertransference in clinical work. In objective countertransference, we actively process all the feelings and thoughts we experience while in the room with the patient. In this way, we are able to understand what the patient is unconsciously experiencing and reliving. In this way, we come to experience what the patient is splitting off from their traumatised, and, thus, dissociated, early experience. In this experiential way, we come to understand and eventually interpret what is being re-lived and projected at the same time. The analyst experiences this through provocation or inducement, or, in Klein's terms, through projective identification.

The capacity to be alone and human development

However, in "The capacity to be alone", Winnicott (1958) is not yet extending his theory into the area of processing objective countertransference. He is merely stating then that we can never develop the fundamental human capacity to be alone without first having a facilitating maternal other, which is being present with us. Further, the facilitating other must be present in a state of relatively pure "being", where compulsive "doing" is suspended. Also, from Winnicott's perspective, the mother's needs must not be imposed on the child. The mother, who is fully present in this "being" capacity, is the one who is full enough within herself, and does not need anything from her child at that moment. Consequently, she can "be" with her child. She can feel with her child, and respond to the child's needs and impulses (the child's omnipotent "gestures" in Winnicott's terms). She both receives from the child and responds to him/her in a state of "being".

In such a state, the mother can be internalised as a psychic presence that sustains and lives within the psyche of the child throughout life. This alive maternal presence is the one that lives on in the child. The facilitating environmental mother promotes an open psychic space and the evolution of creative and loving capacities in the child, as well as the continuing discovery of internal resources. Returning to the subject of Winnicott's dialectic with Klein (as opposed to polarisation), Winnicott's understanding of "presence" can be compared to what Klein describes in her paper on loneliness as the "good object" that can both give and receive love. This "good object"-mother is an external object (or "other") who has an internal balance. She certainly is not the "empty core" mother (Seinfeld, 1991) of the schizoid.

Although many human capacities develop thus from the "alive" presence of the mother, in "The capacity to be alone", Winnicott (1958) is obviously focused on the capacity for independent psychic well-being. He is also addressing the development of the specific primary ability to create and to use solitude. Although creativity and love develop through this "alive" presence of the mother, solitude becomes a path to both. We must be able to be alone with ourselves before we can truly be with another. We also need to be able to have another to be with us, to be able to be alone with ourselves. This dialectical interplay is dependent on a psyche grown to a state of psychic dialectic through the internalisation of a separate other. This dialectical capacity contrasts with a regressive and defensive state of self–other fusion. The later state of fusion harks back a symbiotic unity, prior to separation–individuation. The dialectical capacity emerges through an adequate contact and connection for separation–individuation to take place.

Specifics in Winnicott's "The capacity to be alone"

In his "The capacity to be alone" paper, Winnicott raises the issue of the maturational accomplishment implicit in a psychoanalytic patient's self-reflective silence. He writes of this in contrast to the classical psychoanalytic view of silence being related to resistance in analysis, or, within a Kleinian framework, related to defensive paranoid withdrawal from relationship due to persecutory fantasies.

Here again, Winnicott is speaking in relation to his own maturational process as a clinician, who is thinking in solitude as he writes about solitude. On the first page of "The capacity to be alone", Winnicott declares his manifesto by writing about clinical and psychological phenomena that step beyond Klein, but which also are dependent on Kleinian theory. Winnicott's theories are of dialectical contrast, a dialectical contrast both negating and defining its opposite (see Ogden, 1986). Winnicott writes,

> It is probably true to say that in psycho-analytical literature more has been written on the *fear* of being alone or the *wish* to be alone than on the *ability* to be alone; also a considerable amount of work has been done on the withdrawn state, a defensive organization implying an expectation of persecution. It would seem to me that a discussion on the *positive* aspects of the capacity to be alone is overdue. In the literature there may be specific attempts to state the capacity to be alone, but I am not aware of these. (1958, p. 416)

Further on, Winnicott refers to the specific capacity to "value" and "enjoy" solitude:

> It will be appreciated that actually to be alone is not what I am discussing. A person may be in solitary confinement, and yet not be able to be alone. How greatly he must suffer is beyond imagination. However, many people do become able to enjoy solitude before they are out of childhood, and they may even value solitude as a most precious possession. (1958, p. 416)

Under "Paradox", Winnicott writes,

> The main point of this contribution can now be stated. Although many types of experience go to the establishment of the capacity to be alone, there is one that is basic, and without a sufficiency of it the capacity to

be alone does not come about; *this experience is that of being alone, as an infant and small child, in the presence of mother.* Thus the basis of the capacity to be alone is a paradox; it is the experience of being alone while someone else is present.

Here is implied a rather special type of relationship, that between the infant or small child who is alone, and the mother or mother-substitute who is in fact reliably present even if represented for the moment by a cot or a pram or the general atmosphere of the immediate environment. I would like to suggest a name for this special type of relationship.

Personally I like to use the term *ego-relatedness*, which is convenient in that it contrasts rather clearly with the word *id-relationship*, which is a recurring complication in what might be called ego life. Ego-related-ness refers to the relationship between two people, one of whom at any rate is alone; perhaps both are alone, yet the presence of each is important to the other. (p. 417)

Winnicott then speaks about the state of solitude within the most intimate of relationships, relationships that include sexual intercourse. Winnicott changed his external object connection from his first wife, who was isolated within herself and who was unable to open up and to receive him in sexual intercourse, to a second wife, Claire Britton, who was more fully complete within herself. Unlike Alice Taylor (Winnicott's first wife), Claire Britton was able to open up and surren-der to receiving Donald Winnicott in an intercourse that was sexual as well as deeply emotional. In speaking about "ego-relatedness" in "The capacity to be alone", Winnicott (1958) speaks about "liking" as being different than "loving", based on id relationship and its tension and intensity. He seems to have experienced this combination of "liking" and "loving" with Claire, and so he could speak of the creative dialec-tic between solitude and relationship within sexual intercourse.

Perhaps Melanie Klein never succeeded in sustaining such an inti-mate relationship, in which liking and loving could co-exist along with solitude and interaction. She was divorced and remained single. According to Grosskurth (1986), her mother interfered significantly in her marriage. To the degree that she might not have achieved what Winnicott had in his second marriage with Claire, Melanie Klein may have found herself musing more about loneliness than about solitude. If so, this would suggest that there could have been a psychobio-graphical factor in Klein's focus on the "loneliness" in her patients, which emerged in her 1963 paper, "On the sense of loneliness". (There was, however, at least one significant erotic experience in Klein's history, with a male portrait painter, according to Phyllis Grosskurth (1986).)

In this paper, Klein wrote about an internal world composed of persecutory and depressive psychic fantasies that promoted loneliness, even with others around. Winnicott, on the other hand, writes of solitude rather than loneliness, in the presence of the mother, and even with an intimate other, with whom one has just been engaged in an interpenetrating state of sexual intercourse. (He seems to have found this with Claire, when he could not find it with Alice. Klein might not have found it, at least not on any sustained basis.) In the section "After intercourse", Winnicott (1958) writes,

> It is perhaps fair to say that after satisfactory intercourse each partner is alone and is contented to be alone. Being able to enjoy being alone along with another person who is also alone is in itself an experience of health. Lack of id-tension may produce anxiety, but time-integration of the personality enables the individual to wait for the natural return of id tension, and to enjoy sharing solitude, that is to say, solitude that is relatively free from the property that we call 'withdrawal'. (p. 417)

After the section on the "Primal scene", Winnicott returns to Kleinian terminology to make his points, which are both in conjunction with Klein and in dialectic with her. In essence, in his writing, the solitude is supported by Kleinian presence, perhaps a transferential maternal presence. Winnicott (1958) returns explicitly to Klein and her language in his section on the "Good internal object":

> I will now attempt to use another language, one that derives from the work of Melanie Klein. The capacity to be alone depends on the existence in the psychic reality of the individual of a good object. The good internal breast or penis or the good internal relationships are well enough set up and defended for the individual (at any rate for the time being) to feel confident about the present and the future. The relationship of the individual to his or her internal objects, along with confidence in regard to internal relationships, provides of itself a sufficiency of living, so that temporarily he or she is able to rest contented even in the absence of external objects and stimuli. Maturity and the capacity to be alone imply that the individual has

had the chance through good-enough mothering to build up a belief in a benign environment. This belief is built up through a repetition of satisfactory instinctual gratifications. (p. 417)

Reflecting on Klein's fascination with the internal world, Winnicott makes the point that only with the internalisation of a real good enough mothering object can the internal world be experienced, because only with such internalisation is there an "I" with an "inside" and an "outside". Unfortunately, like Klein, he still uses the word "introjection" to refer to what we today call "internalisation". This can be confusing, because in Kleinian language, introjection also operates as a defence in the depressive position. Like Klein, he refers to an era prior to triadic oedipal developments, when the self, or "ego", develops. This era overlaps with the separation–individuation era of Mahler (1967, 1971) and of Masterson (1976, 1981, 1996, 2000). Like Klein, Winnicott speaks of the internal world when referring to an internalisation process. This process allows one to be a subjective "I", and have a self-contained dialogue with one's internal world, manifesting in states of solitude. Winnicott writes,

> In this language [Kleinian language] one finds oneself referring to an earlier stage in the individual's development than that at which the classical Oedipus complex holds sway. Nevertheless a considerable degree of ego maturity is being assumed. The integration of the individual into a unit is assumed, otherwise there would be no sense in making reference to the inside and the outside, or in giving special significance to the fantasy of the inside. In negative terms: there must be a relative freedom from persecutory anxiety. In positive terms: the good internal objects are in the individual's personal inner world, and are available for projection at a suitable moment.
>
> . . . First there is the word 'I', implying much emotional growth. The individual is established as a unit. Integration is a fact. The external world is repudiated and an internal world has become possible. (1958, pp. 417–418)

Here, Winnicott is certainly in dialectical relationship to Klein, because he refers to an internal world. Unlike Klein, however, Winnicott does not associate this internal world with *innate* psychic fantasies, or even with innate psychic structure predisposed to psychic fantasy as a basic grammar of the mind. (See Ogden, 1986 on

Chomsky's innate neurological blueprint for linguistics, as well as its comparison to innate psychic fantasy proposed by Klein.)

Winnicott speaks of an internal world of good object relations that can only develop through the internalisation of a good enough maternal presence. It is this kind of internal world that promotes solitude, and thus, by implication, can result in loneliness when good object internalisation is not adequate. Growth enhancing internalisations are based on the psychic dialectic between the introjection of the "good" and the assimilation of the "bad" object through symbolic understanding of its derivation and of the impulse towards sadomasochistic enactment that it triggers. The achievement of such psychic dialectic is a developmental achievement, which requires both the good enough mothering presence of Winnicott and the self-digesting psychic capacity of Klein. The self-digesting psychic capacity of Klein assimilates and neutralises hostile aggression, so that it can reach a symbolic level through psychic fantasy. In Bion's (1962, 1963, 1970) terms, protosymbolic beta elements are transformed into alpha elements, while the latter are symbolised psychic fantasies, which can be communicated through language, and which can be interpreted by the analyst in psychoanalysis.

A case vignette related to the loneliness vs. solitude dialectic in Doris

The dialectic of loneliness and solitude, derived from the original writings of Klein and Winnicott, becomes a poignant developmental struggle in psychotherapy patients. For Doris, the struggle was an agony that transformed into her creative individuation. Her case illustrates the fruitful clinical contributions of Klein and Winnicott, when viewed as dialectic, in developmental terms. Doris describes her agony as painful attempts to spend time separately from her boyfriend, to lessen the pressure on her relationship with him. (Doris does not have any structured work at the weekends, while her boyfriend undertakes many independent projects and would like to be free to do them on his own.) Doris tries to explore her desires to create within an area of solitude. Instead of solitude, however, she experiences the pain of emptiness. In fact, she feels a depressed mother inside of her, rather than the alive presence. She never had the "good enough"

Winnicottian mother who was alive within herself, alive within her body self, present with her in childhood for her own internalisation process, as Winnicott describes it. Consequently, Doris could not internalise her mother's presence to help her in times of separation, to engender an area of creative solitude. The following session involves a lengthy monologue from Doris, when she is right in the centre of the poignant pain of loneliness. She cries and sobs throughout the entire session as she speaks of this erupting pain from within.

Doris: I don't have my own interests to go to, no favourite things or things for pleasure that I could have alone. I'm only trying to spend time apart from Henry because I think I should do it! I don't want to do it! I don't have my things! I don't look forward to doing anything! I end up doing the laundry.

Henry has all these things he wants to do! He feels like there's so little time and never enough time to do all that he wants to do. He has so many projects and so many things he wishes he could plan to do! For him the world is a rich full place, but for me it's all dull and dark without him. It's only when I'm with him that I feel alive and like I can have pleasure in anything. It's what we do together that enlivens me. When I try to be alone to find what I might take pleasure in separate from him I just feel dull and depressed—empty. I end up doing the laundry because nothing seems interesting or exciting without him. Once I've told him I want to spend some time by myself to try and find my inner desires I collapse. I fill up the void by doing practical things, like my mother did. She did those things all the time. Life was doing the laundry to her.

I go through the motions of doing the laundry just like she did. She was depressed, but except for a few times when she really broke down after my father died, she would push herself through all her obligatory tasks and get through the day that way.

I realise now, after demanding that you be tuned into me every second, that my mother couldn't tune into me because she was too preoccupied with all the things she had to get done, and preoccupied with her depression. If I played I played alone, and felt anxious and lonely. Only when I did school work did I get her attention. So now I can function at work. But while I'm alone, I feel empty and depressed, just like she was. I fill the void with perfunctory tasks like laundry and vacuuming like she did. What a dreary day!

I tried the drawing classes for a brief time. But unless Henry shares in my drawing by watching me while drawing, I still feel empty. I can never feel like this is something I really desire to do on my own. Only when Henry would come and photograph the drawings would I feel like I could enjoy what I did.

I also can sometimes look forward to decorating and designing things in my house, but all that only comes alive for me when others come over to my house to see what I've done. I can't feel it for myself. Henry's presence also makes it possible, even if he is in another room reading or working on his projects. If he's not there, I can't even feel that small degree of desire I feel to do things on my own around the house to make it look nice. I end up spending the time filled with anxieties about whether he's all right, terrified he won't be home and I'll never see him again. Those anxieties have lessened a little bit with this therapy. Now I can think of our therapy sessions and remember that you will be there again when I come to therapy. When I can grasp and sustain you in my mind, and not kill you off with my rage because you're not there to rescue me when Henry is gone, I can at least do the laundry and not feel like I'm going to jump out of my skin with anxiety. But I still feel depressed.

I ask myself, 'Why am I doing this?' I'm only doing it because I think I should so that there isn't too much pressure on Henry to be with me and to not do his things. I do it so that our relationship doesn't suffer from the tension between us of me holding on to him, but it's no fun! I'm in agony the whole time. I'm lonely! I don't enjoy being alone! I don't know how anyone could like it. I either feel depressed or filled with anxiety and rage. I have to protect Henry from the rage when he comes home because I want to rip and tear him apart! I want to kill him!

At least now I have you. I do feel better after I open my agony up to you, telling you how it is and crying with you. I know you've helped me and I've told you I feel grateful. It came from a deep place when I said that. I'm beginning to allow myself to feel close to you in here, and gradually it is making a difference in the in-between times when I'm alone. It's only because I know I can come here that I've risked asking Henry to let me be by myself sometimes, after he's away at a conference for example. Rather than spend the whole time waiting for him and feeling terrified he won't return I asked him to stay in his house, and to let me finish the weekend alone at my home. I only could do this because I knew I'd be seeing you for a session the next day.

I've finally surrendered all my ways of pushing you away with distrust. I've finally accepted that the disappointment I feel with you is because you can't possibly be totally focused on me every single second like I crave! I still want you there every single second. I still get enraged if I think you look away or look sleepy. But gradually I'm coming to trust that you'll be back. Gradually I'm seeing that you've been with me a lot, a real lot. Maybe it's enough for me to begin to trust that you are here, and that I can have you with me when I cry and rage from this place of lonely emptiness inside of me.

Analyst: If you let me in emotionally, to join you in that empty, depressed, and lonely place, you can begin to feel another is there with you. Then when you're actually alone you can feel me being with you. Gradually this can bring yourself alive when you are alone so that solitude can replace loneliness. You'll still be alone, but I'll be alive inside of you, and you won't have to be alone with your dead, depressed mother inside.

Doris: Yes. Maybe then I can do something besides the laundry. Maybe I can do something I enjoy—if I don't have to become my mother because there's nobody else with me inside. You'll be there even when Henry is not there outside.

Doris was only able to achieve this level of surrender in allowing me into her internal psychic space by first going through many phases expressing persecutory fears in relation to me as the analyst. She herself articulated her beginning ability to surrender after having harboured many suspicions of the analyst, which she agreed were, at least in part, resistances to allowing closeness, which she both craved and feared. Doris was suspicious that I was "not there" in various ways, which she articulated in terms of fears of me being bored with her, or being self-preoccupied, or being indifferent. Such fears, when voiced in therapy, allowed Doris to become less lonely, as her inner ghosts took symbolic form and allowed for connection with the one she feared through communication. In expressing her transferential fears, Doris also was able to associate to memories of her mother's depressed self-preoccupation and indifference. Certainly, she came to trust me through this process of "detoxifying" her persecutory fantasies. Then she could surrender and let me inside, so that she could develop her capacities for solitude and, thus, for self-growth.

It is in keeping with Melanie Klein's thinking that Doris had to become conscious of her negative transference fantasies with its aspect of her aggressive impulses and retaliatory fantasies towards the analyst. Only then could Doris surrender to trusting the analyst to be a "good object", someone who could be related to and who could understand her. Through relating to the analyst, Doris internalised developmentally enhancing object relationships that would build her sense of self. In other words, she psychologically developed an internal psychic structure based on symbolic representations within her internal world.

The clinical case of Semantha

Like Doris, Semantha struggled with her own agony of her need to tolerate being alone, as she decided to leave an early marriage. The alternating feelings of loneliness *vs.* the self growing in solitude are seen in this more extensive case example.

When first entering psychoanalytic object relations treatment, Semantha was twenty-four years old. She was on the verge of leaving a young marriage, and spoke of feeling the need to be single. Yet, she felt highly dependent on her husband, whom she had known since her early teens. She told the analyst that at sixteen, she fell madly in love with this man, but over the years she felt herself growing apart from him. She was seeking some kind of artistic direction and her husband, a young investment banker, was becoming increasingly conservative.

Semantha had studied art and literature. She loved writing and dancing. Her husband did not dance, and he did not take time to read or understand her writing. She spoke of feeling very alone. She thought of going to graduate school, but she was not sure what direction she was going in. Mostly, she yearned for a time when she had studied in Northern Italy. She was afraid to give up the security of her marriage. Yet, Semantha felt stifled within the marriage, in which she was entrenched in financial dependence on her husband. She was indecisive about how to proceed to live on her own. Semantha turned to psychotherapy at a point when she felt torn apart by being taken care of in one minute, and being highly constricted and suffocated by her husband's protective control over her in the next minute. She chose a psychoanalytic approach, where she could examine her highly vivid dream-life.

Hesitant to reveal herself, however, Semantha had a tendency to exhibit her dreams more than to analyse them. Yet, within this exhibitionistic impulse, was a profound desire to express herself and to be truly known. She had rarely been listened to as a child, particularly by her mother. Her exhibitionism seemed to be a protective defence against the fear that if she were to be heard and seen, she would be ripped apart by criticism. She did, in fact, carry within her a highly critical mother, which was a substantial part of her real childhood mother.

Semantha had a dream about the threat of being torn to shreds by a monstrous Chinese bulldog, which sat on top of the gate that confined her in her mother's sphere, and, transferentially, in her husband's sphere. This dream told the story of her wish to escape captivity in a world ruled by her mother. The theme of this dream was now being played out in her early marriage with her childhood sweetheart, whom she had reluctantly let become her husband. So, Semantha was in a dilemma. She wished to be heard and seen, which meant separating from her mother, but her dependence on her mother (or her husband) made her terrified of exposing herself. Because her mother had been internalised as a malevolent critic, who would rip and tear her apart, as in the dream image of the Chinese bulldog with its giant teeth, separating from the external mother could never release her. This was true for the transferential mother that she found in her husband, too. Leaving him could never resolve the psychological enmeshment with her mother. Part of Semantha knew that leaving her husband would not cure her of the inhibiting and sometimes paralysing fears. Nevertheless, her need to leave him, in conflict with her sometimes nightmarish fears of doing so, kept her poised at a point of agonising indecision.

Semantha's initial way of dealing with this indecision was to find another man whom she hoped could release her. She hoped that this other man would lead her to have the confidence to be on her own. Her fantasy was that he could see the emerging woman in her, and that he would see the artist in her that needed to express herself and who had the talent to do so. Semantha was terrified of an encroaching loneliness that was increasing within her marriage as she craved escape. She yearned for a creative solitude, while her inner world pressured for some form of overt expression in the external world. So, she used her encounter with this new man, Paul, as a pivotal point from which to lunge off her home base and make what felt like a death-daring break with her husband. The psychological power of Paul seemed totally related to her need to use him for an external point of motivation. In fact, she only spent a week with him, although she hoped and fantasised that he would return to her. In that week's time, she saw herself differently through his eyes. She projected her own views through his eyes, but in reality, he also looked at her with an adoring admiration for her self-expressive abilities. Since Paul was new in her life, he had not yet been tainted with the projected image of the critical and emotionally elusive mother.

Paul had moved to another country and was only visiting New York, although he had originally been born in that city. At moments, his adoration made both Semantha and him believe that he might return. Yet, Semantha knew that such a hope was precarious. Some part of her knew that she would have to face her fears and her internal demons on her own. Nevertheless, she managed to use her brief encounter with this male mystery figure to propel her decision to leave her husband and to try to face the world as a young single woman, outside the external sphere of both her mother and her husband. Only in solitude could Semantha find the place within herself, where her faith in her own strength resided.

Semantha captured this moment of conflict over loneliness *vs.* solitude on paper. She gave it to me so that I, as her analyst, could understand her decision to leave her husband. Since I did not want her to split off from our sessions the part of herself that she put in her writing, I asked her to read me the seven-page piece out loud within a session, where we both could experience it and inhabit it together. The following is the piece of self-reflective writing she read to me. It came back to me in writing this chapter on Klein's "loneliness" and Winnicott's "solitude", because it is Semantha's "capacity to be alone" that first emerges for her in this writing. The writing also vividly displays the ways that Semantha both wards off and challenges her fears of loneliness. Her writing exposes the haunting persecutory and depressive fantasy presences within her internal world.

Semantha writes and reads a piece of self-expression that she names, "In the Night". It reads as follows.

Under the skylight window—I lay bare and pensive, taken up by the hush of the pre-dawn atmosphere. The surrounding darkness was invaded by precocious light rays, or perhaps by last fledglings of moonlight. All seemed still. I rolled over on the big purple and gay colored, fat and succinctly stuffed pillows, and gazed with remembrances at the sleeping male beside me.

Was it my fate to acquire or maybe to merely yearn for a male muse? I would create great works, not babies (?) A bead of sweat ran down his chest, a glistening streak with the light's reflection. I rolled over with an itchy awareness of more than the night's heat. This was not paradise! A roach crossed the wooden boarded floor. I wondered if I could sleep at all on these pillows. I kept sliding off. Feather-stuffed pillows, like dreams of cotton, are poor platforms for equilibrium.

There was space around us, the open space of hollowed out dance studios—all walls, ceilings, and floors. These were the seductive sirens. They set the atmosphere of a gap waiting to be filled, an abyss waiting to be leveled, a landscape waiting to be painted. I felt shivers of moist sweat turning into tingling dry chills. The silence suddenly became audible.

My eyes shut momentarily, and prisms of color obliterated the straight, clear light rays of out there. The prism melted into forms now. Narrow sunbaked stucco streets, mellowed with the aging hues of time-worn books filled the optical void. What was so terribly haunting about memories and visions of Northern Italy?

Suddenly the narrow durations would burst into large rhomboid or square piazzas. Columned arcades with terracotta pilasters would surge forth into sculptured fountains, and cobblestoned paths would lead to secret places. Stolid Romanesque fortresses stood guard over spots where the laced delicacy of candy land towers flaunted their fragile pride. The oscillating variety was everywhere. Was it true that merchants and blood thirsty papal villains were patrons for the arts?

I leaned over to touch him. He did not wake. I slid my finger over his gently locked eyelids. His lashes brushed me subtly. My own eyes shut away again into images. Florence became a tactile phantom now, speaking in architectural embraces, with rhythmic dynamic. There were the stable pediments of classical adaptation, and the harmonious combination of rounds and angles that solidified hope in the Renaissance. But then there were the propelled imbalances too—the cry for heroic fates of over-expenditure that enflamed the otherwise static refinement. Such was the contrast. Was it creativity or was it decadence insidiously seeping through the membrane of our civilisation?

I looked out into the street. The street lights glared into darkness, mirroring the blinding stare of those threatened by dethroned myths. The sidewalks were empty. The blackened corners of misplaced cornices on the building across the street mocked the art of chiaroscuro contrast. A police siren pierced the air. This was not Florence . . .

I felt chilly, but restless still. I walked back inside and looked at Paul. He lay so casually strewn now, his arm languidly arched upward in a frame around his head, his head tilted back in a seeming ecstasy of oblivion, one black curl dangling on his forehead. If he were blond I could compare him to Christ, I thought, deep in the enthrallment of spiritual passion, etched in white marble by Michelangelo. But he wasn't blond. His hair was black. Perhaps Jesus' hair might have been black, but the symbolic image portrayed was always blond. He kicked his leg slightly.

I found myself walking in circles, with sudden impulses to twirl a few times. How young had I been when I learned to spot with my eyes when I did turns? It was supposed to stop you from getting dizzy, but somehow tonight my last turn would always end abruptly with a backward lurch. That blew the whole thing. Well, was I going to dance?

Can this rhythm go on interminably? I'm long drawn out phrases with short stops at the end.

Paul said he believed in me. In which "me" did he believe? In the dancer me, in the lover me, the person me, or in the professional me that could show up for work? And if he believed in all of them as he claimed, why had he created as an excuse to run from me, to run from ending up as an inspiration, or perhaps running from fighting that?

I lay down and two images paraded my consciousness. They settled side by side, in a bleakly unholy alliance. One was of a stately woman in white, seated in long luxurious robes on a wooden throne, demurely straight of posture, banging on a drum. Seated around her, on the floor, were her students: disciples of her art, salesmen of her pride. They watched her attentively. The other image had the same face, the same persona, but hardly the same spirit. It was of a little old lady, dressed all in black, sitting alone in a booth at a delicatessen, slumped slightly over her plateful of potato knish. She was Jewish but had changed her name for the stage when she was still young enough to dance for the public, and there she was sneaking a knish on the sly. It's funny that she was so proud of keeping her nose that was slightly crooked after she fell on it as a child. Why the name change then? There were all kinds of plastic surgery. Was I to be one of these split female images myself? I could age into a dichotomous mixture of the sublime and the pathetic, the regal and the defenseless: a Zelda Fitzgerald, a Martha Graham.

I began to envision myself at fifteen: running, running, running, down a long dirt-pebbly road—down to the lake or off to the woods—anywhere to escape what felt like the horrendous hoards, the barbarian mass, those with standing-room-only at gladiator jousts. It was camp, the summer of my 15th year, truly the eternal summer. I spent most of it searching for secret pockets of solitude. Sometimes it washed over me like a wave of perennial torture, engulfing me, annihilating me, asphyxiating me—all those adolescent girls I seemed surrounded by day and night. But late, late at night, when everyone else was asleep, I tenderly prized the darkness and peace of my own bed. I lay awake to take hold of it, to feel the enchantment of my own consciousness, the endearing spaciousness of my own identity, even cramped as it was into a tiny bunk-bed, in a corner of a wooden shack. The navel of the night was always a special time for me.

It was that summer also that I danced to preserve the life inside of me from the threat of invasion. Dance had always been a route for me, but that summer it began to be a sacred safety-valve, a form through which the fountain inside of me could be expressed. I danced in the proverbial moonlight before I knew it was proverbial. Night after night I would improvise, sometimes alone, but often with the swimming counselor, who was engaged to the dance counselor, who was not such a great dancer—ruined probably by technique. He said I had a panther-like body. He said that I seemed like an inhabitant of Scarsdale. Was it for him I became a senior lifesaver?

That summer lives hauntingly inside of me for many reasons. I played the dance lead in Finian's Rainbow. I painted still-life in Arts and Crafts, while all my bunk-mates scorned it to play volleyball. Periodically, on erratic days off, I would be driven off in the fiery coach of my friend-soon to be boyfriend—eventually to be husband. He must have worked in a camp that was at least two hours away, but to the dismay of all who happened on the path of his speedy vehicle, he seemed to reappear—my rescuer, my Sir Lancelot. Yet, none of this is engraved so impermeably on my brain as is the one phrase granted to me as a gift by my counselor of that year. As babes speak profundities so did the blithering Polonius speak truth when he first said it to Laertes, and so did Pat as she said it to me: "To thine own self be true." To this day, for all my futzing around and squirming in all directions, I still follow the pied piper who declares this.

The rays of light broadened and streamed more now. I stood in patches of shadow. Soon Paul would wake and we would spend our last day together. How would I deal with the questions he raised for me when he left?

The other night I dreamed of Paul, up on a chair, giving me themes for dance improvisations. We were on the roof of this building, and I began dancing, first to the theme of "direction," and then to the theme of "no direction." As I took off on the second, my toes brushing over the brownish-red roof tiles, the railing on the roof disappeared. I swirled from the center outward, centrifugally taken up in an unyielding tirade of circular gyration. Out further, now further, and still further until other buildings rose up in the distance—I closed my eyes with the terror that I would be smashed against them as wounded seagulls are smashed upon the rocks with a lunging tide. Yet each time the journey was done and I returned to the center, I would choose to spin out again and go even farther than the last time. Perhaps this is the infinite progression of my soul, bound like Sisyphus to an unending struggle. Yet mine is outward from the core rather than upward from the ground, and I carry no boulders, only the weight of my own body. I believe also that my path is not a repetitive treadmill, but is a path that expands in cycles.

The pain of not knowing is appeased by an almost physical sense of what is sacred and profane, or beauty and truth. Deep inside I feel the longing, the lonely abyss. The less lonely I become the more I am aware of the loneliness. There can be no definite decisions tonight, perhaps never. I only know now how much I am my own instrument for sensing an untaught religious sense, and for expressing it as an artist, but mainly as a human being. This night extends into interminable question marks, and at moments asking the right question can bring a comfort of its own, a small soft rug on a cold wooden floor.

I no longer am dreaming of empty rooms to dance in, rooms with marble floors, in a large country house. I no longer have the dream of a garden and lake by its outer edge, with me watering flowers in isolation. Is it something between us that has changed this? Perhaps I'll never know. Yet, as I see him wake as a threat and promise to me, I feel the warmth of his kiss.

As we sit side by side in a garden, seated no one knows how tentatively, seated on this last day together, seated surrounded by life, I feel a settled internal "yes." It seems to speak with an echo, but I'll never know if he hears it too.

This point of self-reflection illustrates Semantha's state of mind at a critical turning point in her young adult life, when the dialectic of loneliness and solitude was pervading her consciousness. Semantha made a decision to leave her husband after a passionate but brief week of romantic encounter with Paul, which culminated in that last night of free associative thinking in solitude, as she anticipated the loneliness to come. After fantasising Paul to be her male muse, she proceeds very quickly to speak to her husband about separating from him, and moves out of the apartment they had been living in together.

After leaving her husband, Semantha worked at a job she liked, and moved into her own apartment for the first time. However, she was emotionally in a suspended animation, as she waited for the muse to return to her. He never did, but perhaps it is fortuitous, as Semantha now turned to psychoanalysis. I became her psychoanalyst, which allowed me to be there as both a witness and a transitional object, when she repeatedly collapsed on the couch in grief. Her grief travelled miles back in her history, as it also travelled deep into the sealed-off core of pain inside her, and into the memories within her psyche.

Semantha's anguish began to erupt as she realised that she had left behind so much, while not knowing what the future brings. She had shut the door on all the financial and emotional security that her husband had provided. She also left behind the fantasy of a "happy-ever-after" life married to her first love. Looking back, Semantha began to recall that at fifteen and sixteen, when madly in love with the younger version of her husband, all she had wanted was to get married and be a mother. She fantasised babies then, as she now fantasised great works as a writer. Now her head swirled with dreams, plans, and fantasies. She felt full of inspiration following every painful piece of mourning related to her life losses and separations. Crying, wailing, and sobbing on the couch, due to her heart breaking from the loss of the fantasy love she dreamed of, first with her husband as a boyfriend, and then later with Paul as her male muse, Semantha always woke up to new modes of creative thought and creative desire. As Semantha faced her losses on the analytic couch, she found out that the loss of her husband was only the tip of the iceberg.

Underneath the agony and grief she felt for the loss of her husband was the most powerful grief—over herself. It was the grief of the loss of her father who died when she was young. In a dream, she found herself trying to resurrect her father's body, as it slipped under the water in the ocean and drowned. She tried to pull the body up to the surface and tried to carry it to the shore. However, her father's body was too heavy for her. It slipped out of her grasp and washed away under the ocean's water, again and again. Not in her dreams or in her life had she been able to succeed at rescuing either him or the heart that had failed him.

Other losses lay in the underbelly of her unconscious. Even beyond the lost husband and dead father, the losses were acutely felt as abandonment, from the period of her toddlerhood when she apparently left her mother, seeking her own autonomy. It seemed that her mother could not stand being left, and she cut off from her two-year-old daughter in unconscious retaliation. Semantha was informed of the significance of her early loss by comments her mother had made when she became an adult. Semantha would later experience this early loss on the couch during the heat of her mourning process, as her mind's layers unfolded. Semantha remembered her mother offhandedly saying, "You were so independent. At two years old, you went on your own and never came back." Semantha had to question her mother's comment, looking back now. Did she not come back, or did her mother cut off from her emotionally, when she dared to walk away from her, to indulge in the normal developmental two-year-old's "love affair with the world" (Greenacre, 1957, p. 57; Mahler, 1971, p. 410)? When she returned to her mother, was her mother not there? She supposed this must have been so. Otherwise, why would she always fear abandonment? Otherwise, why would she have such dreams, where she was forced to orbit outward, to escape an internally dangerous and chaotic world, a world where she might be smashed against buildings as seagulls are smashed against rocks?

Earlier dreams in treatment also revealed to Semantha that she was somewhat severed from her bodily being. She appeared in these early dreams above her body, as if her mind and spirit were trying to transcend it. It felt that Semantha had been forced to disconnect from her body by the emotional block that protected her from the sealed-off pain at her body core. In one dream, she was on a ceiling, looking down at Paul and a girlfriend of his, unable to tolerate the terror and rage in her body as she watched the man whom she had hoped would enter her solitude with her as a male muse now being taken away from her by another woman. Tension and anxiety propelled Semantha out of the body that could not contain abandonment terror and the accompanying rage of primal object loss, which was retriggered with the retraumatisation of losing Paul. Semantha's associations brought us back to her early failure to internalise a secure connection with her mother during her childhood separation–individuation period. In her dreams, Semantha split in terror, and her spirit tried to resurrect above her body. Her spirit tried to transcend her body rather than just submit to being banished from its secure confines by waves of tension that were related to the trauma of being severed emotionally from her mother at two years old. It became clear that she could not cure herself through transcendence, since she could not connect to her body. Without this body connection, Semantha could not have a secure sense of being. Semantha learnt in treatment with me that the only route to cure was through surrendering to her grief, so that she could re-enter the central area of her body self, a place she had been blocked from by the sealed-off pain at her centre. Her unconscious dissociation was a re-enactment. She severed herself from her body, as she had been severed from her mother at two years old. She had been warding off the emotional pain in her body throughout her whole young life.

Yet, as she surrendered to her grief, supported by my presence in the moment, and as she faced the pain that would have been too intolerable to deal with on her own, Semantha started to have dreams in which she was inside her body. Another developmental trend that emerged in her dreams—Semantha was changing the image of her primal internal object, her mother. Along with her own self-integration was the self-integration of her internal mother, which evolved as she remembered the contents of her dreams in treatment. Interestingly, her dream images reflected the same split in her maternal image that she unconsciously depicted through the creative process of her literary piece, "In the Night". Just as she had seen her dance teacher divided into the regal queen as the central authority in front of her class—side by side with the memory of this same female teacher as a small lonely lady in a deli, eating a knish—so, too, in her dreams she depicted her mother in two contrasting idealised *vs.* devalued images. One dream in particular stood out in this regard, in which her mother was first seen as a patrician aristocrat lying on a lounge chair in the drawing-room of a "beaux art" mansion, and then was seen in another part of the dream as a depleted, old, depressed woman who was pushing an iron across a dress on an ironing board with great effort.

The connection to the core child self along with the integration of an internal object

This maternal image transformed into a more whole, more related, and more benign and responsive form, as the images of herself, outside her body, began to transform into images of containment within a body-self. Such self-integration occurred as Semantha faced not only the pain of her marital and parental losses, but also the pain of recognising and owning her abandoned child self.

A critical point in Semantha's treatment came on the day when she burst out crying on the couch after hearing that a homeless man had frozen to death on a bench in the park. All along, Semantha had been opening up her capacities for empathy and concern as she mourned her life losses in her treatment. This mourning process turned Semantha toward the love of her early parents, prior to the time of her mother loss at two, and prior to her later childhood and adult losses. This allowed Semantha to speak with exquisite attunement and sensitivity to the agony that she imagined this homeless man in the park to have experienced in his state of total helplessness.

In her third year of treatment on the couch, Semantha spoke through sobs and tears. She told me that she imagined this man on a park bench, frozen in a state of reaching out his hands towards a fire, as depicted in the news. Apparently, there had been a fire set by a group of homeless people who were sleeping in the park in wintertime, with nothing but newspapers for blankets. But, tragically, the fire had been blown out by the wind or had been put out by other strangers. As Semantha sobbed on the couch, I could feel her experiencing the pain of this man as he froze helplessly, trying to reach the warmth of a fire that had already been extinguished. I imagined that this homeless man must symbolise the fragile and dependent child self within Semantha's internal world. Perhaps, this was the psychic fantasy imprint of the child self that had been cut off from her mother's warmth at two years old, and that had been cut off from her father's warmth as he turned cold towards her at times, and then died.

Through grieving for another with such empathy, Semantha regained a deep sense of empathy for herself. She also could return to a core self connection, a connection with the helpless child within her internal world. This allowed Semantha to begin to love in a way that had formerly been out of reach for her, and, as she became capable of loving, she became able to internalise more love. Eventually, her time being on her own became rich.

Although sometimes still overtaken with moments of excruciating loneliness, when archaic abandonment fears raged, overall Semantha became increasingly content in states of solitude. As she did so, her capacities for relatedness to others improved. She began to date men whom she could now experience as full characters with subjective lives of their own, and for whom she could begin to feel empathy and concern. This was quite different from when she experienced men as idealised fantasy prince figures, or as male muses, who would mainly exist to facilitate her creativity.

Semantha's relationships with women changed as well. She stopped using her girlfriends as sounding boards for her gripes, woes, and exhibitionistic triumphs. She began to listen to her girlfriends. Consequently, she found that her girlfriends had interesting things to say about their lives and their experiences.

Especially important for the subject of this chapter, Semantha's growth in relatedness was accompanied by growth in her capacities to be with herself in states of solitude. Within such states of solitude, she discovered that her feelings and thoughts could evolve into creative thinking and writing. She began to realise the dream of writing as a profession, while she earned money as an editor. She had to suffer much loneliness to be able to psychologically transition into these states of solitude, where she could be alone with herself, without an outside muse or analyst. The suffering of this loneliness involved facing all the kinds of persecutory and depressive fantasies that Melanie Klein (1963) wrote about in her paper on loneliness.

Semantha's dreams depicted some of these fantasies, which involved shame and guilt, as well as terror of attack. One dream was of being on trial on a grand stage within a baseball stadium, a stadium like the ones where her father took her as a young girl. She was on trial before a stadium full of male judges dressed in black. In the middle of the trial, someone betrayed her; someone who had pretended to be speaking on her behalf. Then, the trial was interrupted, as her mother called her and she ran out to a phone booth to receive the call. She came back to the stadium sobbing, having been told by her mother on the phone that her father had just died. Her associations on the couch made it clear that she experienced her father's death as a punishment for her psychic crimes, particularly for the psychic crime of continuing to carry hate and resentment towards her mother.

Along with the mixture of paranoid and depressive fantasies, there were paranoid position fantasies of terror in the face of persecution. She dreamed that she fell into a garbage can, in the shape of a small insect, along with all the filthy and smelly garbage. She felt as if she was garbage, and was small enough to be murdered and suffocated by the garbage around her, with which she was identified. When Semantha remembered the dreams that contained these fantasies, she was able to face her worst fears. Consequently, she less often experienced these fantasies as internal demon objects that haunted her from within. Free of the fear of her internal demons, she was able to tolerate being alone with herself. Thus, she relinquished her belief that she needed a male muse to help her find her own voice for her creativity.

Semantha began to have more tranquil images in her dreams of a peaceful "low key" silence under ocean waves (the waves of her oceanic unconscious). She found peaceful shores to lie on where she could sunbathe. She found peaceful caves under the ocean. These easily could be seen as her images of solitude, having attained the capacity to be alone, after being alone with her psychoanalyst during her developmental mourning process. In fact, Semantha began to have "waking dream" fantasies while on the couch in the analyst's consulting room. She felt as if the female analyst was like a sun beaming down on her as she lay on the beach, and she felt as if she was getting a suntan. Her associations revealed that she was projecting her own newly evolving love towards the analyst on to the analyst and was experiencing her as shining this love back down at her. Of course, there were loving feelings in the analyst as well that were mixed in with her own projected love.

Semantha's experience of joy at these times followed many phases of mourning in treatment, when she would feel the grief pertaining to her early traumatic object loss, and to all the later life losses, particularly that of her father, that followed this. The uncontainable rage and terror had now been transformed, through the containment of the analyst and the holding environment, as described by Winnicott (1986), into tolerable affects of object loss. (See also Winnicott, 1974.) In this way, the analyst could also be a tranquil figure in the room with her, allowing her own "capacity to be alone" to develop.

During the years of Semantha's treatment, I observed how a "developmental mourning" process allows the analysand to develop past a precarious state of solitude that could crash into an agonising loneliness. Consequently, the analysand reaches a fruitful dialectic of solitude and relatedness. As Semantha used me, her analyst, as a transitional object to tolerate early loss in her mourning process, she then could achieve a relative degree of independence from using others as subjective objects (or "self-objects"). Having internalised better relatedness with the analyst, after opening the core of her self through mourning the critical and primal losses in her life, Semantha could relate with mutuality to others, whom she now could experience as full personalities, rather than as demons and muses. Side by side with this growth in her capacity for relatedness was Semantha's growth in her capacity for solitude, since her daily relatedness could now be internalised on a regular basis, allowing her to continually build up her internal world centre from which she drew both comfort and inspiration during states of solitude. In this way, she could feel the full aliveness of the erotic, creative, spiritual, and interpersonal aspects of herself when alone with herself. These aspects of her emerged more fully with each phase of developmental mourning in which Semantha allowed consciousness of her losses, and found insight into the meaning that each lost person had played in her life as she grieved. Consequently, the spectre of loneliness no longer threatened Semantha as in the past, when it had formerly been like a split-off demon forcing her to seek comfort from an external muse.

Loneliness in dialectic with solitude: overall conclusion

This chapter attempts to compare Klein's (1963) paper, "On the sense of loneliness", with Winnicott's (1958) paper, "The capacity to be alone", both written during the same era in the evolution of object relations psychoanalysis, the era which offers a psychologically rich dialogue between the resolution of defence against self-integration and developmental evolution through the mourning process. The overall perspective on self-integration and developmental evolution in psychoanalytic object relations treatment is seen in relation to loneliness being transformed into the capacity for solitude, with its outgrowth of pleasure and creativity. This microcosm of loneliness transforming into solitude exists in reflection of the overall macrocosm of psychic change in a progressive developmental context.

Winnicott's developmental view offers a different perspective from the defence interpretation perspective of Klein. Winnicott's "The capacity to be alone" (1958) explores the capacity for solitude. It speaks of how internalisation of the "other", which is present in a transitional (or "intersubjective") space, develops this capacity for solitude. Klein is focusing on re-owning the intrapsychic projections (which can be symbolically understood) and the paranoid and depressive fantasies related to these hostile aggressive impulse projections. For Winnicott, however, loneliness and its more extreme forms of abandonment and annihilation terrors (as in Winnicott's (1965) "unthinkable anxieties") is the consequence of failure to internalise the "good enough" mother. Winnicott's "good enough" mothering is related to *presence* of the maternal "other" during one's early childhood, when the core self, or potential "true self", is forming (Winnicott, 1953). In speaking of the analyst providing the "facilitating environment" (Winnicott, 1965) of the mother for the patient, Winnicott is speaking of a reparative form of internalisation that compensates for deficits in such internalisation during childhood. Winnicott specifically speaks of the solitude of two individuals after sexual intercourse, when their connection has been profoundly experienced and is, therefore, sustained in an internalised form to allow for the pleasure of solitude.

Winnicott's perspective is in dialectical contrast to Klein's in emphasising the developmental internalisation of a real mother in order to modify loneliness, as opposed to Klein's view on re-owning of defensive projections of aggression put into the mother to modify loneliness. Also, for Klein, loneliness is to some extent always an existential reality, although it can be modified by self-integration through psychoanalytic interpretation of defences. For Winnicott, loneliness can perhaps be alleviated by the secure internalisation of a "good enough" mothering presence that can sustain the person in the face of being alone, so that a pleasurable solitude can ensue. For Klein, the failure of the mother to be a "good object" (which can be securely integrated in the psyche) is predominantly related to innate aggression, as well as to real frustration, disappointment, and trauma in relation to the actual mother. Klein's metapsychology of the death instinct, as seen in "Envy and gratitude" (Klein, 1957), pushes her hypothesis to an extreme. I believe that Klein's "death instinct" metapsychology can be surrendered for the phenomenological truths of her clinical focus.

For Winnicott, the "going-on-being" (Winnicott, 1960a) of the self may be disrupted by internal impulses of both a sexual and an aggressive nature, with aggression due to early trauma being more primitive. Nevertheless, his overall emphasis is on the nature of the actual mother during early development, as opposed to Klein's emphasis on the child's perception of the mother in early development, as influenced by innate paranoid and depressive fantasies.

The two clinical vignettes in this chapter are chosen to illustrate dialectical interplays between loneliness and solitude in relation to the theoretical interests of Melanie Klein and Donald Winnicott. The first case vignette, of Doris, demonstrates the anguish that separation entails for someone whose age-appropriate developmental separation at two years old had been severely compromised by internalising a mother who could not allow separation. Doris feels intense conflict in trying to separate in adulthood from her primary relationship with her boyfriend. She tries to move towards a state where solitude could be tolerable or, ideally, eventually enjoyed. However, she is constantly affected with the anguish of loneliness in the process. The therapeutic relationship with an object relations analyst allows Doris to face the early loss due to a belated developmental separation–individuation process. She is able to psychically integrate her two-year-old child self by facing this loss in the "facilitating" or "holding" environment with the analyst. The analyst consequently becomes a current good enough object, which can be internalised, but only after the working through of many phases of negative transference towards the analyst.

The negative transference work includes paranoid and depressive fantasies being analysed. (NB: this analysis was not included in the session process case vignette.)

The second case is a longer vignette that includes more of a history of the patient during the transformations in treatment. By going further than the clinical movement and process of one session, we are offered insight into the evolution of a struggle around the dialectic of loneliness and solitude. The patient's own words are used to describe the longings for solitude and the agonies of loneliness through the sharing of the patient's self-reflections in a piece of creative writing. Then, dreams are described, as they illustrate the journey through the paranoid and depressive fantasies of loneliness. As these dream fantasies are analysed, this female patient also confronts various levels of primal object loss in her life, and this opens her core self to contact with the analyst, so that new "good enough" internalisations can be made.

The grief experience of many levels of object loss, along with the analysis of paranoid and depressive fantasies, and the reconnection with the core child self through grieving the loss of the child self, are all part of what this author describes as a "developmental mourning process". This developmental mourning process includes both poles of the dialectic between Klein's clinical technique and Winnicott's developmental clinical technique. In addition, it is shown that Semantha moves towards the capacity "to be alone", or towards solitude, with tolerance for increasing states of loneliness, through the analyst's empathic attunement to all levels of grief related to object loss (and disappointment). Through her psychic presence, the analyst also receives the patient's newly developing empathic abilities. Such abilities emerge in the form of empathy with a dying man, who seems to represent a projection of the patient's internal vulnerable child self. The patient surrenders to empathy through the projection of self loss as the grief of object loss has become tolerable. Then, she is able to empathically engage with herself during periods of creative solitude, in which she develops her creative self-expression into the craft of being a professional writer. The developing capacity for empathy and for empathic engagement with her own internal child self is seen to be directly related to a "developmental mourning" process, in which critical early life losses are felt and grieved. In addition, the paranoid and depressive fantasies related to these early losses are analysed and understood.

Conclusion

T his book's theory and clinical illustrations serve to demonstrate how Melanie Klein's theories and Donald Winnicott's theories work together. A look at biographical insights on Klein's life helps us to see that although Klein's death instinct metapsychology might not be essential to understanding her phenomenological theories and their clinical applications, they could colour the impression of Klein among both professional clinicians and the general public, and often in a negative way. Therefore, to clearly view the major and fundamental contribution of Klein's thinking to our clinical work, and to help psychoanalysts and all mental health clinicians to appreciate the vast reservoirs of insights from Klein that they can benefit from in clinical practice, it is necessary to clarify that Klein's clinical theories are seen in a developmental light, distinct from any dependence on a problematic metapsychology that might have roots in Klein's own early life experience.

Klein's phenomenological theory, particularly of the paranoid–schizoid and depressive positions, and of pathological defences, which disrupt self-integration and psychic development, as well as her theories on envy and reparation, is understood in developmental terms. It offers deep mines of clinical riches that we can benefit from, without having to complicate these contributions with her instinct language and her form (different than Freud's) of a "death instinct". The kind of hostile aggression that Klein writes about, which manifests in the transferences in psychoanalytic clinical work, can mostly be accounted for in developmental terms, and can most certainly be dealt with in developmental terms in treatment, despite any innate components to the psychodynamic transactions in psychic fantasy or in this fantasy carried over to the psychoanalytic transference in treatment.

Klein's phenomenological theory that manifests in clinical situations is most consonant with this view, and, in Winnicott's terms, such theory need not be "impinged" on by a metapsychology that might have subjective roots in Klein's personal psychohistory. Klein's brilliant clinical observations are related to her clinical theory, and they can be easily framed in developmental terms. Following the phenomenology and clinical range of Klein's theories allows us to also see how freely they can interact with the clinical and developmental thinking of Winnicott. Understanding these interactions greatly enhances and enriches our possibilities as clinicians, rather than limiting us by polarising Klein and Winnicott and their theoretical perspectives.

Through the chapters in this volume of study, we have seen that Klein's theories of mourning interact with Winnicott's theories on object survival, potential and transitional space, and on the true self and developmental mirroring, as opposed to narcissistic mirroring. We have seen this in clinical cases, and in psychobiographical cases of women writers. We have seen that Klein's views of the depressive position allow us to view a case from a developmental perspective, and that her view of pathology of the paranoid–schizoid position and its defensive operations can also be attributed to developmental disruptions that promote psychic arrest in early pre-oedipal stages of mother–infant bonding.

This allows us to see how important Winnicott's view is of the external side of internal world dynamics that plays itself out in developmental terms, consonant with Klein's observations on psychic fantasy and the internal world. Winnicott's views on the foreclosure and opening of transitional space (potential space) can be seen to operate in parallel with Klein's view of internal psychic space, which expands with the depressive position capacities to process all primal and traumatic feelings of loss, guilt, rage, grief, and longing (see also

Kavaler-Adler, 2006b,c). Winnicott's views of mirroring and the responsiveness of the mother (which determines whether mirroring can be internalised as a healthy developmental function or as the mother's narcissistic intrusion) can be seen to interact with Klein's views of the needed responsiveness of the mother. Mother's responsiveness is looked at in terms of receiving gestures of reparation from the child, as opposed to promoting regressions into depression and the paranoid state from healthy mutuality and give-and-take between mother and child, which allows for healthy developmental internalisations. "Envy and gratitude" (Klein, 1957), with its earlier verbal presentation in the 1930s, was a tribute to Klein beginning to absorb the ideas on internalisation that Winnicott had been promoting. It was in this paper that she spoke of the internalisation of a "good object" experience in a therapeutic session through the "good enough" interpretations of the skilled psychoanalyst, which can be seen in parallel to the mother's part in nurturing and responding to her child in the early stages of development. Traces of this view of internalisation, with compensation for negative developmental internalisations, can be seen in Klein's (1937) paper, "Love, guilt, and reparation".

Where Klein speaks of processing aggression through reaching a symbolic level in psychoanalytic treatment, which allows for the container of psychic fantasy to be consciously constructed and understood (Klein, 1940), Winnicott (1953, 1968) speaks of aggression that is too primitive to be symbolised, and which must be tolerated in a form of enactment (as in "object survival" and "the use of the object") by character disordered "false self" patients. Both theorists give us insights into how dissociated and/or repressed aggression results in a failure of true and authentic self-development. Winnicott focuses on how spontaneity and play are blocked. Klein focuses on how mourning, loss, separation, and, therefore, love, are blocked. Both are speaking about characteristics of true *vs.* false self-development. Both theorists address character defences that result when true self-development is blocked, going beyond the neurotic forms of defences written about by Sigmund and Anna Freud. Klein and Winnicott both see how character defences represent re-enactments of early primal dysfunctions in mothering, or in the child's reactions to, and interpretations of, that mothering.

In the area of loneliness in dialectic with solitude (see Chapter Ten), Klein and Winnicott are again brought together, as Winnicott's view of the internalisation of the benign aspects of the mother's presence in the creation of the "capacity to be alone" is seen as interactive with the states of mothering that leave the child lonely, with consequent re-lived states of *loneliness* throughout life. Klein herself experienced much loneliness in her states of depression, and tried to resolve them with intense commitment to her work, as both a theorist and teacher, and as a clinician. She was, therefore, very sensitive to states of loneliness in her patients, and to how defences against aggressive psychic fantasies toward the transferential mother played a part in promoting such loneliness. On the other side of the dialectic, Winnicott's capacity to be alone allows for the healthy state of solitude, in which love and creativity could be sustained. To polarise Klein and Winnicott here would be to polarise loneliness and solitude, rather than seeing the dialectic between them, with the clinical dimensions related to this dialectic. Loneliness is never cured, but it becomes increasingly tolerable as the capacity to be alone in states of fruitful and peaceful "solitude" is enhanced through the developmental impact of treatment, and through the interpretation of defences against feelings and impulses, not the least of which is aggression.

This book stands as a testament to the fruitful enrichment of our thinking and practice, as we continue to integrate the contributions of Melanie Klein and Donald Winnicott: for example, integration of Winnicottian "capacity for concern" side by side with Melanie Klein's depressive position capacities for empathy and understanding that emerge through the ability to own one's aggression, and to tolerate loss, guilt, and grief.

REFERENCES

Alexander, R. P. (1997). Some notes on the origin of despair and its relationship to destructive envy. *Journal of Melanie Klein and Object Relations, 15*(3): 417–440.

Alvarez, A. (1971). *The Savage God: A Study of Suicide.* London: Penguin.

Bach, S. (1985). *Narcissistic States and Therapeutic Process.* Northvale, NJ: Jason Aronson.

Bach, S. (1994). *The Language of Perversion and the Language of Love.* Northvale, NJ: Jason Aronson.

Bach, S. (2005). *Getting from Here to There.* Hillsdale, NJ: Analytic Books.

Balint, M. (1965). *Primary Love and Psychoanalytic Technique.* London: Butler and Tanner.

Balint, M. (1979). *The Basic Fault.* New York: Brunner-Mazel.

Beebe, B., & Lachmann, F. M. (1988). The contribution of mother–infant mutual influence to the origins of self and object representations. *Psychoanalytic Psychology, 5*(4): 305–337.

Beebe, B., & Stern, D. (1977). Engagement–disengagement and early object experiences. In: M. Freedman & S. Grand (Eds.), *Communicative Structures and Psychic Structure* (pp. 35–55). New York: Plenum.

Bell, Q. (1972). *Virginia Woolf: A Biography.* New York: Harcourt Brace Jovanovich.

Bion, W. R. (1959). Attacks on linking. *International Journal of Psychoanalysis, 40*: 308–315.

Bion, W. R. (1962). *Learning from Experience*. London: Tavistock.

Bion, W. R. (1963). *Elements of Psychoanalysis*. London: Heinemann.

Bion, W. R. (1970). *Attention and Interpretation*. London: Tavistock [reprinted London: Karnac, 1984].

Bollas, C. (1987). *The Shadow of the Object: Psychoanalysis of the Unthought Known*. London: Free Association Books.

Bond, A. H. (1989). *Who Killed Virginia Woolf? A Psychobiography*. New York: Human Sciences.

Boris, H. N. (1990). Identification with a vengeance. *International Journal of Psychoanalysis, 71*: 127–140.

Bowlby, J. (1969). *Attachment and Loss: Volume 1: Attachment*. London: Hogarth Press and the Institute of Psychoanalysis.

Bowlby, J. (1980). *Attachment and Loss: Volume III: Loss, Sadness and Depression*. London: Hogarth Press and the Institute of Psychoanalysis.

Brontë, E. (1908). *The Complete Poems of Emily Brontë*. London: Hodder & Stoughton.

Butscher, E. (1976). *Sylvia Plath: Method and Madness*. New York: Seabury Press.

Caper, S. (1988). *Klein*. Northvale, NJ: Jason Aronson.

Cody, J. (1971). *After Great Pain: The Inner Life of Emily Dickinson*. Boston, MA: Harvard University Press.

Coltrera, J. (Ed.) (1981). *Lives, Events, and Other Players: Directions in Psychobiography*. New York: Jason Aronson.

De Salvo, L. (1989). *Virginia Woolf, the Impact of Childhood Sexual Abuse in Her Life and Work*. New York: Ballantine Books.

Dickinson, E. (1960). *The Complete Poems of Emily Dickinson*, T. M. Johnson (Ed.). Boston, MA: Little, Brown.

Fairbairn, W. R. D. (1952). *Psychoanalytic Studies of the Personality*. London: Tavistock.

Fonagy, P., Gergely, G., Jurist, E. L., & Target, M. (2000). *Affect Regulation, Mentalization and the Development of the Self*. New York: Other Press.

Freud, A. (1936). *The Ego and the Mechanisms of Defense*. New York: International Universities Press.

Freud, S. (1905d). *Three Essays on the Theory of Sexuality*. S.E., 7: 125–245. London: Hogarth.

Freud, S. (1915c). Instincts and their vicissitudes. S.E., *14*: 111–140. London: Hogarth.

Freud, S. (1917e). Mourning and melancholia. S.E., *14*: 239–258. London: Hogarth.

Freud, S. (1920g). *Beyond the Pleasure Principle. S.E., 18:* 7–64. London: Hogarth.

Freud, S. (1927e). Fetishism. *S.E., 21:* 152–158. London: Hogarth.

Freud, S. (1940a). *An Outline of Psychoanalysis. S.E., 23:* 141–207. London: Hogarth.

Gerin, W. (1971). *Emily Brontë: A Biography.* New York: Oxford University Press.

Glendinning, V. (1981). *Edith Sitwell, A Unicorn among Lions.* New York: Alfred A. Knopf.

Glover, E. (1945). Examination of the Klein system of child psychology. *Psychoanalytic Study of the Child, 1:* 75–118.

Gordon, L. (1984). *Virginia Woolf, A Writer's Life.* New York: W. W. Norton.

Greenacre, P. (1957). The childhood of the artist: libidinal phase development and giftedness. *Psychoanalytic Study of the Child, 12:* 47–72.

Grosskurth, P. (1986). *Melanie Klein: Her World and Her Work.* New York: Knopf.

Grotstein, J. S. (1996). Bion's "transformation in 'O'", "the thing-in-itself" and the "real": toward the concept of the "transcendent position". *Journal of Melanie Klein and Object Relations, 14:* 109–141.

Guntrip, H. (1968). *Schizoid Phenomena, Object-Relations and the Self.* London: Hogarth.

Heimann, P. (1950). On countertransference. *International Journal of Psychoanalysis, 31:* 81–84.

Horner, A. J. (1984). *Object Relations and the Developing Ego in Therapy.* New York: Jason Aronson.

Horner, A. J. (2005). *Dealing with Resistances in Psychotherapy.* Lanham, MD: Jason Aronson.

Isaacs, S. (1943). The nature and function of phantasy. *International Journal of Psychoanalysis, 29:* 3–97.

Joseph, B. (1989). *Psychic Equilibrium and Psychic Change: Selected Papers of Betty Joseph,* M. Feldman & E. Bott Spillius (Eds.). London: Routledge

Kahr, B. (1996). *D. W. Winnicott: A Biographical Portrait.* London: Karnac.

Kaplan, L. (1991). *Female Perversions: The Temptations of Emma Bovary.* New York: Talese/Doubleday.

Kavaler-Adler, S. (1985). Mirror, mirror on the wall . . . *Journal of Comprehensive Psychotherapy, 5:* 1–38.

Kavaler-Adler, S. (1986). Lord of the mirrors and the demon lover. *American Journal of Psychoanalysis, 48*(4): 366–370.

Kavaler-Adler, S. (1987). Nightmares and object relations theory. In: H. Kellerman (Ed.), *Nightmares: Biological and Psychological Foundations* (pp. 33–57). New York: Columbia University Press.

Kavaler-Adler, S. (1988). Diane Arbus and the demon lover. *American Journal of Psychoanalysis, 48*(4): 366–370.

Kavaler-Adler, S. (1989). Anne Sexton and the demon lover. *American Journal of Psychoanalysis, 49*(2): 105–114.

Kavaler-Adler, S. (1990). Charlotte Bronte and the feminine self. *American Journal of Psychoanalysis, 50*(1): 37–43.

Kavaler-Adler, S. (1991a). Emily Dickinson and the subject of seclusion. *American Journal of Psychoanalysis, 51*(1): 21–38.

Kavaler-Adler, S. (1991b). Some more speculations on Anna O. *American Journal of Psychoanalysis, 51*(2): 161–171.

Kavaler-Adler, S. (1991c). Object relations insights concerning the female as artist. In: E. Segal (Ed.), *Psychoanalytic Perspectives on Women*. Monograph No. 4 in *Current Issues in Psychoanalytic Practice* (pp. 100–120). New York: Brunner Mazel.

Kavaler-Adler, S. (1991d). A theory of creative process reparation and its mode of failure: the case of Katherine Mansfield. *Psychoanalysis and Psychotherapy, 9*(20): 134–150.

Kavaler-Adler, S. (1992a). Mourning and erotic transference. *International Journal of Psychoanalysis, 73*(3): 527–539.

Kavaler-Adler, S. (1992b). The aging decline of two untreated borderline geniuses: Virginia Woolf and Edith Sitwell. *Psychoanalysis and Psychotherapy, 9*(2): 134–150.

Kavaler-Adler, S. (1992c). The conflict and process theory of Melanie Klein. *American Journal of Psychotherapy, 53*(3): 187–204.

Kavaler-Adler, S. (1992d). Anaïs Nin and the developmental use of the creative process. *Psychoanalytic Review, 79*(1): 73–88.

Kavaler-Adler, S. (1993a). *The Compulsion to Create: A Psychoanalytic Study of Female Artists*. London: Routledge. Third edition published as *The Compulsion to Create: Women Writers and Their Demon Lovers*. New York: ORI Academic Press, 2013.

Kavaler-Adler, S. (1993b). Object relations issues in the treatment of the preoedipal character. *American Journal of Psychoanalysis, 53*(1): 19–34.

Kavaler-Adler, S. (1995). Opening up blocked mourning in the preoedipal character. *American Journal of Psychoanalysis, 55*(2): 145–168.

Kavaler-Adler, S. (1996). *The Creative Mystique: From Red Shoes Frenzy to Love and Creativity*. London: Routledge [reprinted New York: ORI Academic Press, 2013].

Kavaler-Adler, S. (1998). Vaginal core or vampire mouth: the visceral level of envy in women: the protosymbolic politics of object relations. In: N. Burke (Ed.), *Gender and Envy* (pp. 221–238). London: Routledge.

Kavaler-Adler, S. (2000). The divine, the deviant, and the diabolical. A journey through an artist's paintings during her participation in a creative process group an evolution of "developmental mourning". *International Forum of Psychoanalysis, 9*: 97–111.

Kavaler-Adler, S. (2003a). Lesbian homoerotic transference in dialectic with developmental mourning: on the way to symbolism from the protosymbolic. *Psychoanalytic Psychology, 20*(1): 131–152 [reprinted in J. Schaverien (Ed.), *Gender, Countertransference, and Erotic Transference* (pp. 157–183). London: Routledge, 2006].

Kavaler-Adler, S. (2003b). *Mourning, Spirituality and Psychic Change: A New Object Relations View of Psychoanalysis.* London: Brunner-Routledge.

Kavaler-Adler, S. (2004). Anatomy of regret: a developmental view of the depressive position and a critical turn toward love and creativity in the transforming schizoid personality. *American Journal of Psychoanalysis, 64*(1): 39–76.

Kavaler-Adler, S. (2005a). The case of David: nine years on the couch for sixty minutes, once a week. *American Journal of Psychoanalysis, 65*: 103–134.

Kavaler-Adler, S. (2005b). From benign mirror to the demon lover: an object relations view of compulsion versus desire. *American Journal of Psychoanalysis, 65*: 31–52.

Kavaler-Adler, S. (2006a). My graduation is my mother's funeral: transformation from the paranoid–schizoid to the depressive position in fear of success, and the role of the internal saboteur. *International Forum of Psychoanalysis, 15*: 117–130.

Kavaler-Adler, S. (2006b). From neurotic guilt to existential guilt as grief: the road to interiority, agency, and compassion through mourning (Part I). *American Journal of Psychoanalysis, 66*: 239–260.

Kavaler-Adler, S. (2006c). From neurotic guilt to existential guilt as grief: the road to interiority, agency, and compassion through mourning (Part II). *American Journal of Psychoanalysis, 66*: 333–350.

Kavaler-Adler, S. (2007). Pivotal moments of surrender to mourning the parental internal objects. *Psychoanalytic Review, 94*: 763–789.

Kavaler-Adler, S. (2009). Object relations perspectives on "Phantom of the Opera" and its demon lover theme: the modern film. *American Journal of Psychoanalysis, 69*: 150–166.

Kavaler-Adler, S. (2010). Seduction, date rape, and aborted surrender. *International Forum of Psychoanalysis, 19*: 15–26.

Kavaler-Adler, S. (2013). *The Anatomy of Regret: From Death Instinct to Reparation and Symbolization through Vivid Case Studies.* London: Karnac.

Kernberg, O. (1975). *Borderline Conditions and Pathological Narcissism.* Northvale, NJ: Jason Aronson.

Kernberg, O. (1980). *Internal World and External Reality.* Northvale, NJ: Jason Aronson.

King, P., & Steiner, R. (Eds.) (1991). *The Freud–Klein Controversies 1941–1945.* London: Tavistock/Routledge.

Klein, H. S. (1974). Transference and defense in manic states. *International Journal Psychoanalysis, 55:* 261–268.

Klein, M. (1932). *The Psychoanalysis of Children.* London: Hogarth.

Klein, M. (1937). Love, guilt and reparation. In: J. Rickman (Ed.), *Love, Hate and Reparation. Psychoanalytical Epitomes,* No. 2 (pp. 37–119). London: Hogarth, 1981.

Klein, M. (1940). Mourning and its relation to manic-depressive states. *International Journal of Psychoanalysis, 21,* 125–153 [reprinted in *The Writings of Melanie Klein,* Vol. 1, 1975].

Klein, M. (1946). Notes on some schizoid mechanisms. *International Journal of Psychoanalysis, 27:* 99–110.

Klein, M. (1957). *Envy and Gratitude and Other Works (1946–1963).* London: Tavistock.

Klein, M. (1963). On the sense of loneliness. In: *Envy and Gratitude, and Other Works 1921–1945* (pp. 300–313). New York: The Free Press.

Klein, M. (1975). *Love, Guilt and Reparation and Other Works 1921–1945.* London: Hogarth.

Kohut, H. (1968). The psychoanalytic treatment of narcissistic personality disorders—outline of a systematic approach. *Psychoanalytic Study of the Child, 23:* 86–113.

Kohut, H. (1971). *The Analysis of the Self.* New York: International Universities Press.

Kohut, H. (1977). *The Restoration of the Self.* New York: International Universities Press.

Laing, R. D. (1990). *The Divided Self: An Existential Study in Sanity and Madness.* London: Penguin.

Leonard, L. S. (1982). *The Wounded Woman: Healing the Father–Daughter Relationship.* Chicago, IL: Swallow Press.

Leonard, L. S. (1984). *The Father–Daughter Wound.* Boston, MA: Shambhala.

Lorenz, K. (1974). *On Aggression.* New York: Harvest Books.

Mahler, M. S. (1967). Child development and the curriculum. *Bulletin of the American Psychoanalytic Association, 23:* 876–886.

Mahler, M. S. (1971). A study of the separation–individuation process and its possible application to borderline phenomena in the psychoanalytic situation. *Psychoanalytic Study of the Child, 26:* 403–424.

Mahler, M. S. (1979). *Selected Papers of Margaret S. Mahler*. New York: Jason Aronson.

Mahler, M. S., Pine, F., & Bergmann, A. (1975). *The Psychological Birth of the Human Infant*. New York: Jason Aronson.

Masterson, J. F. (1976). *The Borderline Adult*. New York: Brunner Mazel.

Masterson, J. F. (1981). *Narcissistic and Borderline Disorders*. New York: Brunner Mazel.

Masterson, J. F. (1985). *The Real Self: A Developmental, Self, and Object Relations Approach*. New York: Brunner/Mazel.

Masterson, J. F. (2000). *The Personality Disorders: A New Look at the Developmental Self and Object Relations Approach. Theory, Diagnosis, and Treatment*. Phoenix, AZ: Zeig, Tucker, & Hiesen.

McClatchy, J. D. (Ed.) (1978). *Anne Sexton: The Artist and Her Critic*. Bloomington, IN: Indiana University Press.

Middlebrook, D. W. (1991). *Anne Sexton, Biography*. Boston, MA: Houghton Mifflin.

Modell, A. H. (1976). The holding environment and the therapeutic action of psychoanalysis. *Journal of the American Psychoanalytic Association, 24*: 285–307.

Newman, C. (Ed.) (1971). *The Art of Sylvia Plath*. Bloomington, IN: Indiana University Press.

Nicolson, N., & Trautmann, J. (Eds.). (1975). *The Letters of Virginia Woolf, Vol. 1: 1888–1912*. New York: Harcourt Brace Jovanovich.

Nin, A. (1974). *A Spy in the House of Love*. Chicago, IL: Swallow Press.

Ogden, T. (1986). *The Matrix of the Mind*. Northvale, NJ: Jason Aronson.

Ogden, T. (1994). *Subjects of Analysis*. Northvale, NJ: Jason Aronson.

Panken, S. (1987). *Lust of Creation*. Albany, NY: SUNY Press.

Phillips, A. (1988). *Winnicott*. London: Fontana.

Plath, S. (1965). *Ariel*. London: Faber & Faber.

Plath, S. (1981). *The Collected Poems*, T. Hughes (Ed.). London: Harper Perennial/HarperCollins.

Rinsley, D. B. (1982). *Borderline and Other Self Disorders: A Developmental and Object-relations Perspective*. New York: Jason Aronson.

Rinsley, D. B. (1989). *Developmental Pathogenesis and Treatment of Borderline and Narcissistic Personalities*. Northvale, NJ: Jason Aronson.

Riviere, J. (1936). A contribution to the analysis of the negative therapeutic reaction. *International Journal of Psychoanalysis, 17*: 304–320.

Rodman, F. R. (2004). *Winnicott: His Life and Work*. New York: Perseus.

Rose, P. (1978). *Woman of Letters: A Life of Virginia Woolf*. London: Oxford University Press.

Rosenfeld, H. (1971). A clinical approach to the psychoanalytic theory of the life and death instincts: an investigation into the aggressive aspects of narcissism. *International Journal of Psychoanalysis, 52*: 169–178.

Rosenfeld, H. (1987). *Impasse and Interpretations.* London: Tavistock.

Safan-Gerard, D. (1998). Bearable and unbearable guilt: a Kleinian perspective. *Psychoanalytic Quarterly, 67*: 351–378.

Salter, G., & Harper, A. (1956). *Edith Sitwell: Fire of the Mind.* New York: Vanguard.

Segal, H. (1964). *Introduction to the Work of Melanie Klein.* London: Heinemann [republished London, Hogarth, 1973, reprinted London: Karnac, 1988].

Segal, H. (1986). *The Work of Hanna Segal.* New York: Jason Aronson.

Seinfeld, J. (1990). *The Bad Object.* Northvale, NJ: Jason Aronson.

Seinfeld, J. (1991). *The Empty Core.* Northvale, NJ: Jason Aronson.

Seinfeld, J. (1993). *Holding and Interpreting.* Northvale, NJ: Jason Aronson.

Sewall, R. (1974). *The Life of Emily Dickinson.* New York: Farrar, Straus and Giroux.

Sexton, A. (1981). *The Complete Poems.* Boston, MA: Houghton Mifflin.

Silverman, M. A., & Will, N. P. (1986). Sylvia Plath and the failure of emotional self-repair through poetry. *Psychoanalytic Quarterly, 55*(1): 99–129.

Socarides, C. W. (1966). On vengeance—the desire to "get even". *Journal of the American Psychoanalytic Association, 14*: 356–375.

Spillius, E. B. (1993). Varieties of envious experience. *International Journal of Psychoanalysis, 74*: 1199–1212.

Stern, D. (1985). *The Interpersonal World of the Infant.* Northvale, NJ: Jason Aronson.

Stevenson, A. (1989). *Bitter Fame.* New York: Houghton Mifflin.

Stolorow, R., & Lachmann, F. (1980). *The Psychoanalysis of Developmental Arrests.* Madison, CT: International Universities Press.

Sutherland, J. D. (1989). *Fairbairn's Journey into the Interior.* New York: Free Association Books.

Tessman, L. H. (1982). A note on the father's contribution to the daughter's ways of loving and working. In: S. Cath, A. Gurwitt, & J. M. Ross (Eds.), *Father and Child: Developmental and Clinical Perspectives* (pp. 219–238). Hillsdale, NJ: Analytic Press.

Van Buren Kelley, A. (1971). *The Novels of Virginia Woolf, Fact and Vision.* Chicago, IL: University of Chicago Press.

Winnicott, D. W. (1945). Primitive emotional development. *International Journal of Psychoanalysis, 26*: 137–143.

Winnicott, D. W. (1947). Hate in the counter-transference. In: *Through Pediatrics to Psychoanalysis* (pp. 194–203). London: Hogarth and the Institute of Psychoanalysis, 1975.

Winnicott, D. W. (1953). Transitional objects and transitional phenomena —a study of the first not-me possession. *International Journal of Psychoanalysis, 34*: 89–97

Winnicott, D. W. (1958). The capacity to be alone. *International Journal of Psychoanalysis, 39*: 416–420.

Winnicott, D. W. (1960a). The theory of the parent–infant relationship. *International Journal of Psychoanalysis, 41*: 585–595.

Winnicott, D. W. (1960b). Ego distortion in terms of true and false self. In: *The Maturational Processes and the Facilitating Environment: Studies in the Theory of Emotional Development* (pp. 140–152). London: Hogarth, 1965.

Winnicott, D. W. (1963). The development of the capacity for concern. *Bulletin of the Menninger Clinic, 27*: 167–176.

Winnicott, D. W. (1965). *The Maturational Processes and the Facilitating Environment: Studies in the Theory of Emotional Development.* London: Hogarth.

Winnicott, D. W. (1967). Mirror-role of mother and family in child development. In: P. Lomas (Ed.), *The Predicament of the Family: A Psychoanalytical Symposium.* London: Hogarth and Institute of Psychoanalysis [reprinted in D. W. Winnicott, *Playing and Reality.* London: Tavistock, 1971].

Winnicott, D. W. (1968). The use of an object and relating through identifications. In: *Playing and Reality* (pp. 86–94). London: Tavistock, 1971.

Winnicott, D. W. (1971a). Transitional objects and transitional phenomena. In: *Playing and Reality* (pp. 1–25). London: Tavistock.

Winnicott, D. W. (1971b). *Playing and Reality.* London: Tavistock.

Winnicott, D. W. (1974). Fear of breakdown. *International Review of Psychoanalysis, 1*: 103–107.

Winnicott, D. W. (1975). *Through Pediatrics to Psychoanalysis.* London: Hogarth.

Winnicott, D. W. (1986). *Holding and Interpretation.* London: Hogarth.

Wolff, C. G. (1986). *Emily Dickinson.* New York: Alfred A. Knopf.

Woolf, V. (1915). *The Voyage Out.* London: Duckworth.

Woolf, V. (1919). *Night and Day.* London: Duckworth.

Woolf, V. (1925). *Mrs Dalloway.* London: Hogarth.

Woolf, V. (1928). *Orlando: A Biography.* London: Hogarth.

Woolf, V. (1927). *To the Lighthouse.* London: Hogarth.

Woolf, V. (1929). *A Room of One's Own.* New York: Harvest/Harcourt.

Woolf, V. (1931). *The Waves*. London: Hogarth.

Woolf, V. (1937). *The Years*. Orlando, FL: Harcourt Brace.

Woolf, V. (1941). *Between the Acts*. London: Hogarth.

Woolf, V. (1953). *A Writer's Diary*, L. Woolf (Ed.). New York: Harcourt Brace Jovanovich.

Woolf, V. (1978). *Moments of Being: Unpublished Autobiographical Writings*, J. Schulkind (Ed.). London: Hogarth.

Wright, K. (1991). *Vision and Separation*. Northvale, NJ: Jason Aronson.

Wrye, H. K., & Welles, J. K. (1998). *The Narration of Desire: Erotic Transferences and Countertransferences*. Hillsdale, NJ: Analytic Press.

INDEX

Rose, P., 150, 154
Rosenfeld, H., xiii, 104

sadism, xvii, 18, 22, 49, 62, 75, 94, 106,
    151, 219 *see also*: aggression,
    behaviour(al), fantasy, phantasy,
    rage
  actions, 109
  active, 16
  control, 75
  eroticised, 32
  impulse, 100, 109
  passions, 109
  paternal, 216
  revenge, 217
  torture, 50
  wish, 62, 88
Safan-Gerard, D., 102
Salter, G., 29
Segal, H., xiii–xiv, 3, 58, 71, 89, 110
Seinfeld, J., xii, xxvii, 29, 66, 72, 106,
    235
self (*passim*) *see also*: conscious(ness),
    development(al), narcissism,
    object(ive), recognition,
    subjective, unconscious(ness)
  -absorbed, 139, 218
  -abusive, 103
  agency, 99–100, 104, 146
  -aggrandisement, 61
  -anchoring, 127
  angry, 75
  -annihilation, 50, 91–92, 217
  -assault, 213
  -assertion, 100, 145
  -assured, 128
  -attack, 214
  -aware, 126, 146
  bad, 86, 104, 142
  -blame, 106
  body, 142, 154, 163, 254
  -boundaries, 168
  child, 123, 172, 215–216, 224, 232,
    254–255, 259–260
  cohesive, 104, 161, 167–168, 217
  -concept, 188

-confidence, 144
-constellation, 123
constructed, 104
-contained, 111, 239
contrived, 206
core, xxv, 101, 120, 132, 147, 255,
    258, 260
-destructive, 79, 102, 217
-digesting, 240
disorders, xxiii, xxvi
-disruption, 91
-division, 217
-doubts, 20, 168
emerging, 93
-esteem, xxv
-evolving, 194, 196, 210
-exhibition, 212
-experience, xxvi, 76, 161, 206
-expression, 161, 164, 192, 194, 196,
    213–214, 246–247, 260
-extensions, 14, 28, 172, 210
false, 62, 77, 104, 117, 186, 209–211,
    214, 218–220, 222, 263
-feeling, 79, 133, 200
female, 37, 219
-formation, 37, 44, 91
fragmenting, 168
-gesture, 214
grandiose, xxiv–xxv, 206, 210, 215,
    220, 228
-growth, 244
-harm, 159
hate, 217
-hood, 218–219
idealised, 12, 70, 210
-identity, 104, 167
-image, 117, 167, 188, 199, 210,
    212
-important, 198
inadequate, 16, 104
individual, 199
infant, 10, 67, 175, 232
-initiated, 191
inner, 119, 214, 216–217, 222
-integration, xv, xviii, xxvii–xxviii,
    4, 29, 32, 72, 77, 79, 97, 100,